635

D0324149

USDA Plan[t]
Hardiness
Zone Map

Gardening in the Heartland

Who loves a garden still his Eden keeps,
Perennial pleasures plants, and wholesome
harvests reaps. ❧

Amos Bronson Alcott, 1868, *Tablets*

Gardening in the Heartland

Rachel Snyder

Illustrations by Bob Holloway

UNIVERSITY PRESS OF KANSAS

© 1992 by the University Press of Kansas

All rights reserved

Published by the University Press of Kansas (Lawrence, Kansas
66049), which was organized by the Kansas Board of Regents and is
operated and funded by Emporia State University, Fort Hays State
University, Kansas State University, Pittsburg State University,
the University of Kansas, and Wichita State University

LIBRARY OF CONGRESS CATALOGING-IN-PUBLICATION DATA
Snyder, Rachel
Gardening in the Heartland / Rachel Snyder ; illustrations by Bob Holloway.
p. cm.
Includes bibliographical references and index.
ISBN 0-7006-0516-9
1. Gardening—Middle West. I. Title.
SB453.2.M53S6 1991
635'.0977 — dc20
91-19183
CIP

British Library Cataloguing in Publication Data is available.

Printed in the United States of America
10 9 8 7 6 5 4 3 2 1

The paper used in this publication meets the minimum requirements
of the American National Standard for Permanence of Paper for
Printed Library Materials z39.48-1984

Design: ACME DESIGN COMPANY

Contents

Preface

The subject of gardening deserves regional treatment. That is the underlying premise of this book. When the region has such distinct climate, soils, and topography as this one, here called "the Heartland," the case seems especially strong.

Other gardening books have appeared for regions all around us. It is time for one here. A few other books about gardening in mid-America have pioneered the way over bygone years— but none remains in print or, to my knowledge, is as comprehensive as *Gardening in the Heartland.* Gardeners here have complained, justifiably, that most garden books seem based on, or are directed toward, gardens elsewhere—in the East or Far West, or even in England or Europe. This one really is for the Midwest.

Of course, a line drawn around a cluster of states means nothing so far as plants, wind, and weather are concerned. Therefore, "the Heartland" as here assumed to be within the bounds of Nebraska, Iowa, Missouri, and Kansas is admittedly an arbitrary concept. The book can readily serve a much wider area than within these imaginary lines. Gardeners through most of the Midwest, if in plant hardiness zones addressed here (4, 5, and 6), will find much applicable information. But these four states are where the material was gathered and toward which the information is particularly directed.

Do not expect this book to answer your every garden need. Some aspects of the huge field of gardening have little to do with location or environment, and so I have omitted them. Such topics as indoor and container plants, greenhouse growing, water gardening, propagation, arranging or drying flowers or using them in crafts, gardening structures, tools and appurtenances—these receive no more than passing mention. Many excellent books on all of these special topics are available in bookstores and libraries. Nor will you find ultimate details about individual types of plants such as roses, tomatoes, oaks, or hostas that can be covered completely only in more narrowly focused plant books. *Gardening in the Heartland* will not take the place of a gardening encyclopedia, although checking the index should lead you to basic information about a large number of plants and gardening topics. Pesticides and other product recommendations were all available at the time of writing, but there is no guarantee they will remain so in the future. Some vanish from dealers' shelves, and new ones take their places. Local dealers are your closest link to reality in this situation.

My hope in writing this book is to show possibilities for great Heartland home gardens and suggest how to achieve them. My hope is to prevent the early mistakes that often discourage gardeners in our region. My hope is to fire your enthusiasm and back it up with relevant advice.

Gardening is one of the oldest and most honored of human activities. It is unique among humanity's pastimes in the many kinds of personal rewards it brings. There is no need to name them—gardeners soon discover the dividends for themselves. People in the Heartland relish the benefits as fully as gardeners anywhere. I hope that your Heartland garden will reward you with satisfaction and joy.

Many individuals and organizations have contributed over a long time to the information included here, too many to acknowledge by name. My sincere thanks goes to them all.

The following organizations and people were particularly helpful in

providing comments or information, answering questions, or inviting me into their gardens for photography and study: the Cooperative Extension Services of Iowa, Missouri, Kansas, and Nebraska; All-America Rose Selections; Bartlett Arboretum; *Flower & Garden Magazine* library; Horticultural Services, Inc., of Manhattan, Kansas; the Lawn Institute; Powell Gardens; Charles Brasher; Wilbur Dasenbrock; Mr. and Mrs. J. Robert Flynn; Mrs. Verla Heitman; Mr. and Mrs. Walter Hiersteiner; Joe Holtzman; Mrs. Sally Keach; Mr. and Mrs. Andrew Klapis; Mrs. Cynthia Kunkle; William Lanning; Mrs. Eleanor McClure; Mrs. Mildred Meinke; Dr. and Mrs. H. B. Overesch; Mrs. Elvira Ratliff; Mrs. Lynne Tavener; Misses Sarah and Virginia Weatherly; and Arnold Webster.

To Frank Good, garden editor of the *Wichita Eagle*, and Dr. Ray Rothenberger of the Department of Horticulture, University of Missouri, special appreciation for reviewing the final manuscript and heading off some mistakes and omissions. The errors that remain are, I fear, my own responsibility.

RACHEL SNYDER
Mayetta, Kansas
January 1991

CHAPTER ONE

Where We Garden

*"Heartland" is a self-bestowed name
for this landlocked central region where we
garden. Although the word has many
meanings, for the people who live here the
primary one refers to our location at the
geographic center of the contiguous United
States. But we also like to think of ourselves
in the sociopolitical sense as the steadily
working, producing center that sustains
much of the rest of the nation.*

However that may be, we are undeniably at the middle of things, not only at the center of the "lower forty-eight," but also very near the center of the North American land mass. This reality we cannot and ought not ignore. We are far from climate-tempering influences—no oceans or great lakes are nearby, no mountain ranges to divert the winds, not even any great forests to help cool our summers or warm our winters.

We are speaking of latitudes from about 36 degrees in the south to 44 in the north, and from the Mississippi River on the east to near the foothills of the Rocky Mountains on the west. States involved are Nebraska, Iowa, Missouri, and Kansas. Most of this vast area was in prairie until a little over a century ago; a bit of it still is. The far-

ther east one went, the higher the grasses grew, in step with the increase in rain as the land emerges from the "rain shadow" of the high western mountains, which wring water from eastbound air before it reaches our side. Consequently, the High Plains are semi-arid with only 15 to 20 inches of precipitation a year.

Farther east, the Heartland becomes a mixing ground of cold air plunging down from Canada and warm moist air rising from the Gulf of Mexico—spawning majestic storms that may roll all the way to the East Coast. Wild extremes of temperature are commonly experienced within a short time. Rises or falls of 60 degrees in eight hours are not unheard of. When a cold wave sweeps across to vanquish a balmy interval in autumn, riding a bitter gale and spreading sleet in its path, we call it the "Siberian Express."

Our region is susceptible to cyclic long-term droughts. Although scientists cannot agree on their causes or reliably predict their frequency, they do know from tree rings that such cycles have gone on for at least thousands of years. Droughts of course are broken by intervals of rainy years. When we look at the miles-wide flat valleys now bordering such rivers as the Platte and Missouri, we can imagine the ancient floods that formed them and laid down those rich soils. The next time you fly over these valleys, study the still visible meandering channels these streams have taken. The creation process continues today despite efforts to control it.

A jousting ground for giant air masses

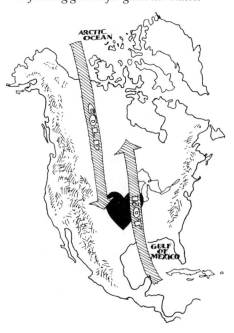

SOILS

Before settlement, most of the Heartland supported boundless coverings of prairie grasses. Wind-driven fires regularly laid bare the ground, but with returning rains the grasses grew again with fresh vigor. These fires kept trees from overgrowing the prairies, even far eastward where moisture was plentiful. Humusy deep soils formed under the prairies, although soil types differ widely from place to place. In the north, the region bears a blanket of transplanted, "till" soils left by glaciers that visited and receded over the ages. In the wake of the melting glaciers, windblown dunes of silt and sand hundreds of feet deep piled up in some areas. These soils, called "loess," are much different—in texture, mineral components, and workability—from others that may lie only a short distance away.

With mountains as old as any on the continent, the Ozark region of southeastern and southern Missouri, occupying nearly a third of the state, has had a dramatically different geologic history from the region to the north. The great variety of stony outcrops largely determine the types of soil coverings. Where limestone prevails, soils may be alkaline; where sandstones, chert, and granite prevail, acidic soils are likely to occur. Much of the soil formed while the surface was forested; but in some areas, long tongues of prairies extended up the slopes, resulting in different, deeper soils. Gardeners in the hillier parts of the Ozarks are likely to find topsoil of any sort in fairly small supply. The readiness with which trees establish and grow in the region proves that the elements are present to produce good gardens. You can expect generally reliable rainfall (the highest averages in the region), good drainage, and often more acidic soils than are found elsewhere in the Heartland. Glaciation was not a part of the soil history in either southern Missouri south of the Missouri River or in Kansas more than a few miles south of the Kansas River.

If you are new to your gardening site, one of your first get-acquainted projects should be to dig a 2-foot-deep hole and study its "profile": the layers of colors and textures visible from top to bottom. If you are in a river valley, you may find a dark, silty loam on top, blending down to paler levels of sandy loam. If you pour in water, you will probably find that it drains away fairly soon. If you are on high ground, you may find a heavy black loam thinly covering a subsoil of sticky tan clay that drains poorly and turns gummy when wet. Or you may encounter rocks, rubble, or other surprises.

The Soil Conservation Service (SCS) has mapped nearly every section of land in the region and undoubtedly has a map showing the general soil types of the ground in which you are gardening. For a small garden it may not be practical to buy the book (each county has one), but you could ask at your county SCS office to look at it. You will probably be amazed by it. The soil survey book tells other data specific to your location, such as spring and fall freeze dates and temperature and precipitation averages. It is a good way to gain fundamental understanding of the climate and soil you

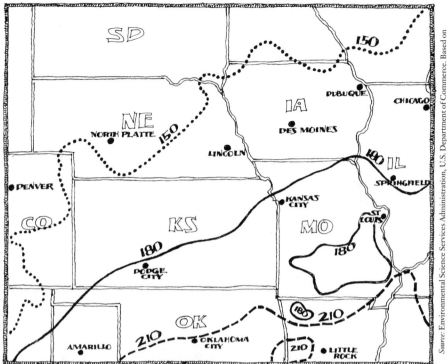

Source: Environmental Science Services Administration, U.S. Department of Commerce. Based on thirty-year period, 1921–1950.

Mean length of growing season (number of freeze-free days)

confront as you create your garden.

You can learn about your soil in yet another way. You can have it tested in a laboratory (see Chapter Two for more about this). Such a test saves money that might be wasted on unneeded or inappropriate fertilizers, and it usually leads to successful gardens.

Much of the Heartland is underlain by limestone. Sedimentary limestone layers interspersed by shales—seen in many deep road cuts—are the result of primordial seas that rose and fell through geologic ages. The limestone presence affects gardening here by bringing most of our soils into the alkaline or neutral part of the pH range.

Also, our water supplies are alkaline. A soil that is strongly acidic is hard to find here, with calcium (an element linked to alkalinity) constantly weathering out of the limestone into the environment. Since some plants—for example, the rhododendrons or azaleas—do poorly in alkaline soils, Heartland gardeners must go to extra efforts to grow them. Undaunted, many succeed.

WATER AND ITS CONSERVATION

Water shortages, past, present, and future, are also realities of our area. We cannot ignore the growing possibility that some day, perhaps not far off, there will be no water available from municipal or district supplies for watering gardens. In response to this

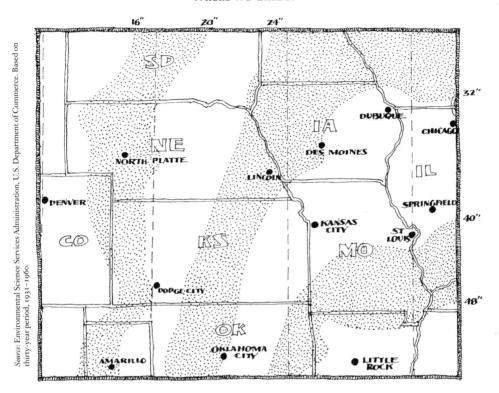

Source: Environmental Science Services Administration, U.S. Department of Commerce. Based on thirty-year period, 1931–1960.

Normal precipitation (inches per year)

threat, the concept of xeriscapes has emerged. The word "xeriscape" means dry garden. It was an idea largely developed at the Denver Botanical Garden to describe man-made landscapes that use only water-conserving plants and methods. Although Colorado is even less endowed with water resources than the Heartland (having even lower average rainfall and being a long way from any abundant water source such as the Missouri or Mississippi rivers), we have no cause for complacency. With our groundwater table lowering year by year, demands increasing steadily, and dry weather patterns seeming always to recur, water is obviously too precious to justify using

it on the landscape. Summertime bans on lawn and garden watering, car washing, and so on are already commonplace and we can expect them to increase.

The xeriscape concept combines several strategies. The plants used have low water needs and high drought tolerance. Natives—both woody (trees and shrubs) and nonwoody, or herbaceous (grasses and flowers)—are high on the list of plants with modest water requirements. There are also nonnative plants from parts of the world closely matching ours in what nature provides. Although many of these drought-resistant plants are still strangers to most of us, the rising interest in and demand for them have increased the supply. Get acquainted with them at every opportunity and with what they might do in your own Heartland garden.

As for practices that save water, some of the basics are to limit the space you devote to highly maintained lawns; concentrate on soil improvement and the use of mulches; and organize plantings so kinds with similar needs are grouped together for efficiency in handling (called "zoning"). We can learn how to conserve water and how to make better use of the water we do have (for more about such ideas see Chapter Twelve).

MICROCLIMATES

Aside from latitude and longitude location and the broad aspects of climate, nearly every garden also has those special pockets of circumstances called

"microclimates." Watch for these situations and take advantage of them. A high place and a low one only 50 feet apart may differ markedly in temperature, soil moisture, or air circulation, and the soil may vary in texture, minerals, or drainage characteristics, making a difference in what will thrive in each spot. Nooks with reflected warmth from structures or protection from winds may afford havens for plants that could not survive in the raw open country nearby.

In making decisions for your realm to aid and abet the natural forces, you need to "think like a plant" and realize the possibilities offered by special places. Besides intuition, there are some standard guidelines. Be aware that cold "runs" downhill and settles in low spots or against barriers that impound and

Mean date of last frost in spring

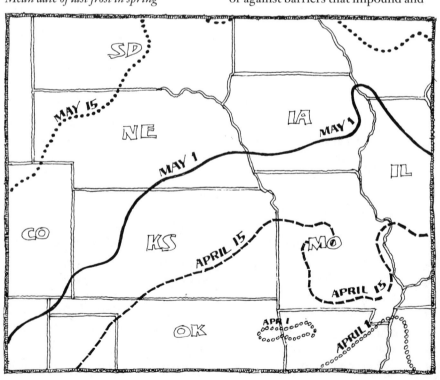

Source: Environmental Science Services Administration, U.S. Department of Commerce. Based on thirty-year period, 1921–1950.

hold the chilled air. Therefore, you should place the more tender plants and those needing longest growing seasons in the warmer levels away from frost pockets. Save the coolest areas for the latest-blooming and cold-hardiest kinds.

North-facing slopes versus those facing south, and to a lesser extent those facing east versus those facing west, present possibilities of stretching bloom seasons of daffodils and tulips and many other kinds of plants. South slopes are where you see earliest seedlings or sprouts of any kind. They come nearly as soon on west facing slopes. North-facing slopes are slower than other exposures to bring plants into bloom; spring is still going on there after high summer is in command elsewhere. On north-facing slopes, the soil even re-mains moist much longer than on other slopes. East-facing slopes are similar to north-facing ones, although to a lesser degree.

Orchardists in the Heartland traditionally prefer a north- or east-facing slope for fruit trees on the principle that blooms may open just a few days later than elsewhere, thereby escaping the devastating late freezes of a capricious spring. Regardless of the direction faced, a slope is better for fruits than a flat bottom field, because in the latter a crop may be frozen out year after year.

PLANT HARDINESS ZONE MAPS
Gardeners anywhere in this country soon encounter plant hardiness zones. Seed and plant catalogs, nurseries, and

Mean date of first frost in autumn

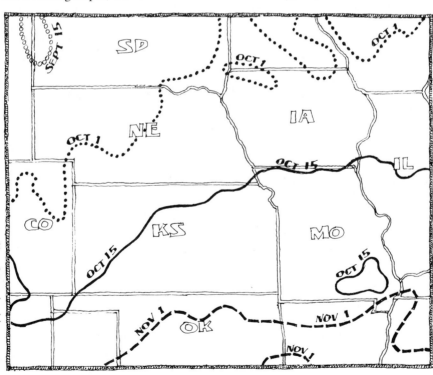

Source: Environmental Science Services Administration, U.S. Department of Commerce. Based on thirty-year period, 1921–1950.

most of the literature published on gardening (including this book) refer you to hardiness zones as indications of where plants can be expected to survive. And since these zones are based primarily on average lowest winter temperatures, the maps particularly indicate the likelihood of the plant to survive the winters. If you protest that *summers* in the Heartland are also a test of tolerance, you are absolutely right, but unfortunately there are no hardiness maps that address this particular problem.

Zone maps can be confusing because there are so many of them, all slightly different. The idea started in the 1920s with the publication of a map created by the Arnold Arboretum, Jamaica Plain (Boston), Massachusetts, and used in Alfred Rehder's classic *Manual of Cultivated Trees and Shrubs.* Both the book and the map were reprinted many times and are still in use. Rehder keyed all his plant listings to the map's eight hardiness zones, which covered much of North America. His zones were based on the lowest mean temperatures of the coldest months, and they represented differences of 5 degrees. Later, this same map was used by Donald Wyman, then of the Arnold Arboretum, in his several widely read books including *Wyman's Gardening Encyclopedia.* Many other publications, including some nursery catalogs, have used it.

In 1960 and again in 1965, the U.S. Department of Agriculture published a "Plant Hardiness Zone Map." It gained wide acceptance and was probably the prevailing plant zone map for the next thirty years, even though the government let it go out of print in 1981. It is reproduced in many catalogs and books, and most nurseries have keyed their plants to it to indicate hardiness. The map's zones were based on average annual minimum temperatures; each zone represented a 10-degree difference from its neighbors, and was divided into "a" and "b" subzones of 5-degree differences.

In 1990, the U.S. Department of Agriculture, through the U.S. National Arboretum, issued yet another Plant Hardiness Zone Map from newer, more comprehensive studies of climate data. The new map (see endsheets) uses the same 10-degree differences between zones, but the boundaries have shifted south, reflecting recent data that indicate winters have been bringing colder lows over much of the country. Heartland gardeners who once considered themselves in Zone 6 may now find that they are in Zone 5. Those once in Zone 5 may now be in Zone 4, and so on. Large urban areas may carry a warmer zone designation than the surrounding countryside, because of the microclimate created by heat-retaining buildings and paving. Elevation differences in some places also create "island" zones carrying a different zone designation. The large 4-by-4-foot size of this 1990 map made it possible to include the outline and name of every county in the United States, so readers can identify their precise zone locations.

Cold hardiness is only one of several factors affecting the survival of plants. Heat tolerance, the pH of soil, water or rainfall amounts, day length, and radiation (or light intensity) are other factors affecting whether or not a plant will prosper under given circumstances. But as cold hardiness is such a major criterion, and as average annual winter minimums are readily measured and mapped, hardiness maps such as these have been a logical development. The new map should improve our ability to select plants suited to our locations. It is available from the Superintendent of Documents, U.S. Government Printing Office, Washington, D.C. 20402-9325. Ask for Miscellaneous Publication No. 1475.

Study the new map to find where you are, and fix your hardiness zone firmly in your mind. Study its lists of indicator plants for each zone, especially for Zones 4, 5, and 6, which cover the Heartland. Catalogs and books that have rated plants according to past hardiness zones will retain those ratings into the future, but in applying those old ratings you may find plants you once thought appropriate for your area no longer among the recommended ones, because your zone has changed.

STORMS

Wind- or thunderstorms are what everyone thinks about when "storm" is mentioned. But there are other kinds as well—ice storms, hailstorms, cloudburst rainstorms, dust storms, and even those times when the sun seems to fill the sky and produce an inferno, or "heat" storm. A single season is likely to produce an example of each, perhaps more than one.

Storms of any sort move across the region in a generally west-to-east di-rection. Spring and summer may bring dozens of windstorms, of various strengths. It is sometimes hard to tell the difference between a windstorm and the ordinary winds that often blow for days on end, especially in spring. Trees are the plants most affected by wind. Aside from the expected breakage, trees buffeted by winds do not grow as tall as their counterparts in calmer regions and sometimes lean to leeward. Visitors from less windy climates often notice this trait in our trees and wonder about it.

Allow for storms in your garden building and your plants. Build structural elements so they will withstand blows and downpours. Make trellises strong, fences durable, and drains ample. Put overhead wires underground where possible (low-voltage garden lights make this easy). If tree breakage is common in ice storms, safeguard your trees in advance, especially those prone to breakage, by using cables, bracing, or preventive pruning. If lightning strikes are regular occurrences in your area (yes, lightning can and does strike the same place twice or more), you can protect valuable trees or buildings with lightning arresters. Trees that tower above others in the landscape are especially susceptible—and many foresters think that oaks and cottonwoods are more vulnerable to lightning than most other kinds.

Ice storms are common in Heartland winters. You can count on one every few years. Immense damage to trees may occur in only a few hours, and little can be done to prevent it.

Surveying the scene afterward, you can learn which kinds are the most damage prone and which get off relatively unscathed. Trees that present the most surface to which ice can cling are those that split and come crashing down from the weight. A prominent example is the Siberian elm, *Ulmus pumila* (mistakenly) called the "Chinese" elm by many. Years after the event, ice-caused damage can be seen in many of these trees across our region. It is why they are no longer much planted. Because they keep their leaves all winter, evergreens of different kinds are also very susceptible to ice damage. Ice-laden limbs may be peeled from white pines and other needle evergreens. If the evergreen is of a formal, erect type, such as an upright yew or arborvitae, it is practical to support it against ice breakage by wrapping a spiral of twine around the branches up to the tip. This idea is also useful for foundation shrubs you want to protect against snowy avalanches from the roof, or landscape evergreens likely to feel the weight of snow shoveled or blown over them in clearing sidewalks or drives. If twine seems inadequate bracing, burlap wrap or wood structures can be positioned over valuable shrubs in particularly vulnerable places. March is the month most likely to bring the combination of conditions producing ice storms, although of course they can happen anytime through winter or spring.

HAIL

Most parts of the Heartland typically get two or three hailstorms a year. They can come at any time but do the most damage in spring and summer while plants are in full leaf and growth. Often they come with such wind and fury that the icy pellets are driven like bullets. A gardener can do little to diminish hail damage. Leaves are scoured from trees, and large-leaved garden plants are turned to lace. Wind-driven hail can debark trees on the windward side. Ice piles up against tender plant stems and they are frosted, even in the flush of summer. If hailstones reach the size of golf balls—not unusual—they pummel and pound the soil, driving the air out of it and turning it into stonelike solidity when the sun comes out. Although compaction of soil is one of the pervading damages done by

---

Things Nobody Ever Tells You

❧ The moisture content of snow varies, but a rule of thumb for gardeners is 10 percent. So if the snow depth is 5 inches, count it as ½ inch of precipitation. You should measure snow depth while the snow is fresh.

❧ As it falls, snow gathers nitrogen from the air. The nitrogen is carried into the ground as snow melts and is like a shot of fertilizer to the plants. Rain also gathers nitrogen from the air, with the most added during thunderstorms.

❧ Well water and river water used for municipal supplies is usually quite alkaline (has high pH) in this region. Although it fluctuates, in summer it often shows a pH rating of 9 or more (highly alkaline), which creates problems when you use it to water acidity-requiring plants like blueberries or azaleas.

hail, it is seldom recognized because of all the other more-visible devastation. The best way to avoid hail compaction damage is to use a good airy mulch that cushions the blows—and this should be reason enough for every Heartland gardener to become a mulcher.

RADIATION

Light, especially sunlight, is the energizer for the process by which plants grow. The Heartland has plenty of sunlight—sometimes too much. In the southwestern part of our area, you will find as much sunshine in the month of July as you can find almost anywhere in the continent, with the possible exception of the deserts of California and Arizona. Winter sunshine is also comparatively abundant in our region, as we have more sun than any area east of us except for southern Florida. The western parts of our region are comparable in winter sunshine with Denver and Albuquerque.

Though all this sunshine is a real plus for farmers growing corn, wheat, milo, and soybeans and for vegetable gardeners growing squash and tomatoes, it makes a difference in the ornamental plants we can grow and how we grow them. Plants that come from misty, cloudy places do not react well when placed in the full glare of the Heartland sun. This is a principal reason why our list of broadleaf evergreen shrubs and trees is so short. Even though some kinds like hollies or euonymus are technically cold hardy

enough where we plant them, the combination of frigid weather with brilliant sunshine—perhaps magnified by snow glare—often leads to browning of leaves in late winter and defoliation in spring. Although the plant may survive, it must struggle. For such plants, selecting the proper site is very important. Our forceful summer sun is why we need to shade newly set-out transplants, even peppers and tomatoes, and why certain plants (for example, New Guinea impatiens) listed as "sun plants" in other regions do better in full or partial shade here. We learn by experience.

Over the long pull, gardeners in the Heartland are well advised to graciously accept the limitations set by climate and soil and to channel their efforts into areas where they can not only succeed but excel. There are enough promising possibilities to keep any gardener happy for a lifetime. We live in a land of agricultural plenty that has been the envy of the world. It is only a thin line between agriculture and horticulture, and of the two, horticulture offers by far the greatest interest and personal reward. The current trend toward using native plants in landscapes and flower gardens is a step in the right direction. The natives can teach us secrets of plant success here in their homeland. Among the natives are many beautiful plants discovered long ago by European explorers who valued them highly. In Europe they became garden favorites. Now we are buying some of them back as cultivated varieties.

CHAPTER Two

Soil Matters

*Soil is the anchorage of your garden.
A lawn, a tree, a flower bed, a row of potatoes,
whatever—the plants are rooted in the
mineral mantle of earth called "soil." Not
many people study their soil before they begin
gardening in it. Most of them accept
what they find and hope for the best. But
soil conditions play a major role in the success
and enjoyment of the garden or, on the
other hand, in discouragement and failure.
Fortunately, most soils can be
improved.*

There is no generalizing about soils in the Heartland. We have some of the best soils for gardening to be found anywhere, and some of the worst. The ideal for most gardens, especially vegetable, is a "friendly" soil that warms up early in spring, is easy to till or cultivate, absorbs and retains moisture reasonably well but not too well, and naturally offers a rich store of nutrients plants can use. Nature does not endow many places with such soil, but approximations can be created and maintained.

Realities about the soil's true nature do not appear until you actually begin to plant plants, turn the soil with a spade, and rub it through your fingers while it is wet and again while it is dry.

In a newer housing development you'll be lucky if you get the original topsoil. Grading machines may have peeled it off, leaving the subsoil "basement" clay, which makes good bricks —and will do so if you work it while it is wet. A conscientious developer will provide at least a few inches of topsoil, reserved during excavation or brought in from elsewhere, to give a base for lawn grasses or a possible place for vegetables, shrubs, trees, or flowers.

As described in Chapter One, geologic origins account for broad differences in our soils. A vast area generally north of the Missouri and Kansas rivers and east from the Blue River in Kansas carries a covering of soil brought in by glaciers and then topped by soils that formed under prairie grasses. In this area the rolling, scenic hills are mantled with a heterogeneous "till" that includes clays, loams of different types, sands and gravels, and even boulders that were part of the glacial debris. These were and are fertile and productive soils, but in places where the ground has long been plowed and cropped, the soils' tendency to erode has resulted in the disappearance of much topsoil and exposure of the underlying clay.

Southward, in Missouri, the land was shaped by the ancient Ozark Mountains and although the gently rounded hills now belie the usual idea of mountains, you can assure yourself of the truth by digging a planting hole in the stony hillside. Yet on the broad Ozark Plateau the land flattens out in an upland with deep topsoil that formed under prairies. Rivers draining this area carved valleys both wide and narrow, depending on the terrain, but offering readily worked agricultural land with deep soils excellent for gardening.

A little farther west the Ozark upland blends into the cuestas of southeastern Kansas, gently tilted limestone ridges generally running north-south, that owe their formation to the shallow inland seas that came and went over this region, laying down the ledges that are bedrock, along with the intervening shales. It was a land of rich prairies interrupted here and there by steeper, higher hills. This region is drained southward and eastward by rivers that have overflowed often, each time delivering a new topping of silty loam along their valleys.

The Flint Hills in Kansas owe their preserved grasslands to the abundance of chert or flint that impeded the plow—until recent advances in machinery changed the situation. The chert or flinty outcrops were poor places for gardens, but the stream valleys offered bottoms that were rich and productive, as settlers discovered.

In both Kansas and Nebraska, progressing west, the land flattens and the sky widens with the imperceptible rise toward the Rockies. This land owes its character to the shallow seas that once covered it, to the uplifting mountains to the west that have drained across it and brought an outwash of soils and gravels, to the plants that have grown over it through eons, and to the climate. The winds sweeping these landscapes, from Texas to the Dakotas and beyond, have carried and shaped the soils and sands. Dunes lie deep under prairie grasses in the Nebraska sandhills and elsewhere. In western Kansas and Nebraska the soil thought by early explorers to be desert proved that it can grow about any sort of crop, provided there is enough water. Scattered across this area are marks of other events—volcanoes to the southwest that erupted and sent clouds of ash our way; the wearing down of minerals of many kinds; and always the work of water draining from higher elevations and forming eastbound rivers that still run aboveground and, in greater continuous volume, deep underground in a gravelly aquifer.

LOOK AT YOUR SOIL

Your first task as a gardener is to discover just what kind of soil you have. Soil is not static; it is always being formed. You can affect the process in your own garden in a relatively short time. Almost any soil can be improved somewhat, even one that already seems good. Soil is a combination of mineral elements, organic components, air, and water. But it is not a simple matter. The mineral particles exist in various sizes, each giving soil a different nature, and the organic components create a maze of chemical reactions. Changing climates affect soil behavior from year to year, and of course the water flowing over the ground or down through it can alter the topography, the chemistry, and the mechanical behavior.

With a simple jar-of-water test you can preview the main components. Into a clear-glass quart jar put a pint of water and a quarter cup of representative garden soil. Stir or shake this actively for a minute, then set it aside to settle. After the water clarifies (possibly a day later), look closely under good light at the layers showing through the glass. They will not be sharply defined, but gradations of colors and granules may be visible. At the bottom you should make out the coarsest mineral particles or sands, which are visible to the unaided eye. As particles become smaller they are not visible without magnification. The next smaller category is called silt (smaller than the smallest sand). The finest particles are microscopic—some of them will probably still be suspended in the water; these make up the clay component. Soil professionals recognize many more textures, but if you understand the basic three—sand, silt, and clay—you are on the way to understanding your soil. Compare the various layers to judge the proportions of each. If over half of the total is sand, it is a light, sandy soil. If it is over half silt, without much clay, it would be called a heavy silt soil. If the clay layer, usually yellowish brown, tan or reddish, appears to make up one-fourth of the total and there is a sizable amount of silt, you should call it a clay soil. If it seems to be about two-fifths sand, two-fifths silt, and the rest a narrow band of clay, you can call it a good loam. It is the kind of soil every gardener hopes for. The kinds to dread are heavy silt and clay.

Light, sandy soil is easy to work, warming up early in spring, but it is not very fertile and plants growing in it need boosting with fertilizer more often than in a heavier soil. Also in a light soil you will plant seeds and bulbs a little deeper than is generally recommended for an "average" soil. A heavy silt or clay soil is more difficult to work, is slow to warm up in spring, and may shrink and crack in summer; but it retains moisture and nutrients longer than the sandy soil. Because heavy silt and clay soil are more dense, bulbs and seeds are set more shallowly than is routinely recommended for the "average" soil.

In the water jar test of your soil, you may notice another component resting atop the clay, floating or suspended in the water, or clinging to sides of the jar—organic material. The more of it, the better. Organic material helps almost any soil. It makes a dense soil lighter and more water absorptive. It makes a light, sandy soil spongier and

able to hold moisture. Therefore, one goal in soil improvement is to increase the organic material. Generally the farther west you go in our region, or the hotter and drier the area, the less organic matter your soil contains.

Another easy soil test can tell you when soil may safely be worked in spring. Scoop up a small handful of it and form it into a walnut-sized lump in your palm. Then press it to see how readily it breaks apart. If it forms a gummy ball that does not break, postpone tilling to a later date. If it breaks apart into several fragments, it is ready to work. This is a good test to know, because it applies to any type of soil. It is particularly important to avoid working a too-wet clay or heavy silt loam soil in spring, because the effect of doing so is long lasting. The clods formed as a result will remain most of summer. It is best even to avoid treading or running machines over such soils while they are wet.

COMPOSTING

Actually a very easy process, composting is merely a system by which once-living (organic) plant material is returned to the soil to replenish the organic components and ultimately the humus. Humus is the end product of the breakdown of once-living tissues. As a storehouse of nutrients and a life-sustaining engine of the soil, humus is invaluable to plants. There are two main methods to create humus: surface composting and the compost pile.

SURFACE COMPOSTING. Surface composting simply means spreading undecayed plant refuse such as autumn leaves or grass clippings over the surface of the soil and digging or tilling it in. Autumn, after the year's garden is cleared away, is the best time to do this. The soil provides abundant bacteria to break the material down quickly, with the help of moist winter conditions. By spring planting time in our region, most of the plant remains will have disappeared. This is a favorite practice for vegetable gardens and is easiest to accomplish if you have a power tiller.

A variation of this idea, "green manuring," is to plant a crop such as winter rye or annual ryegrass specifically for this purpose. Typically the ryegrass would be planted early enough in autumn for it to make growth before winter, and then it would be plowed or spaded under or tilled into the ground the next spring as soon as the ground could be worked. Often in the Heartland it is April or May before soil dries enough to work, and the rye may be knee high before it can be plowed down. Consequently, only a late garden is usually possible in an overwintering green-manured area. Buckwheat, on the other hand, can become a summer green manure in crop rotation schemes—sown in early summer, allowed to grow four or five weeks or until it starts to bloom, then tilled under to improve the ground for a late planting of beans or for the spring garden.

COMPOST PILES. A compost pile is a collection of plant debris heaped together to encourage it to decay before it is spread over the garden. You can find many designs and instructions for making compost piles. Some gardeners organize their compost collections by age into two or three heaps, each with its own bin. The oldest heap is the one ready to use. The intermediate is pitched over into the vacant space left from using the oldest stuff. The newest heap moves to the middle stack, and the fresh material goes into the beginning bin. Fertilizer and water added to these heaps hasten the breakdown, and the very act of restacking them occasionally mixes the material, encouraging decay.

If you have no space or inclination for the three-bin idea, you can make perfectly good compost with a single pile of plant trash. Once or twice a year, simply rake off the covering of most recent additions to reach the older material underneath. Dig out and use the "made" compost from the bottom of the pile. In restacking, put new material on the bottom and mix some of the older compost into and over it as "starter." Make the pile large (at least 4 by 5 feet) and high (3 to 4 feet) to promote heating and quick breakdown. Leave the top slightly dish shaped to collect rainwater that will soak into the pile.

Compost is ready to use when it is dark and crumbly and the ingredients are unrecognizable. Shovel your made compost into a wheelbarrow or cart and deliver it to parts of your garden most in need of improvement. Perhaps it is the asparagus bed; or a border of perennial flowers; or along rows of tomatoes; or around your roses as a mulch. The favorite time for spreading compost is early spring just ahead of new growth. Do not be afraid to pile it lightly over the crowns of hostas, daylilies, true lilies, and many other perennials, or to scatter it over ground covers such as pachysandra, epimediums, and English ivy. New foliage will soon overtop the compost, shading and concealing it, and speeding its final decay and disappearance into the soil. Its effect will be long lasting. Repeated treatment with compost can transform poor or difficult soils into good ones.

The best location for a compost pile is in a shaded area out of view. A compost pile is not a thing of beauty, but it should be accessible. Keep out woody ingredients—sticks and brush—unless you expect to put the compost through a shredder. Some gardeners, real perfectionists, sift compost before spreading it. Avoid composting seed-laden weeds such as crabgrass and purslane or you will compound your weed problems.

PROBLEM SOILS

Clay has the tiniest particle sizes of any soil type and thus presents the most difficulties. A heavy silt soil is nearly as bad. When these soils are wet, they are as sticky as glue. When they are handled, air is driven out, making them even more dense and difficult. Working clay or heavy silt soils while they are wet results in clods that last through the growing season. Clay shrinks when it dries, resulting in deep cracks that sometimes break or dry root systems. When dry, clay is hard to dig, coming up in blocks. There is a brief period between too dry and too wet when clay or heavy silt soils may be plowed or otherwise tilled; exploit that interval if you can.

Since clay is often practically devoid of humus, adding any sort of organic material will help it. A 3-inch layer of moist peat moss or compost tilled into the top 6 inches will make it more workable. If sand is added to lighten a heavy clay or silt, a layer at least 2 inches thick should be worked into the top 6 inches of soil. Finely milled pine bark mixed into clay is also helpful in making it more workable. Spread the bark like a mulch 2 or 3 inches deep and dig it in. Vermiculite and perlite are two other amendments sometimes added to dense soils to lighten them and introduce air, thereby aiding plant growth.

On the positive side, clay and silt soils are generally rich in mineral nutrients and they hold moisture well, far longer than a sandy loam.

Extremely light, sandy soils likewise are helped by adding compost, moist peat moss, or other organic matter to keep them from drying out too quickly, and to store nutrients a little longer.

It helps any problem soil, whether a dense clay or silt or a light sand, to keep it covered in summer with airy mulch to shade it and retain moisture. For the short term, a "dust mulch" maintained by regular shallow cultivation is better than nothing.

EROSION PROBLEMS

Gullies can happen even in civilized gardens. A slope long enough or steep enough for a stream to gather momentum and begin carrying off soil is a setup for erosion. A certain amount is to be expected and can be tolerated.

But rills that regularly uproot your strawberries or wash out lawn areas or parts of your flower beds deserve corrective effort. The classic remedy is a terrace created across the contour (horizontal) of the slope to slow the runoff and give it an outlet across some grassy area that resists washing.

Where space is too restricted for this, an alternative is to level and raise the beds, so that water can drain off gently and harmlessly. Cover connecting paths between such beds with grass or a nonfloating mulch such as crushed rock to halt erosion there. In perennial beds, organic products such as fir or pine bark make good mulches on mild slopes and will not float away if they are worked lightly into the upper soil layer. Pine needles also are an excellent soil-anchoring mulch.

On slopes of newly seeded grass, it pays to prevent erosion while seedlings get established by installing a landscape netting over the seeded bank. When the netting finally rots away, after a year or so, the grass will be established.

DRAINAGE PROBLEMS

To spot areas that do not drain well, go out after a hard rain and look around. Areas with poor surface drainage will loom like lakes. Usually the problem is simply that in grading, low areas were left with no outlet. Regrading should solve this.

Another solution would be to raise the beds. By elevating the beds a few inches—using landscape timbers, railroad ties, stone or brickwork, or whatever other means may be at hand—you can overcome even the "down-through"

problems of a dense clay soil. The soil you fill into the raised portion of the bed should by all means be improved by adding organic material. This in itself guarantees a better moisture situation in the upper few inches of soil where most of the plant roots are. Also, raised beds tend to be more intensely worked than planting areas in open ground; the frequent deep incorporation of various soil amendments creates better conditions for plant roots.

Areas with poor "down through" drainage typically occur in clay soils underlain by hardpan that creates a "dam" 2 feet or so below the surface. This layer is so packed and impermeable that roots and water cannot penetrate. Sometimes trees and shrubs planted into such places die, because "tubs" of water drown the roots in wet seasons even though the planting site seems high and dry. If you suspect this, dig up the tree and examine the roots. If they are wet, your easiest response is to avoid planting in that spot. However, if the whole design hinges on having trees there, you could install special drainage lines leading out and down from the planting hole to drain off excess groundwater. This is a major job, and I advise you to hire a professional landscaping firm that will guarantee the success of future trees in that place.

Another possibility for solving such a drainage problem is to use a regular soil auger to drill holes down through the bottom of the excavation to reach a more permeable lower layer. To keep the drainage channels open, put a layer of coarse gravel in the bottom before planting.

NUTRIENT ELEMENTS AND WHAT THEY DO

Of the nutrients or elements essential to plant growth that are taken up from the soil, three stand out as primary because they are needed in large amounts: nitrogen, phosphorus, and potassium—symbolized chemically as N, P, and K. There are also some secondary elements (sulfur, calcium, and magnesium) needed in lesser amounts, and a list of "trace" elements (iron, boron, manganese, zinc, copper, molybdenum, chlorine, and possibly others) that are needed only in extremely small amounts. The primary three are regularly added to garden soil as fertilizer to boost plant growth. The others seldom if ever need to be added, as they are already present in the soil in adequate amounts, or occur as impurities in the primary fertilizers.

Nitrogen aids in photosynthesis and promotes leafy growth. Phosphorus is important in root growth, flowering, and fruiting and helps keep plants healthy. Potassium helps a plant grow strong roots, or tubers, and plays a part in plant health.

When you buy a bag, box, or bottle of commercial fertilizer, these three primary nutrients and the percentages they represent in the total formula are shown on the container by three numerals always giving the proportion of N, P, and K in that order.

A fertilizer you buy for your lawn is likely to be strong in nitrogen, the first number. For example, a 10-6-4 is a popular formulation for lawn food—with 10 percent nitrogen, 6 percent phosphorus, and 4 percent potassium.

You might encounter products with higher numbers—in which case a smaller amount would be needed to cover the same area; or lower numbers—in which case you would need more for the same area. Nitrogen is almost always scarce in soil, as it is easily washed away.

Commercial lawn foods come in bags that have instructions telling you how to set the spreader to get the right amount for that particular formulation. Follow these instructions carefully. To apply the correct amount, you need to know the size of your lawn areas in square feet.

A fertilizer sold for vegetable gardens, or for a special crop such as tomatoes, is likely to be strongest in phosphorus (the middle number)—perhaps with a formulation such as 5-10-5. Phosphorus, remember, promotes flowering and fruiting as well as good root growth. It is because of the latter benefit that soluble high-phosphorus fertilizers are often sold for "starter solutions" used to water new transplants into place. Bulb foods also are usually high-phosphorus formulations. As phosphorus tends to remain where it is placed rather than move downward in soil, it is important to work it well into the ground during soil preparation so it will be available down where the roots are.

Potassium is seldom the leading component in a balanced fertilizer, but as a promoter of starch and sugar formation and of general good health, it is usually included in formulations intended for flowers and vegetables and trees and shrubs.

There are organic sources for all of these primary nutrients. Sewage sludge and various animal manures are well known for containing nitrogen. Bonemeal is a time-honored source of phosphorus. Wood ashes have abundant potash (potassium). Sometimes with organic fertilizer products such as these, the percentage of actual nitrogen, phosphorus, or potassium is not known—so it is hard to judge the proper amount to apply. Since they break down slowly, however, there is little risk of burning plants with them. From the plant's standpoint, it makes no difference whether the nutrient comes from a chemical factory or a barnyard, as the final form taken up at the roots is the same. One precaution with wood ashes—not only are they loaded with potash, but they also are highly alkaline. This brings us to another concern: soil pH.

THE pH PUZZLE

Heartlanders cannot garden long before they hear about pH (pronounce both letters separately). The chemical symbol means "potential hydrogen," but in practical gardening terms it means the acidity-alkalinity (opposite factors) balance of soil.

The pH scale consists of fourteen units, with 7 as the midpoint, or "neutral." Numbers above 7 express alkalinity; numbers below 7 express acidity. Each point on the scale represents a multiple of ten upward or downward. For example, pH 6 is ten times more acidic than pH 7 (neutral); pH 5 is ten times more acidic than pH 6, or one hundred times more acidic than pH 7.

Most plants grow well in the slightly acidic range of pH 6 to 7 (see the list on page 23). Fortunately, most of our Heartland soils are in this range. Places with high rainfall generally have a lower soil pH than places with low rainfall. From this it follows that the farther west we are, the higher the pH level of our soils will probably be. Alkalinity is strongly related to presence of calcium, an element abundant throughout our region. Our groundwater and even water drawn from our rivers is loaded with lime (calcium), as evidenced by the lime deposits in our plumbing fixtures. Also, our water supplies are usually highly alkaline, in the pH 9 range. Thus every time we irrigate from the spigot, we are administering a mild dose of alkaline calcium.

To learn just what pH condition you have in your soil, it pays to get the soil tested. Most of our county or area horticultural extension offices run by the state universities offer a soil testing service at reasonable cost. Their test of your sample will probably also give you a reading on the nitrogen, phosphorus, and potassium levels in your soil. There are home soil testing kits of various types and accuracies, as well as electronic pH meters that give you a reading merely from inserting the probe into the soil.

Once you understand the pH condition of your soil, you will be able to tell the possible from the impossible in terms of plants. For example, you will know what you are up against if you want to grow acid-loving plants such as azaleas in an area that oozes alkalinity. You can detect pH problems by watching your plants. For example, if pin oaks or birches show yellowing leaves, they may be signaling a pH imbalance. The yellowing leaves (called chlorotic) are caused by unavailability of iron. The soil may contain plenty of iron, but if it is too alkaline the iron is "locked" and will not dissolve in water. The plant cannot absorb it and so it "starves" in the midst of plenty. The symptoms can take a variety of forms, and other elements besides iron may be unavailable.

Large plants such as trees cover so much space that it is practically impossible to change their soil from alkaline to acid. It is best to stay with plants that can take the soil you already have.

In the short term and for smaller plants, it is possible to reduce alkalinity (lower the pH) by treating the soil with sulfur, aluminum sulfate, or other acidifying materials such as cottonseed meal, acid peat, or pine bark mulch. The chart on page 24 suggests amounts of a few acidifying substances to use in soils of moderate density. Keep in mind that higher amounts are needed for denser soils; lesser amounts for lighter or sandier soils. It will be an ongoing process, the price one must pay for trying to grow plants in a region nature apparently never intended to grow them. Nevertheless, it is a challenge cheerfully accepted by many Heartland gardeners.

Things Nobody Ever Tells You

➷ Two types of commercial peat are sold for adding to gardens. One kind is sphagnum peat moss, which is brown and fibrous, and the other is sedge peat, which is black and powdery. The one that is best for gardens is the sphagnum peat. It is long lasting whether you incorporate it into the soil as a conditioner or use it as a surface mulch. Either way, it should be moistened before using. To do this, slit one side of the bag or bale cover and pour 1 gallon or more of hot (even boiling) water over the moss. Allow this to soak in overnight. The next day you can add more water to bring moss to the level of moistness you want. Peat packed perfectly dry resists wetting, and if it is mixed dry into the soil, it may draw moisture from it; or if it is spread as mulch on the surface, it may blow away before nature moistens it enough to stay down.

➷ Wood shavings or sawdust are good mulches if they are aged outdoors for a year before they are applied. Sprinkle them with nitrogen fertilizer to hasten their breakdown.

➷ Irish potatoes develop scab when they are growing in soil that is too alkaline.

Preferred pH Ranges of Sixty-Two Plants

FRUITS

Apple 5.0–6.5
Blackberry 5.5–7.0
Blueberry 4.0–5.0
Gooseberry 5.0–6.5
Grape 5.5–7.0
Hazelnut 6.0–7.0
Peach 6.0–7.5
Pear 6.0–7.5
Raspberry, black 5.0–6.5

SHRUBS AND TREES

Azalea 4.5–5.5
Barberry, Japanese 6.0–7.5
Bittersweet, American 4.5–6.0
Boxwood 6.0–7.5
Dogwood, flowering 5.0–7.0
Euonymus 5.5–7.0
Forsythia 6.0–8.0
Fringe-tree 5.0–6.0
Hawthorn 6.5–7.5
Holly, American 5.0–6.0
Holly, Chinese 5.5–6.5
Ivy, English 6.0–8.0
Lilac, common 6.0–7.5
Magnolia, star 5.0–6.0
Maple, Japanese 6.0–8.0
Oak, pin 5.0–6.5
Pine, white 4.5–6.0
Redbud 5.5–6.5
Rhododendron 4.5–6.0
Russian olive 6.0–8.0
Willow, pussy 6.5–8.0
Wisteria 6.0–8.0
Yew, Japanese 6.0–7.0

PERENNIAL FLOWERS AND PLANTS

Bleeding-heart 6.0–7.5
Daylily 6.0–8.0
Epimedium 6.0–7.5
Fern, Christmas 6.0–7.5
Fern, cinnamon 4.5–5.5
Fern, sensitive 5.5–7.5
Gaillardia 6.0–7.5
Gayfeather, Liatris 5.0–6.0
Helleborus niger 6.0–8.0
Hosta 6.0–7.5
Iris, tall bearded 6.5–7.5
Lily, regale 6.0–7.0
Pachysandra 5.0–8.0
Peony 6.0–7.5
Phlox, creeping 5.0–6.0

VEGETABLES

Asparagus 6.0–8.0
Beans, most 6.0–7.5
Beet 6.0–7.5
Broccoli 6.0–7.0
Fennel 5.0–6.0
Leek 6.0–8.0
Lettuce 6.0–7.0
Muskmelon 6.0–7.0
Pea 6.0–7.5
Potato 4.8–6.5
Tomato 5.5–7.5
Watermelon 5.5–6.5

GRASSES

Bluegrass, Kentucky 5.5–7.5
Fescue, tall 6.5–8.0
Buffalo 6.0–7.5

How to Lower Soil One Unit of pH to Make It More Acidic[a]

I SQUARE YARD   MEDIUM SOIL

Aluminum sulfate, or   6 oz. ($\frac{2}{3}$ cup)
Iron sulfate (copperas), or   7 oz. ($\frac{3}{4}$ cup)
Sulfur[b]   2$\frac{1}{2}$ oz. ($\frac{1}{3}$ cup)

How to Raise Soil One Unit of pH to Make It More Alkaline

I SQUARE YARD   MEDIUM SOIL

Ground Limestone   8 oz. (1 cup)

[a]Scatter on surface, work in 2 or 3 inches.
[b]Use pelletized or flaked sulfur for easier spreading.

A Realistic and Satisfying Design

At first thought, the subject of design seems too universal to have many regional aspects. But when the design is for a garden, it is different. Instead of brush or pen strokes, you are working with living plants. Each kind has its own attributes and requirements. Your garden will be outdoors under the Heartland sun, buffeted by the rain and wind, unprotected from heat and cold. Moreover, the vision you have of the garden you hope to create is not static. It will change with the seasons and with the years.

Like gardeners everywhere, we Heartlanders strive to make our gardens attractive and livable all year, to have a procession of colors, pleasing forms and textures, and points of interest year-round. But the "ground rules" and overall circumstances, the combination of factors directly affecting the outcome, are unique to our area. We are forced to admit that for part of both our summer and winter, we often seek haven indoors from climatic elements that are less than kindly or inviting. Even at those times, we want to look out on a pleasing scene.

WHERE TO BEGIN? LISTS!

Put yourself into an objective mood and analyze your actual garden situation and your hopes and dreams for it. Start with lists. If you are overhauling an old, established garden, your first list should be of the plants you want to keep and the permanent features you want to retain. Even in a brand-new "clean slate" garden you will probably need to jot down permanent factors to be recognized—for example, utility lines (above- and underground), easements, driveways, and walks.

Next, review questions every gardener should ask: Am I creating this garden for many years, for just a few, or for just a summer? How will I care for it? And how much time can I devote to it? Honest answers will help with the realistic aspects of your design.

Now for the creative part—make another list of things your garden should contain. Again, starting with realities, put down the "needs," the utilitarian or lifestyle features that

must be worked in. Doghouse or run? Playground area for children? Badminton, horseshoe, or croquet courts? Woodpile? Trash storage area? Drying yard? Basketball backboard? Turnaround or parking area for cars? Tool, potting, or equipment shed? It is best to plan on these from the start instead of adding them later. Next, put down the "wants," the aesthetic or amenity features you would like your garden to contain. Fish or lily pool? Vegetable or fruit garden? Ornamental beds of flowers or shrubs? Garden area to display hobby plants such as irises and roses? Outdoor dining or entertaining area? Keep this basic list posted in a prominent place as you move to the final phase: creating the plan.

Before that, however, make a "wishes" list of plants you want to include. You probably have some favorites. Visits to local nurseries, parks, public gardens, or botanical gardens are the best way to learn about plant possibilities. Catalogs are another source to study. In noting down "wishes" from catalogs, pay special attention to how they rate in hardiness. By shopping at local nurseries, you may assume that the kinds offered are hardy or they would not be there (not an infallible guide, however).

CREATING THE PLAN

You will need a "bare bones" diagram of your property showing boundaries, immovable features such as house, garage, utility lines (above- and underground), paved or established drives and walks that won't change, mature trees that will remain. This diagram should be to scale and should show actual dimensions. Perhaps there is a plat with your house deed or purchase papers that shows all this. If so, copy it to use as your "master." Enlarge it if necessary to a practical size. Otherwise make up your own basic plot plan based on stepped-off or actual measurements. Get a supply of tracing paper to lay over your master as you "doodle" with your plan. Use pencil to develop ideas, and don't be afraid to toss out a flawed version and start over.

Another idea when you are planning just a portion of your landscape, such as the house front or entrance, is to photograph that area and have an enlargement made. Use this as your master while you try out different treatments using sketches or cutout forms. This elevation approach is especially helpful in visualizing how combinations of plants may look in relation to your architecture.

The objective is to develop a permanent overall plan on paper of your whole place that will guide your progress and keep it on target. Always the total plan divides itself into three basic parts: the public area (the front yard, especially the part leading up to the front door); the utility or service areas containing all those necessary elements you put on your needs list; and the living or private area containing the amenities on your wishes list.

BASIC PLANNING CONSIDERATIONS FOR LANDSCAPES IN THE HEARTLAND

Strive for a landscape that will be easy to maintain. For example, lawns should be accessible to the mower. This means that the mowing pattern should be smooth and continuous and that trees (even orchards) and shrub and other planting beds should be positioned to ease mowing. For difficult areas, consider putting in ground covers (either plants or mulches) that need not be mowed, remembering, however, that they will still need occasional weeding. For sun-baked areas, consider putting in dryland grasses (such as buffalo grass) that need no watering and infrequent mowing. To reduce maintenance further, keep to a minimum attention-requiring features such as topiaries, clipped hedges, and beds that will need repeated edging throughout the season.

Today's trend is toward using plants that perform well without a lot of moisture. Native plants are getting more emphasis. Only lack of availability of nursery-grown native plants has held back their wider use; but this situation is changing.

The concept of "zoning," or grouping plants according to their moisture and light requirements or tolerance, is a good strategy for reducing maintenance. If you cannot resist including some plants that you know will need special attention, at least you can place them all in the same area so they can be tended at the same time.

Arrange your landscape to improve the seasons. This means planning to temper the extremes. Allow for winter sun to enter areas where its warmth will be welcome; arrange for shade on summer afternoons and evenings in places where people gather at day's end. If you position deciduous (leaf-shedding) trees to the south and west of the house, both goals will probably be served. Provide windbreak plants to slow down cutting winter gales; needle evergreens to the north and northwest of the house are good for this. Avoid planting evergreens where they would shade walks and drives in winter, thereby delaying snow and ice removal.

Emphasize our most pleasant season, autumn, in your landscape planning. One important way is to favor trees and shrubs that develop bright foliage as days shorten. Another is to plan fall gardens containing late-blooming flowers such as dahlias, asters, goldenrods, and chrysanthemums.

Group plants for screening effect. Select shrubs for color interest through a long season (spring flowers and fall foliage). Shrubs are most effective used in groups of several of the same kind. Vines on trellises and fences are useful for screening.

In structural elements, use durable materials. Native stone, especially limestone, always seems compatible with the Heartland scene. Crushed limestone or gravel in various grades are appropriate for paths and drives, although they do not make for easy walking. Bricks used for terraces and walks harmonize well with our gardens. Be sure to select the hard-fired kind to avoid having them spall in our freeze-thaw winters. In glaciated parts of the Heartland, the rounded pink-buff quartzite boulders have been used well for low walls, cobblestones, and garden accents. Asphalt is suitable for paths but is not so good for surfacing terrace and patio areas because of its heat-holding nature. For constructing garden fixtures made of wood—gazebos, decks, garden seats, screens—choose pressure-treated lumber that will last. Footings for any major structures should go below frost level. If footings are not below frost level they may be heaved out of position or cracked by freeze pressure. This depth will, of course, increase with latitude northward, and even in the south of our region it is probably more than you would imagine. Call your county engineer's office for this statistic.

Plant to emphasize good existing views. Or if there is an objectionable view, plant to screen it out. With their year-round foliage, needle evergreens such as pines, spruces, junipers, and yews are good choices both for framing a view and for hiding one.

Allow enough space between permanent plants (trees and shrubs) to avoid the need for future thinning or removal. (See Chapter Ten for information on the mature sizes of most permanent plants grown in the Heartland). Avoid planting tall growers under telephone or electrical wires. Also avoid planting thirsty-rooted kinds such as willows too close to sewer or drainage lines. By the same reasoning, avoid planting vigorous-growing vines such as wisteria and trumpet vine on inadequate trellises or structures that might be damaged by their weight. Wisteria has been known to pull down guttering, and trumpet vine has pried siding off of houses.

Position major shade trees (deciduous) with attention to summer and winter shade patterns. For example, an ash or oak renders its greatest service when placed where it shades the house in the heat of a summer day—mid-afternoon—so a spot to the southwest or west of the house is practical. Major evergreens such as pine trees give greatest climate-modifying help when they are used as winter windbreaks— this means locating them to the north or northwest of the house or outdoor area you wish to protect.

Adopt a timetable for your garden development to determine priorities. In the first phase, include the layout and planting of lawn areas, major trees, and shrub groups and the installment of utilities such as garden lighting and the watering system. Drip irrigation systems are efficient and economical for watering shrub borders and foundation plantings. They should be designed and installed at the time the shrubs are planted. Next, put in the structures and pavings, if any are included in the plan, and block out areas intended for flowers, herbs, or vegetables. Finally, develop the gardens themselves, a process that need not be hurried.

Designing Flower Beds

Traditionally, flower beds or borders have been placed against a backdrop such as a fence or wall or shrubs. But this is not a law. Free-standing or "island" beds of perennials or annual flowers make attractive landscape accents.

Aim for plantings that provide a succession of color or interest over a long season. (Details about the kinds of annual flowers useful for landscape effects are in Chapter Seven. Perennial flowers are described in detail in Chapter Eight.)

To achieve the greatest impact in the landscape, plan on using groups of each kind rather than single individuals. In planning the arrangement, pay attention to the expected heights of the flowers, so that each is properly displayed and visible from the front. Beds viewed from both sides should have the tallest plants at the center. There is leeway in this for artistic expression, and the plants themselves may take a hand. Mat-forming types such as thymes and *Stachys byzantina* (lamb's-ear) of course are best in the foreground and make pleasing transitions with lawn, paving, or whatever adjoins the bed.

Handling of colors is largely up to your artistic judgment. Gray-foliaged plants such as *Nepeta* (catmint) and *Artemisia* (mugwort, dusty miller) are useful for blending colors peacefully together. Ornamental grasses incorporated into the planting give long-season effect as "blenders," and some of them have a magical light-gathering quality.

Professional colorists use a star or wheel concept with six spokes to evaluate colors and their relationships (see the diagram on page 30). The three primary colors, red, yellow, and blue, are paired with their opposites on the wheel, secondary colors green, violet, and orange. These pairs, called complementary colors, are always pleasing

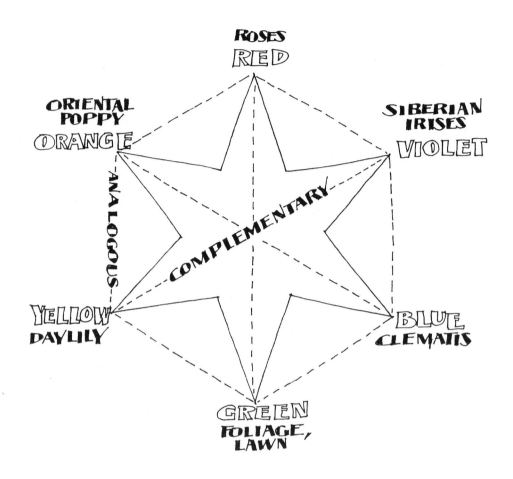

ROSES
RED

ORIENTAL
POPPY
ORANGE

SIBERIAN
IRISES
VIOLET

ANALOGOUS

COMPLEMENTARY

YELLOW
DAYLILY

BLUE
CLEMATIS

GREEN
FOLIAGE,
LAWN

The Color Wheel is a useful tool for showing relationships between colors and for arranging them to good effect.

together—for example, violet and yellow or blue and orange. They are exciting combinations and create strong accents in a garden; however, you might want to use them sparingly to avoid a jarring effect. A calmer, yet pleasing, plan with the warm colors

(red, orange, and yellow) is to use a limited sequence of adjacent tones together—such as yellow, gold, and salmon—in various intensities with emphasis on lighter tones. As warm colors are "advancing" colors (that is, foreshorten the space), they are used with restraint in small areas. In those, you would instead choose the receding cool colors—blues, violets, and greens—which seem to expand the space. Working out color theory with living plants, and even with cut flowers in a vase, is a complex business. It requires knowledge of when things bloom and what to expect from them. It is part of the challenge and the reward of flower gardening.

Bold-foliaged plants are helpful for texture contrasts and for accents or focal points. Yucca, for example, provides season-long (actually, year-long) service in that way, in addition to its spires of creamy flowers in early summer. In shaded areas, hostas give great bold textural lift, and those with variegated cream or gold touches also help with color. They grow well in the Heartland.

A few seasons of experience are the best guidance in growing and designing with perennial and annual flowers. Each added year will give you new insights and widen your range of possibilities.

ABOUT WILDFLOWER "MEADOW" GARDENS

The idea of planting wildflower "meadow" gardens has grown phenomenally in recent years. It seems based on desire for the natural self-sustaining blend of flowers and grasses that nature sometimes creates in the wild. In part the enthusiasm for meadow gardens might be motivated by revolt against maintaining the monoculture lawn. Seed companies have responded to the demand by marketing wildflower seed mixtures, the best of them consisting of kinds chosen for the region in which they will be sold. Usually they contain at least a

dozen different kinds of seeds, part of them annual types that will come up fast and make an early show the first season and part of them longer-term plants that should live over winter and return the following spring. A few seeds of various grasses are often included to fulfill the meadow expectations of purchasers.

Most of the meadow mixtures on the market should be planted in a sunny area. Purchase ones designated for the central United States, the Midwest, or something similiar, so you know that attention has been paid to including kinds adapted to this region and likely to stay with you for many years, either because they are perennials or because they are self-seeding annual types. Follow the package directions. All will recommend that you till the intended area to remove existing grass or other vegetation before you scatter the seed thinly over the coverage area. For example, an ounce of a realistic mixture for the central United States is expected to cover 440 square feet. To get even distribution, mix the seed into a pint of dry sand or soil before scattering it. Rake lightly to cover and then mulch thinly with shredded bark or other mulch. Also, a light watering might be needed to speed germination.

As seedlings emerge, there will probably be weeds (things you did not plant) among them, but it is best to leave them alone and let nature take its course—at least until the various plants are mature enough to be identified. If tree types come up in your "meadow" you will need to remove them promptly to prevent shading out of the wildflowers. About the only care suggested for such a planting is to mow it in autumn after a hard frost and leave the clippings where they fall. Thus any seeds produced are brought down to the ground where they have a chance to sprout the next spring and thicken the stand.

Public reaction to these wildflower gardens is mixed. They do not have the groomed look of a lawn, and some complaints may be heard about the "weeds." Such a planting always looks better if it is surrounded by a mowed area so the demarcation is clear, and the public understands that you intended to have it this way.

ABOUT HIRING A PROFESSIONAL DESIGNER

A trained, experienced landscape designer can save you lots of time and uncertainty and possibly money as well. It is best if the person you hire has no commercial arrangement with a nursery (as you do not want anyone motivated to "push plants"). Of course, the person should also be thoroughly experienced with your area as to climate, soil, and plant hardiness. Ask to see local examples of his or her garden designs.

If you hire such a professional, explain fully what you want your garden to be and do. If you have special plant enthusiasms such as perennial flowers or a certain type such as daylilies tell the designer so that these plants are prominently worked into the scheme.

Once you adopt the designer's plan, he or she may also be prepared to over-see installation of the garden if you wish. For those who want the garden as soon as possible but who are unsure of their own expertise with plants, the services of the professional are a good idea. Local nurseries usually know of such people in their communities, or you could find them listed under "Landscape Architects or Designers" in the Yellow Pages of directories in larger cities.

You need not "swallow whole" the

Things Nobody Ever Tells You

❧ Daffodils (*Narcissus* species) are among our most reliable and long-lived spring-flowering bulbs, but unlike most they have a "front" and "back." They tend to face the sun, which means that the blooms usually are showiest when viewed from the south. Therefore, when planning bulb layouts, place your daffodils along the north side of east-west paths so the trumpet flowers will not turn their backs on passersby.

❧ Walnut trees are incompatible with certain other plants. The roots release a toxin that adversely affects some kinds, especially tomatoes and their relatives. It is unwise to position a vegetable garden within root reach of a walnut tree. A number of ornamental plants also suffer ill effects from nearby walnuts. On the other hand, grasses do very well around them.

❧ Standard space allowances for home driveways: 10 feet per lane. For entrance-to-home sidewalks: 4 feet minimum. For placement of stepping-stone paths: 2 feet on centers.

professional's entire plan. You can select the parts you really like and reserve the rest. Or adapt your own ideas aroused by the professional's suggestions. By and large, the professional with education and experience is worth his or her pay in saving you from expensive blunders or, worse, dissatisfaction with the resulting garden.

BOOKS ON HOME LANDSCAPING

Many excellent books are available detailing basic guidelines for designing and installing landscapes of home grounds, although they are not particularly directed to the Heartland. Inquire at your public library or at your nearest botanical garden or civic garden center. The following brief list of recommended books was selected as especially appropriate for home gardeners.

Landscaping Your Home, by William R. Nelson, Jr. (Urbana: University of Illinois Press, 1963 and later editions).

Garden Design Illustrated, by John A. Grant and Carol Grant (Portland, Ore.: Timber Press, 1987; reprint of 1954 edition).

All about Landscaping, by Ortho Books Editorial Staff (San Ramon, Calif: Ortho Books, 1989).

New Budget Landscaping, by Carlton B. Lees (New York: Holt, Reinhart and Winston, 1979).

Southwestern Landscaping with Native Plants, by Judith Phillips (Santa Fe: Museum of New Mexico Press, 1987)

CHAPTER FOUR

The Lawn Question

*Environmental concerns have brought
many people across the continent to rethink the
subject of lawns. We in the Heartland
are no exception. In fact, we may be in the
forefront of rethinkers, since we face
chronic summer water shortages. We have
too often seen our green lawns of spring
turn straw-colored in July.*

The concept of the velvety lawn is ingrained in those who inherit Western cultural ideas. We cannot part with it lightly. Lawns have long been the frame and setting for English and European gardens; American gardeners have adopted them as the natural system of things. The lawn is functional as well as decorative. It keeps you out of the mud in wet seasons, free of dust in dry times, cool and clean all summer. It retards soil erosion and runoff and makes a safe and pleasant playground for games and other outdoor activities. Not the least of its virtues, it contributes beauty in itself, especially when it is well maintained.

The question nowadays centers on how perfect the lawn must be and how much of it to have. Particularly in dry Heartland summers when watering restrictions are slapped on and grasses turn brown, we struggle with frustration and even with guilt as we pour on water. Not to be overlooked is the economic fact that a huge service industry revolves around lawn and turf care, reaching right down to neighborhood teenagers who mow lawns as their first jobs.

If you didn't have that space in lawn grasses, what else would you put there? Some have tried paving or graveling, but those ventures are short lived. Paving over tree roots eventually kills the trees, and then the summer sun turns the yard into a broiler. If graveled, the area collects seeds of many kinds that sooner or later sprout, presenting an ongoing weed problem. Some have seized on the meadow idea with wildflowers, a concept not as simple as it

seems. In a variation on this theme, some have created wildlife habitats with berried plants and similar features to attract birds, rabbits, squirrels, and other animals. These interesting alternatives have satisfied some owners and made them gardeners in the process. Many owners do not want their grounds covered by shrubs because of security reasons and because they like some openness.

Small areas are ideal for groundcover plants. This is a diverse group of usually low-growing perennial plants that will blanket the space, giving variety in texture and color to the landscape. As they do not need to be mowed, they are relatively low in maintenance once established. (See Chapter Eight for more on this category of plants to substitute for lawns.)

Most municipalities enforce codes favoring lawns and discouraging high grasses or "weeds" (wildflowers?) in the belief that such conditions are trash catchers, possible fire hazards, and a threat to the safety and welfare of the community. History probably justifies this stance, although many imaginative home owners with unconventional ideas of how they want to plant their grounds condemn such ordinances and want them changed.

All these considerations underlie our thoughts on lawns as we cast about for alternatives to the manicured turf. We search for something as readily maintained, as cool, safe, quiet, and serviceable, and as pleasing in the landscape. Until the time comes—if it comes—when summer watering of lawns is regularly curtailed and other

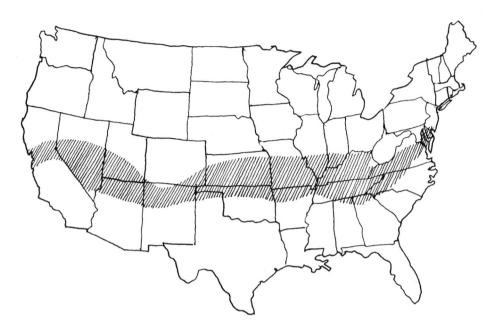

A transition zone crosses the southern third of the Heartland where winters are too cold for warmth-needing grasses and summers are too hot for the best performance of cool-favoring kinds.

maintenance methods (such as using herbicides to get rid of weeds) are restricted, most owners will probably go on keeping fine lawns.

They might strike a compromise by dividing their space as golf courses do, into low- and high-upkeep zones—with a perimeter (the "rough") mowed higher and less often, allowing some diversity (weeds) to the area if within limits, and left unwatered. The high-upkeep lawn zone, equivalent to greens and fairways, would be restricted to such vital but smaller areas as entrance courts and borders of outdoor living areas.

When dedicated gardeners under-

take projects, they usually want to achieve the best results they can. Therefore, I provide in this chapter state-of-the-art recommendations for creating and keeping good lawns. Having stated the pros, cons, and possibilities of Heartland lawns in the future, I leave the final decisions to you.

WHAT KIND OF GRASS SHALL IT BE?

Not long ago it was a foregone conclusion that lawns in the Heartland would consist of bluegrass in the northern parts and probably zoysia or Bermuda in the southern parts. Today we have a wider range of choices in grasses to match our conditions and purposes.

Across the southern part, approximately south of the thirty-ninth parallel, runs a transition zone too cold in winter for best performance of warmth-needing grasses and too hot in summer for cool-favoring kinds (see the map on page 37). True, there are many instances of crossovers, but not without climate-related problems.

The five main seed-started Heartland lawn grasses are Kentucky bluegrass, turf-type tall fescues, fine (or red) fescues, buffalo grass, and perennial ryegrass. Our two main kinds started from plugs or sprigs are Bermuda grass and zoysia.

KENTUCKY BLUEGRASS (*Poa pratensis*) is available in a number of named strains (varieties)—for example, 'Adelphi,' 'Classic,' 'Glade,' 'Merit,' and 'Sydsport.' The list changes year by year. Many experts recommend using mixtures of two or three different strains rather than a single kind to widen tolerances against diseases or other difficulties. Old-fashioned "common" Kentucky bluegrass, which is more or less a "field run" harvest from plants not of any particular improved variety, has inherent genetic spread and is often recommended for its health and utility as well as economy. For shaded areas, a different species of bluegrass, *Poa trivialis*, has long been used; recently an improved variety, 'Sabre,' was introduced and can be found in mixtures for shady lawns. 'Sabre' is also used as a winter grass for overseeding dormant Bermuda grass in southern areas.

PERENNIAL RYEGRASS (*Lolium perenne*) has been much improved. The more recent strains, such as 'Manhattan,' give a richer green color, finer texture, and more even appearance when mowed than older strains. Even so, there are better grasses for our permanent lawns. The speed with which perennial ryegrass germinates and grows makes it a good choice for temporary repair of areas that have been disturbed, as for excavations. It is a bunch grass and does not tiller to form a sod, so thin or bare spots require overseeding to fill in. It is one of the few grasses that establish well from spring seeding, although September is the ideal time. Use perennial rye to get a "quick fix" cover, especially when you need it in spring time, but do not expect it to become the permanent lawn of your dreams. You can also use it as a "nurse grass" mixed with Kentucky bluegrass (one part rye to four parts bluegrass).

TURF-TYPE TALL FESCUES (*Festuca arundinacea*) are called turf type to distinguish them from the coarser, older K-31 or Alta tall fescues commonly used for pastures, roadsides, and athletic fields. The finer-textured turf-type tall fescues, fairly recent developments, can also take summer heat and drought without browning. Some of the current varieties are 'Houndog,' 'Rebel' and 'Galway.' Dwarfer varieties recently introduced include 'Twilight' and 'Shortstop.' As these fescues are naturally clump forming, they have not usually been mixed with other types of grasses in lawns but instead have been used in solid stands. The newer turf-type varieties do not clump as conspicuously as the older kinds such as K-31. Therefore, today it is common practice to mix some of the new varieties together at planting time for greater genetic diversity. Do not mix them with the old clump-forming varieties. These fescues are perfectly winter hardy throughout our region. So far they seem disease and insect resistant. They tolerate shade and stay green into early winter.

FINE FESCUES (*Festuca rubra* and *Festuca ovina*) have been developed in improved varieties that are often included in lawn seed blends because of their shade and drought tolerance. Their fine texture merges well with bluegrass, and since seed comes up quickly, the plantlets help the slower bluegrass get established. Fine fescue seed is generally offered only in prepackaged mixtures. A typical good mixture blended for light shade may contain 40 percent or more of improved fine fescue. Sow such mixtures at rates given on the package.

BUFFALO GRASS (*Buchloe dactyloides*) is a tough, undemanding native short grass from the High Plains. It makes a low fine-textured gray-green sod that withstands heat, cold, and drought unassisted. It tolerates mowing and quite a lot of traffic but not shade. It could well be considered for covering sunny areas where watering is impossible and maintenance is low. Improved seed, treated to give a high rate of germination, is now available. Another recent development has been introduction of a vegetatively propagated variety, 'Prairie,' with promising qualities as a lawn grass.

Buffalo is a warm-season grass that does not green up until about tulip time or later; but then it grows fast in a running habit and needs no fertilizer or watering. Plant it in late spring after the soil is warm, about when you would set out tomatoes. Though occurring naturally mostly west of the one-hundredth meridian, buffalo grass will grow throughout the Heartland in dry, well-drained places—the very conditions that stress most other grasses. It should be used more, in ways and places that show off its special qualities. If in poorly drained soil or if kept too moist, it thins out and is overtaken by weeds. It is slow to establish from seed and faster from sod or plugs where such are available. Plant seed on prepared soil at the rate of ½ pound pure live seed (abbreviated PLS on labels) per 1,000 square feet. Usually this means using nearly double that much as it comes from the bag (almost 1 pound per 1,000 square feet) to allow for the presence of chaff and nonviable seeds in the overall seed lot as sold.

Pure live seed is equal to the percent of pure seed multiplied by the percent of germination. For example, if the label shows that the seed lot consists of 80 percent pure seed, and the germination is 75 percent, then .75 × 80 = 60 percent PLS. Seeds of native grasses that cannot be cleaned entirely of their husks, fluff, or other chaff are usually sold under this formula so the buyer knows what he or she is getting.

Cover buffalo seed with soil ½ inch deep and firm it by pressing or rolling to assure good contact. If weather is dry at seeding time and thereafter, water the area to keep it moist until seedlings show (in about two weeks) and again every few days for another fortnight as roots develop. Once established, buffalo grass needs no watering.

Keep it mowed at about 1½ inches for good appearance. It should not need mowing often.

BERMUDA GRASS (*Cynodon dactylon*), an Old World native, is widely used across the South; some forms of it are winter hardy well into Zone 5 (down to about -15 degrees). A warm-season grass, it turns tawny brown in autumn and does not green up again until midspring. Bermuda is usually not seeded but instead is plugged or sprigged into place to assure that the resulting lawn has the same good qualities of the superior parent varieties, which are sterile (seedless) hybrids. These plants spread by runners, forming a dense drought- and heat-resistant cover. Bermuda can be mowed as closely as 1½ inches. It is used most often in lawns along the southern parts of the Heartland. As a low-maintenance, self-sufficient turf it might be used more than it is, except for its reputation as an invasive spreader that creeps into flower beds, through fences, and over to neighbors' yards. It is unsuited for shade. A recent development in Bermudas is a seed variety, 'Guymon,' which promises improved lawn-grass qualities.

ZOYSIA JAPONICA is a warm-season grass introduced from Asia that has had heavy promotion and wide use, especially the variety 'Meyer.' In the Heartland, it is more appropriate in the south. It spreads by creeping stems just beneath the ground surface, forming a dense sod that is relatively weed free, seldom requires watering (after established), and needs mowing less frequently than bluegrass. The turf effect is deep green, dense, and luxuriant. It turns brown with autumn's first frosts, remaining so until oaks leaf out in spring. Zoysia lawns are started by planting growing plugs of it in spring. Depending on the length of growing seasons, it needs two to three years to fill in entirely from plugs set about 12 inches apart. It does not thrive in shade. In the Heartland, zoysia lawns are usually fertilized twice in the growing season—first in early May and again in early August—using a high-nitrogen lawn fertilizer such as 10-6-4 at about 20 pounds per 1,000 square feet each time. Mow zoysia at 1½ inches. As the clippings resist decay, they tend to build up a thatch, which may need to be removed by power raking early each summer, about June. The grass suffers less injury at this time than if it is power raked earlier at green-up time, once a widespread practice.

GROUNDWORK FOR LAWNS

It can truthfully be said of lawns anywhere, and not just in our region, that effort spent on ground preparation pays off in a more successful lawn. Grade the soil to the right slopes with no humps or low spots. Remove debris—no buried boards, roofing, stumps, cans. If no topsoil is left after grading, the easiest plan is to buy enough, from a reliable source, to cover your grade 5 to 6 inches deep. The alternative is to improve the soil you have by adding lots of organic matter. Compost, peat moss, leaf mold, sewage sludge—anything that will improve the humus content will help. If you are working with a poor-draining clay, generously add sand

How Grasses Rank in Drought Tolerance[a]

Buffalo ....Excellent
Bermuda ....Excellent
Zoysia ....Excellent
Fine fescue ....Good
Turf-type tall fescue ....Fair
Kentucky bluegrass ....Fair
Perennial ryegrass ....Fair

Recommended Summer Mowing Heights in the Heartland (in inches)

Bermuda 1½
Buffalo 1½
Fine fescue 2
Kentucky bluegrass 3
Perennial ryegrass 2½
Turf-type tall fescue 3
Zoysia 1½

Recommended Seeding Rates per 1,000 Square Feet (in pounds)

Buffalo ½–1
Fine fescue 3–4
Kentucky bluegrass 1½–2
Kentucky bluegrass–
 fine fescue mixture 2–3
Perennial ryegrass 5–6
Turf-type tall fescue 7–8

[a]Arranged in order of tolerance

and/or vermiculite or perlite. This is a good time to get soil tested so you know what fertilizer is needed. Add it now and work it in with the final tilling. A rotary tiller is ideal for this preparation. Finally, rake it all to a smooth, firm seedbed charged with nutrients and organic material.

SEEDING

Mid-August through September is ideal for seeding lawns in the Heartland. A few showers often fall around mid-September to provide needed moisture for germination. Cooler days then favor grass growth.

Measure the area you want to seed so you know how much to use. Write this figure down for future reference. See chart for the seeding rates of different kinds purchased as bulk seeds. Commercially packaged mixtures should show seeding rates on the box or bag. Weigh out the proper amount for the size of the area and divide it into two equal lots. Whether you use a mechanical seeder or spread the seed by hand, go over the area twice, traveling the second time at right angle to the first for even coverage. For larger seeds like tall fescues, rake lightly to cover; small seeds like bluegrass should not need covering. On slopes it pays to install a landscape netting to anchor both seeds and soil while grass establishes. Cheesecloth is a suitable substitute. Landscape netting is sold by garden supply stores.

WATERING NEW SEEDINGS

For the critical time while grass germinates and gets its roots down, approximately the first month, you'll need to attend to watering faithfully. Unless you get rains, daily watering with a fine spray from hose or sprinkler is essential. The surface should never dry out. As soon as grass is 1 inch high, you can relax a bit, but still don't let new grass completely dry out or you will lose it. Shortening days in autumn work in your favor in this—an important reason why fall is by far the best time for seeding.

MOWING NEW SEEDINGS

As soon as the new grass blades reach 2½ inches, mowing can begin. Mowing encourages the grass to thicken and spread out. If winter weeds begin to show (chickweed or henbit), wait until the following spring to control them with lawn weed killer rather than risk damaging the young grass.

LAWNS FROM SPRIGS, PLUGS, OR SOD

Bermuda grass and zoysia lawns that have been started from small vegetative plugs and turf sod of any sort should have the same soil preparation as described for seeding. For these, however, the work is done in spring instead of fall. It is important to allow the plants plenty of time to establish roots before going into winter. Ask the nursery where you obtain the plugs for a "plugger" tool to open planting holes. Plugs are usually spaced 12 inches each way, but can go closer for faster fill-in if you want. Count on two summers for plugged zoysia lawns to fill in. Bermuda sprigs usually cover a little faster; of course, the farther south, the quicker they grow.

CARING FOR ESTABLISHED LAWNS

Mowing, controlling weeds, fertilizing on schedule, and watering when dry are the four basic parts of maintaining lawns. There is yet a fifth job, raking, if your lawn becomes submerged under tree leaves every autumn. Where they collect heavily, leaves need to be removed or they will smother the grass.

MOWING. The chart on page 41 shows recommended mowing heights for different lawn grasses in the Heartland. The hotter our summers, the higher we let the grass grow, with the objective of having extra growth to protect and shade the soil and discourage weeds. This principle applies mainly to cool-season types—bluegrass, fescues, perennial rye grass. The rule of thumb is to time the mowing so you remove no more than one-third the length of the blade. For example, if you intend to mow bluegrass to 2 inches, do the job as soon as the blades reach 3 inches. If this rule is observed, it should be unnecessary to catch and remove the clippings. Catching and bagging clippings is not only a time-consuming and laborious part of the mowing job, it also raises environmental concerns about wasted energy and space in landfills. When you consider that the clippings, if rightly handled, could be "recycled" as compost to the benefit of all—including the lawn—it is impossible to justify hauling them off. At the very least, you could spread them out to dry for a day, and then distribute them around the garden where mulch is needed. The answer to the whole problem is merely to mow at the proper time and height, so there will be no "hay crop" to gather.

As days grow shorter in September, lower the mowing height a bit at a time (down to 2 inches for bluegrass and tall fescue) as autumn leaves are coming down. Be sure to keep your mower blade sharp. Dull mowers fray grass edges and discolor them as if they were diseased. Zoysia and tall fescues especially have tough leaves that require a sharp mower.

CONTROLLING WEEDS. Weeds are inevitable as nature works to restore diversity to the monoculture of a fine lawn. Dandelions, henbit, chickweed, plantain, shepherd's purse, buckhorn plantain, and knotweed are the main broadleaf invaders of lawns in the Heartland. The worst wild grass invaders are crabgrass, goosegrass, and foxtail.

The broadleaf types (meaning they are not in the grass family) are susceptible to chemical control with 2,4-D type herbicides, whose great advantage is that they are selective and do not kill the grass. The great *disadvantage* of these 2,4-D type herbicides is that they do not distinguish one broadleaf plant from another and thus are capable of killing or damaging your (or your neighbors') roses, grapes, tomatoes, or other sensitive and desirable garden plants if any of the spray or fumes reaches them. If you are unfamiliar with using this herbicide or are unwilling to take time to read the label over and over and follow it carefully, it is better to hire a commercial lawn firm to come spray your broadleaf weeds. Those people are experts in how to do it right.

In the Heartland, October and November are good months to spray with 2,4-D for overwintering lawn weeds such as dandelions and chickweed. At that quieter season those growing weeds are more susceptible than the maturing trees, shrubs, and other desirable garden plants—so the possibility of accidental damage is reduced. There should then be no need for spring spraying.

The grassy weeds, the worst of which are annuals that come up from seed each spring, are easy to control in lawns by using one of the chemical seed germination preventers called preemergents. Garden supply stores offer these as granular preparations that you apply to your lawn with a lawn spreader in late March or early April. Follow directions on the bag. If you can prevent crabgrass or foxtail from going to seed for two or three consecutive years, seeds remaining may be so few that further treatments are not needed.

Two other weeds not fitting either of the previous categories come up in Heartland lawns and cause anguish to their owners. The first, appearing from late winter through spring, is wild onion. The other is called "nut grass" or "water grass," even though it is really a sedge rather than a grass. It comes up after the soil is warm and spreads underground by rhizomatous runners that produce bulblets ("nuts").

Wild onion shows up in bright green clumps while grass is still tan and dormant. Digging it out is the surest control. Be sure to get bulbs and all and dispose of them in the trash. Do not put them on the compost or you will inadvertently spread them. Kleen-up or Roundup (glyphosate herbicide products) in repeated applications will kill not only wild onion but also surrounding lawn grass if any touches the grass plants. Instead of spraying, you can carefully "wipe" the solution on, using rubber gloves and a sponge but don't spill any on the grass or it will be killed in that spot.

You can also use Kleenup or Roundup in the same way for nut grass (nutsedge), wiping it on to avoid getting any on desirable grass. It is hopeless to try to pull or dig out nutsedge, because the nutlets attached to the roots will break off and remain, only to send up new growth.

FERTILIZING. Regular boosting with nitrogen fertilizer is a key practice in keeping good lawns. The total-care lawn services usually apply fertilizer in liquid form. Their tank truck arrives containing a fertilizer-water solution blended for the type of lawn and the time of year. The operator sprays it on, and the grass is instantly foliar fed. At garden stores and catalog suppliers, you can get hose-end feeders with the soluble fertilizers to deliver a similar foliar feeding in spray-on form. This may be the wave of the future in lawn feeding.

Most do-it-yourselfers today still apply lawn fertilizer as a dry granular product put on with a drop-through or broadcast spreader. This method is surely easier for calculating just how much you are putting on. Lawn experts fairly well agree that cool-season lawns (bluegrass, fescues, perennial ryegrass)

should get 3 to 4 pounds of *actual* nitrogen per 1,000 square feet per year. The word "actual" requires explanation. Remembering that nitrogen is the first number on the bag and supposing that the N-P-K formula is 10-6-4, let us see how much actual nitrogen is in a 40 pound bag of the mixture. Ten percent times 40 pounds comes out to 4 actual pounds. The 6 percent phosphorus and 4 percent potash make up another 10 percent, or 4 pounds. The remaining contents, 32 pounds, are "carrier," an inert medium that makes the chemicals easy to spread.

So, in that bag of fertilizer is enough nitrogen for 1,000 square feet of lawn for one year. But to put it all on at once would overdose and damage the grass. The limit is about 1 pound per 1,000 square feet per application. Therefore, we spread the contents of the bag over a wider area, usually as recommended on the bag—perhaps 4,000 square feet—and plan to repeat applications three more times, totaling four, and bringing the year's application up to requirement. The nitrogen is the most important bit of information to know about any balanced fertilizer, one containing all three of the essential elements.

Lawn experts are less in agreement as to when fertilizer should be applied to do the most good. Cool-season lawns are fertilized differently from warm-season ones. It is not considered a good idea to fertilize bluegrass or fescue lawns in the hottest months of summer (June, July, and August). Assuming you make four applications, you might time them as three in autumn—September, October, and November—and one in March. If you limit the applications to three, they could be about Labor Day, Columbus Day, and Thanksgiving Day. Or the third feeding can come in early March to give grass a spring boost, which is especially helpful if you have a tree-shaded lawn where you want to get grass going well before tree-root competition hits its peak.

It is possible to maintain a cool-season lawn such as bluegrass with less fertilizer, perhaps as little as 2 or even just 1 pound a year of actual nitrogen per 1,000 square feet. The lawn will not be as dark green, dense, or attractive; but on the plus side it will need less mowing. If you can feed it only once a year, do it in September.

Warm-season grasses (zoysia, Bermuda, and buffalo) are dormant for five to six months, during which time of course fertilizer is of no use to them. Buffalo is a low-maintenance grass and needs no fertilizer at all. Zoysia is usually fertilized moderately after green-up starts in spring, again in six weeks, and a final time six weeks later. Too heavy fertilization results in thatch buildup on zoysia and subsequent dead patches. Bermuda, like buffalo, can be kept at a low-maintenance level with little or no fertilizer, but it responds to feeding with greener color and more vigor. Fertilize after first green-up in May, again mid-June, and a final time in mid-August.

MAINTENANCE WATERING. Established lawns of bluegrass, turf-type tall fescues, perennial ryegrass, and to some extent zoysia usually need watering through our summers if they are to be kept to picture-book perfection. The rule for bluegrass, and pretty much for the rest, is 1 inch of moisture total per week—whether it falls from the sky or is supplied or supplemented by you. July and August are normally dry months in the Heartland. There have been dry periods of many weeks, often accompanied by heat in the high 90s or more. Coping with these elements is a test of resolve. It is why so many fine lawns in the Heartland are equipped with watering systems automated to provide the needed water on a predetermined schedule without the owner giving it a thought or lifting a hand. Without supplementary watering, cool-season grasses (bluegrass and fescue) often go into summer dormancy through the prolonged hot dry weather. First the grass darkens to blue green. When you walk over it, your footprints show. Growth ceases and color gradually fades from the blades, leaving them tawny brown. While the appearance of the lawn in this state suggests total disaster, all is not lost. This summer dormancy is nature's way of going "on hold" until better times. Even though it looks dead, the sod retains a spark of life; when cooler nights and a few cloudy days finally arrive with refreshing showers, green begins to show. Within two weeks the lawn may be as fresh and green as it was in May.

Certainly the desertlike look of a summer-dormant lawn is not beautiful, but recognizing the condition is better than thinking the lawn is dead. When the lawn is in this state, protect it from foot traffic and any heavy use. Avoid the temptation to sprinkle it sporadically, for to do so will encourage crabgrass to overrun it, which may happen anyway. Mowing is seldom needed during summer dormancy but weeds such as crabgrass should be cut and prevented from seeding if possible. When a summer-dormant lawn begins to revive in fall, let it grow a little taller than normal before mowing and then set your mower to cut as high as possible.

Other rules for lawn watering: Thorough soakings are better than frequent light sprinklings. Aim to apply 1 inch of water at a time (this means letting the sprinkler run two hours before moving it). Early morning is the most efficient time to water, because evaporation is lower, and the safest from the disease standpoint, because the wetness is of short duration.

DISEASES AND INSECTS

Grasses get their share of maladies, both diseases and injurious insects. Some horticultural scientists have made distinguished careers in learning how to combat them. Professional turf keepers use spray-on fungicides to subdue leaf spot and other diseases and insecticides to control insect outbreaks such as sod webworms and chinch bugs. In the home garden, however, one wonders how far it is practical to go in trying to treat these lawn problems, especially in light of environmental concerns. The positive steps of providing a good root base for the lawn, planting the best available varieties for our climate, and carrying out regular good maintenance will do as much as anything to neutralize the harm inflicted by disease or insect organisms.

The current trend toward lower

Things Nobody Ever Tells You

❧ At the very beginning, calculate the square footage of each separate area of your lawn and then the total. Write these figures down where you can refer to them whenever you buy or apply fertilizer or lawn-grass seed.

❧ A fast way to measure a ground area is to step it off. First measure how far you travel with each average step. (Men average 2½ feet; women average 2.) Walk the length and width of the area, counting your steps. Simple multiplication does the rest: first convert steps to feet and then multiply the width by the length, which gives you the square footage of the area. It will be almost as accurate as measuring by tape.

❧ Keep mower blades sharp. Otherwise, you'll beat grass off instead of cut it, and it will show in the bleached, drying shreds at the tips. Sharp blades are particularly important if you have zoysia or tall fescue—both of which are tough to cut.

❧ Fertilizer corrodes anything metallic except stainless steel. Always wash out your spreading equipment after using fertilizer in it or you will soon need new ones.

maintenance and reduced watering of lawns could actually pay dividends in slowing disease and insect damage. Grasses not kept to unnatural levels of lush growth are not such easy targets for disease spores and insect explosions.

RENOVATING LAWNS

Almost every Heartland cool-season lawn is ready for some degree of renovation by late August or September. Unfortunately, the lawns may be more ready than their owners, whose enthusiasm wanes over the long hot summer. Early fall is by far the best time for renovating lawns, just as it is the best for starting new ones. Early spring, when most owners decide to renovate, is also a possible time, although second best. However, for renovating zoysia and other warm-season grasses, spring is the only time. Low-maintenance buffalo and Bermuda lawns rarely need anything in the way of renovation. But in the Heartland, zoysia often does.

Aeration, fertilizing, and sometimes reseeding are key elements in reviving a tired lawn. Some lawns that have accumulated a lot of thatch (the stemmy debris that does not break down readily) may need core aeration (done with a machine that punches holes that allow water and fertilizer to penetrate) or verticutting (done with a machine that slices through and loosens the material so you can rake it up). Close inspection of the lawn will tell you if this is necessary. If the thatch is so thick water doesn't penetrate and seed wouldn't contact the ground when you plant it, then one of these treatments is probably in order. You can rent machines to do them. In urban areas you can hire out the whole process—not a bad idea for such a dirty job.

After you have treated the surface so you can see the ground again, it is ready for fertilizer. Then, where grass is thin and sparse or in dead areas, overseed it. Use seed of the same kind, and variety if you know it, as your lawn. This avoids a patchy appearance.

In the case of zoysia lawns, larger bare spots may need to be replugged (done only in spring); for this I recommend that you obtain fresh plugs from a grass nursery rather than borrow from elsewhere in your own lawn, which may harbor some sort of disease organism that killed the patch in the first place.

CHAPTER FIVE

Your Garden of Vegetables and Herbs

*Vegetable gardens were among
the first things planted by westering pioneers,
but theirs were not the first vegetable
gardens of the Heartland. The prehistoric
inhabitants of the region, and the immigrant
tribes after them, grew corn, squash, and
other crops long before settlers of European ancestry arrived in the 1800s. It was good
land then also, providing well for those
who made it their home and
came to know it.*

The elements of successful food gardens in the Heartland are the same today as they were for earlier gardeners: a sunny, fairly level site with available water and away from tree roots and areas susceptible to flooding; a place convenient to tend and protect; a friendly, tillable soil. If you expect to grow vegetables only for your family's use, the space need not be large. About 500 square feet per person can provide a full spectrum of harvests from asparagus to zucchini, with plenty to give away.

If possible, lay out the garden so rows run north and south. This arrangement gives maximum light to the plants. If the garden area slopes, arrange to contour it to prevent washing or too-rapid runoff. Plan to put tall growers such as okra and corn toward the north to avoid shading lower crops; this will be more important late in the season as shadows lengthen than it is in high summer. If you have mechanical cultivating equipment, allow space to run your machine, with rows separated enough for clearance and turning room at the ends.

Do you need to fence the garden? There may be good reasons for doing so—roving animals, children, intruders. If so, put up the fence at the beginning, with a gate wide enough for your wheelbarrow, garden cart, tiller, or whatever else you use.

Do you plan to elevate the beds for drainage, access, appearance, or higher production? If so, do this also at the start. There are several approaches to raising beds, ranging from temporary to permanent. Landscape timbers or old railroad ties are popular for framing permanently raised beds. Avoid newer ties, as they may contain enough creosote to affect plants; old weathered ties present no problem. Some gardeners temporarily raise beds by shoveling out soil from intervening paths onto the adjoining area so the planted (raised) area is elevated a few inches. In wet springs this technique proves very helpful, preserving seedlings that might otherwise drown. Ordinarily, raised beds are made about 3 or 4 feet wide, so middles can be reached without stepping into them. Seeds are sown broadcast rather than in rows; transplants are set in checkerboard fashion. Lettuces, onions, carrots, beets, and turnips are a few of many vegetables lending themselves to this strategy.

The gardener by his or her own efforts can improve or preserve the goodness of the soil. (See Chapter Two for general recommendations on soil improvement.) In an area like a vegetable garden where you will be sowing seeds over an extended interval in spring, a certain amount of tillage is necessary so the soil is receptive to the seeds and so you can open drills (seed rows) for kinds needing them. Tillage can be done in either spring or fall. If your soil is clay or heavy silt, it is best to plow (turn) or hand spade it in autumn after crops are cleared off and leave it rough over winter. Use the occasion to dig or turn under any leaves or old mulch to add organic matter. Freezes and thaws will mellow it and snow melt will sink into the hollows and air spaces. By the time early spring seeds such as peas should be sowed, you can have the seedbed ready merely by raking it. Fall plowing or spading thus saves time and frustration early in spring when heavy soil is too wet to be worked. If you have a fast-draining sandy, light soil, on the other hand, you have much wider latitude and can probably run a tiller through it early in spring to prepare ground for those first things planted. In any case, do not overdo the tilling. Overtilling damages texture, creates a "pan" under the tine level, and leads to erosion.

CHOOSE WHAT TO GROW

The most fun in laying out the garden is deciding what to grow. For peak pleasure, get out catalogs and work on this some stormy January night. When dreams give way to reality, base your selections on growing kinds you and your family like to eat and will use. After you list these, the rest consists of arranging and scheduling them.

With minor exceptions, we can grow almost anything in the catalog. No place on earth can grow tomatoes, corn, potatoes, green and lima beans, peppers, melons, pumpkins, okra, sweet potatoes, cucumbers, or squash better than the Heartland. Among herbs, our notable successes are with basils of all kinds, fennel, dill, chives (and any other kind of onion), summer savory, sage, thymes, borage, and all sorts of mints.

Our hot summers work against some of the traditional vegetables of European origin—cauliflower, broccoli, brussels sprouts, cabbages, peas, spinach, and head lettuce. The "cole" crops and others, developed in regions of cool, steady temperatures suffer in the blasts of hot Heartland winds from April on. Nevertheless, it is possible to grow them and gather edible harvests—though they may not reach the superb quality they would in a more suitable place, at least as spring crops. We can do better growing some of them in fall, when winds are quieter and temperatures steadier. For example, at that season we can grow excellent Chinese cabbage.

Kinds *not* suited to our region are broad (fava) beans (our summers are too hot for them) and globe artichokes (they do not survive our winters in the open). Radicchio, the red-heading chicories, are difficult. If planted in spring, they bolt to seed or collapse when the weather gets hot. Midsummer sowing for late fall harvests might be better. Celery generally makes a poor showing and is scarcely worth the effort.

In planning, think about possible "second cropping." Our seasons are long enough to permit some succession crops. Beans can follow where spring lettuce and radishes come off. Kale or turnips can occupy space where potatoes or peas were harvested. Where space is scarce, things can be combined: early lettuce and spinach can snuggle up to tomatoes or peppers and be out of the way by the time the larger-growing plants begin to expand. Squash hills can be seeded into a patch of early sweet corn to take it over after the corn comes off.

PERENNIAL VEGETABLES

Three worthwhile perennial vegetables for our gardens are asparagus, rhubarb, and Japanese bunching (winter) onions. All can remain in the same spot for a decade or more, so place them at one side of the garden where they are out of the way of other activities. All should be in a well-drained spot, especially the rhubarb. As it takes time for them to become productive, particularly asparagus, they should be the first things planted.

ASPARAGUS is probably the most permanent, carefree, and welcome vegetable you will ever plant. Those first tender spears of April fully justify whatever effort went into the planting. Choose a location in full sun where water drains through or off quickly. Improve the ground by digging compost or peat in deeply. A dozen plants from the nursery will plant a 3-by-10-foot bed, enough for most home needs. In this area, open two wide rows, 18 inches apart. Make each planting trench 6 inches deep and about the same width, so the roots may be spread out at that level. Space the crowns (bud or growth end up) about 18 inches apart zigzag style up each trench; then fill in soil over them. Let the plants grow uncut the season of planting. The next spring you can harvest spears the first two or three weeks, then allow following ones to grow. From the third year on, you can reap a full harvest, taking the spears as they appear, up to early June. Then let plants "go to fern," maturing their tops and restoring strength for the next season. If volunteer seedlings, from seeds dropped by mature plants, appear in your planting, pull them out while they are small. Otherwise, seedlings will crowd the original plants and quality suffers. Hybrid all-male (seedless) varieties of asparagus have recently been developed and are worth seeking out, as they circumvent the problem of volunteers. They are also highly productive. Harvest asparagus spears by cutting or snapping them off above ground level.

RHUBARB comes from a cooler part of the world than ours and thus suffers from the summer heat and drought, especially in our southern areas. But it comes up in spring before almost anything else and yields the very first dessert crop you can harvest. Spring pickings are better in quality than those of later summer. "Pie plant," an old name for rhubarb, derives from its providing the first "fruit" pies of the year. Plant rhubarb crowns in early spring, 3 feet apart in well-tilled, rich soil, bud end up, covering the crown 1 inch deep. A place in full sun is best, but in our hottest areas, afternoon shade is acceptable. Provide extra water through droughts, especially while new plants get established. Let plants grow without harvesting the first year. As rhubarb grows, it sends up bloom stems bearing fluffy white flowers. Remove these bloom heads as soon as you see them, as they divert vigor from the rest of the plant, the part you really want. Every third or fourth year, as crowns become crowded and leaf and stalk sizes dwindle, divide the plants. Do this in early spring. Either lift the entire crowns and cut them into quarters for replanting, or slice down through the crown in the ground with a sharp spade and pry off and remove one side of it. After this renewal, the stems will be larger and more vigorous. Harvest rhubarb stalks by breaking them out from the base rather than cutting them. Trim off leaf parts immediately to curtail wilting. Rhubarb leaves, incidentally, are poisonous, so don't be tempted to add them to anything you plan to eat, even as a garnish. The stem part is edible and delicious when cut into short segments and cooked briefly with sweetening.

JAPANESE BUNCHING, OR WINTER, ONIONS are seldom seen today but grandmother knew and relied on these plants for flavoring and something fresh to eat even in the depth of winter anytime they could be pulled or dug. They make scallions (known to older gardeners as "green onions"), never bulbs. Clumps increase rapidly in summer and may be divided. These perennial onions require little space. Compared with the mild, seed-grown scallions of spring, their flavor is strong, but when added to soups, casseroles, meats, or salads, they are as good as any onion and are always conveniently at hand in your garden. Plant the seed in spring, and you will have plants from that summer on. Keep seed heads cut off (they mature in early summer) to prevent unwanted seedlings from becoming weeds. For sources, consult catalogs for "bunching" or "evergreen" onions. They are winter hardy in our region.

ANNUAL VEGETABLES
SPRING THROUGH FALL
The chart on page 65 gives the basic planting sequence of our main vegetables. Study the maps in Chapter

One showing the last expectable spring frosts and first expectable fall frosts. From this you can learn the usual number of days in your growing season. This information is important in selecting varieties, as many of them are rated in catalogs or on seed packets according to the number of days they need from seed to maturity. There is no use in planting some variety of cantaloupe or squash, for example, that will not mature within the remaining length of your growing season.

Each new spring you'll understand better how to synchronize your garden with our climate. It helps to keep a journal of significant weather events (unusually high or low temperatures, droughts, floods, and storms). Also jot down dates you planted things for future reference.

The earliest vegetables are peas, radishes, lettuces, cabbage, onion sets, and potatoes, which need a cool growing season to mature before summer heat strikes. For these, much depends on your ability to prepare soil. Begin in February to watch for opportunities, and be ready to seize any dry, open interval for whatever ground work needs to be done. Winter is sure to revisit in March, but by midmonth, if the ground is ready, planting should be possible for peas and potatoes through most of the Heartland. You need not leave everything to chance. You can warm the soil or dry it slightly by covering it with a plastic tarp (black is best for this) for two to three weeks. Some gardeners install temporary sun traps (for example, tunnel cloches of clear or translucent plastic sheeting or spunbonded "floating" garden fabrics) over the intended area. (See more about these on pages 186–87.)

Neither potato sets nor pea seeds—nor any other kind of vegetable—will begin to grow until soil warms to a certain temperature. Little is gained and all can be lost by planting too far ahead in a cold, slow, wet spring. Potato sets may rot and fail entirely in such conditions. So also may too early sowings of beets, lettuces, spinach, parsnips, chard, and others in the "early" category.

Cabbage transplants, if "hardened off" (subjected ahead of time to outdoor weather), can be set out in most of the Heartland from mid-March to mid-April. It is good insurance to install Hotkaps (individual reinforced paper tents) over them; these provide shelter against the icy elements, wind, and even early insects and help plants get established through difficult times. Broccoli and cauliflower transplants can also be set out as early as cabbage and likewise benefit from Hotkap protectors. Remove them as soon as killing frosts seem over.

Extending the growing season in autumn is done much more on an ad hoc basis than similar efforts in spring. As soon as the first fall freeze is forecast, the gardener flies into action to save late harvests of tomatoes, peppers, eggplants, beans, and similar tender kinds that are still bearing. Often two to three more weeks of growing weather will follow that first cold snap, so if protection is successful, you are rewarded by an extended harvest. Many sorts of coverings can be used to hold earth warmth down around the plants—newspapers, bed sheets, plastic sheeting. Coverings that sag from rain or whip in wind may do as much harm as good to the plant beneath. The new feather-light, or "floating," covers allow both moisture and air to penetrate and so get good marks as plant protectors in autumn cold snaps.

In the Heartland, autumn vegetable harvests are the finest of the year in quantity and quality for several reasons. Fall rains have pepped up the plants; longer nights bring cooler temperatures, resulting in greater succulence; and the shortening days send signals to plants that they had better shape up "or else." Particularly good kinds for fall harvests are snap beans, Chinese cabbage (which may be stored in a refrigerator long into winter), most lettuces, summer squashes such as zucchini and golden crookneck or straightneck varieties, spinach (far better now than in spring), kohlrabi, broccoli, beets, and turnips. See the planting sequence chart on page 65 for suggested sowing dates of these for fall crops.

Some vegetables planted in spring have long growth seasons and are normally harvested in late fall or early winter—for example, parsnips, winter squash such as hubbard and butternut, leeks, kale, brussels sprouts, and winter-keeper beets. All do well in Heartland conditions. Parsley reaches its stride in autumn. Leave it in the garden all winter to provide occasional snippets for the cook. Mulch it and the plants may still be alive the next spring.

CARE THROUGH THE
GROWING SEASON

MULCHING. Mulching is the one most effective thing you can do to help vegetables through summer. Apply mulch as soon as plants are well up and growing. Grass clippings from your lawn make good mulch if you first spread them out to dry for a few days. If applied fresh they might ferment and heat, injuring plants. If clippings are from a lawn recently treated with weed killer, allow extra days of airing to be sure any herbicide has dissipated. Shredded leaves or any garden refuse put through a shredder are excellent. Apply mulch thinly at first; build it up as the supply permits.

Mulch preserves soil moisture; inhibits weeds, making cultivation unnecessary; steadies the soil temperature; and in breaking down it builds the organic content of the soil. Also, in a mechanical sense, mulch keeps the garden cleaner and more accessible in wet weather. In our region, mulches also have value as hail insurance—they may not fend off the pelting ice, but they do cushion soil against compaction that usually follows a hailstorm, driving out the air and slowing regrowth. In autumn, dig mulch into the ground to improve organic levels for the future.

CULTIVATING. If you can't mulch, you'll probably cultivate somehow by hoe or tiller to keep weeds down and the soil surface loose. The loosened surface is called a "dust mulch." Although no substitute for a real mulch of organic material, it does hold down weeds, impede soil drying, and steady

soil temperature. Its disadvantage is that you must recultivate after every rain. It also wastes some soil moisture. If you cultivate too deeply or too close to plants, roots may be damaged. Think of cultivation as an alternative or contingency measure when you are unable to lay down a real mulch.

WATERING. Where water is plentiful and you can be lavish, you have a wide range of methods and hardware for applying it. But in most of the Heartland, water is increasingly precious. We look for ways to conserve it. Drip irrigation, a concept and system developed in arid Israel, is a modern method we could well adopt. It uses plastic (polyethylene or polyvinyl chloride [PVC]) tubing and special emitters to deliver small steady amounts of water directly over the root area of target plants. None is wasted to evaporation or runoff. Various hardware items are available for vegetables grown in rows or in other ways. The systems are simple to assemble, and they may be moved out of the way for ground preparation or stored over winter. Although they are expensive, they last for years. Automated controls for self-maintaining programs are also available. Serious gardeners here in the Heartland can profit greatly from the drip irrigation concept and should look into it. The systems are widely available through garden supply catalogs or from local dealers.

Vegetables growing in rows are efficiently watered by the trench method—simply a shallow trench opened with a wheel hoe down the row "middles," with water from the hose started down

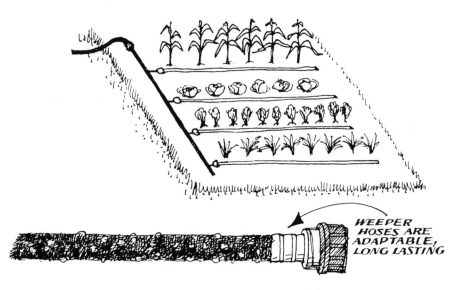

SIMPLE DRIP IRRIGATION SYSTEMS ARE EASY TO ASSEMBLE

WEEPER HOSES ARE ADAPTABLE, LONG LASTING

one end of it. You can guide and extend the stream as the water works along; little is wasted. Weeper or "leaky pipe" hoses also are variations on the trench idea; they are labor saving, movable, and adaptable to slopes.

Avoid overhead sprinkling if you can. Sometimes in early spring it is justified when you need to soften a soil crust to induce seedlings to emerge. But it wastes water by evaporation and by applying it where it is not particularly needed. If you *must* use an overhead sprinkler on your vegetables, observe these rules:

🌢 Sprinkle early in the morning to minimize evaporation and allow drying by noon.

🌢 Run the sprinkler long enough in one place to water thoroughly, then do not repeat until the ground dries.

🌢 Measure the water applied by the

sprinkler: set a straight sided shallow tin can under the spray area and let it collect at least ½ inch before shutting off or moving the sprinkler to another area. This eliminates guesswork.

STAKING/SUPPORTING VEGETABLES. "Indeterminate" (climbing) tomatoes, pole beans, tall-growing peas, and cucumbers are a few of the kinds needing some sort of support, both to aid performance and to save space.

Tomato systems abound, ranging from manufactured supports ("cages"), to homemade wood frames or trellises. Decide first whether you want to prune tomatoes to one stem or allow two or more—or even the full natural growth of the plant. Training to one or a few stems is more work but gains more perfect fruits, and since you can space individual plants closer together, you can get higher production from the given area. Only tomatoes of "indeterminate" type are suitable for training to single stems and staking. Every "sucker" that arises from leaf axils should be pinched out, leaving the main stem to continue upward. Tomatoes trained to single stems this way can be spaced as closely as 18 inches. For these a single pole or two-by-two from a lumberyard will do. Simply tie the main stem to it as it grows upward. Some gardeners use a permanent post-and-wire trellis across the garden, with three horizontal wires and a twine strung from top to bottom above each plant on which the stem is led upward. Most home growers compromise by pruning ("suckering") plants to two or three stems early in the season and then letting them go their destined ways in August. For these the cage supports are best. The "determinate," or bush-type tomatoes, with their naturally low and branching habits, need no staking.

Pole beans form heavy vines that need sturdy support. Three or four six-foot poles of any reasonably straight description should be tied or wired together near the top, tepee style, with the legs spread 3 feet apart for stability. Space seeds around the base of each leg. Or sow seeds in two rows, 30 inches apart, and position the pole tepees along the double rows.

Peas and cucumbers have much smaller tendrils and climb best on woven-wire or string-mesh trellises. Cucumbers make vigorous vines and need a trellis 5 feet high or more. Pea netting can be as low as 36 inches. The main idea in trellising cucumbers is to enable the fruits to hang and thus be straight and symmetrical. Long salad types are the main ones trellised. The mesh should be large enough so you can draw the fruits through in picking from either side. Pickling-type cucumbers are seldom trellised unless the purpose is to save space. Bush-type cucumbers do not lend themselves to trellising.

Basella, or climbing spinach, is a subtropical vine sometimes sold as an ornamental or vegetable novelty. Hot Heartland summers suit it well. Give it a string- or wire-mesh trellis at least 4 feet high. Use basella leaves either in salads or as a briefly cooked pot herb like spinach.

COPING WITH PESTS. Whether in urban or rural areas, a garden with tempting edibles is almost sure to draw wildlife you possibly did not know was

Tomatoes of "indeterminate" type are suited for training to single stems tied to stakes. Every "sucker" that arises at a leaf axil is routinely pinched out, leaving the main stem to continue upward. Don't confuse a "sucker" with bloom stems.

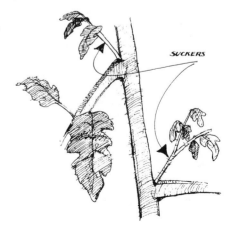

SUCKERS

around—deer, rabbits, squirrels, raccoons, crows, woodchucks, even turtles. In civilized surroundings you cannot resort to force or poisons. First see if it is possible to fence the garden to hold the vandals out. Wire poultry mesh with the bottom edge buried a few inches in the ground is considered the best fencing to keep out rabbits, which are probably the most damaging animals because they are the most numerous.

Repellents are the next weapon, and these occur in wide variety. At your garden store you will find them marketed for repelling rabbits, deer, and squirrels. Some of them contain mainly paradichlorobenzine (pdb), the ingredient of mothballs, so mothballs should do as well, although they probably will not last as long outdoors. Another repellent reliably reported to scare off rabbits and possibly deer is

---

Human hair, swept from barber and beauty shop floors, scares off rabbits and deer most of the growing season. Tie it into small mesh bundles and scatter the bundles throughout the vegetable garden.

human hair, the sweepings of barber or beauty shop floors. Proprietors may save hair for you; only a little is needed. Tie the hair into small net bundles to tuck among plants being victimized. Or in the case of row plants such as beans and peas, merely place tufts of hair along the row and anchor them with a little soil. Bar soap, used by arboretums to repel deer, can work as well in your vegetable garden. Use the motel-size bars *in their wrappers,* drill a hole in the center to thread a string through, and tie them to the fence or stakes where you want deer to turn away. The wrapper enables the soap to last longer; apparently the smell is what spooks animals.

Scarecrows, imitation owls and snakes, and noisy or glittering scare devices such as aluminum pans dangling from stakes are familiar ways of repelling bird pests and animals until the novelty wears off—long enough for seedlings to establish themselves. With low-growing crops such as beets, lettuces, and bush beans, the new lightweight row covers spread over them will keep foraging animals away through critical periods.

When sweet corn ears are reaching their most edible stage, they are irresistible to squirrels and raccoons. To repel squirrels, red pepper sprinkled on the ripening silks is said to work fairly well. Hardly anything will deter raccoons—which are night raiders—but some gardeners claim success by running portable radios dialed to all-night talk shows; leaving a lighted lantern in the patch; or tethering a barking dog nearby. These methods may arouse neighbors if any live within earshot.

If all else fails, you can capture these pests in humane traps available from garden suppliers and transport them to a park or unpopulated area for release.

When cantaloupes are reaching sweet perfection in your melon patch, it pays to make some chicken-wire cylinders to place over them and prevent roving Carolina or ornate box turtles from harvesting them first. These shy, normally helpful, insect-eating creatures can hardly be blamed if they select your choicest melons for their dessert. You may wonder what is making holes in the melons, until you catch the turtle in the act. The Heartland is home to either or both of these land turtles.

CONTROLLING WEEDS

The Heartland's summers bring forth truly impressive flushes of weeds. Vegetable gardens are especially vulnerable because the open ground presents ideal conditions for weed seeds to germinate, and the sunlight stimulates growth. Many a vegetable garden that was picture perfect in May can scarcely be identified amid the blanket of crabgrass and other weeds by September. The gardener's flagging enthusiasm has something to do with this. New gardens have the worst problem because the ground is probably richly seeded by weeds of previous years. Each year that you control the weeds, the closer you come to a weed-free garden without great effort. The best vegetable gardens are those free of weeds.

Mechanical, chemical, and biologi-

cal weed control weapons are at your command, but all require commitment and vigilance. A really passionate hatred of weeds provides the needed motivation. It is not that you hate the plants themselves, but that they reproduce too well and out-compete other plants you are trying to grow. A single one allowed to drop seeds costs future time and effort that would be better devoted to a more productive goal.

Start early in the season to apply mulches around the crops that are already up and growing. The mulch prevents many weeds from starting and smothers or shades down any already started. Grass clippings and black plastic are good laid between rows. Where weeds already have a good start, root them out with a cultivator, hoe, shovel, or any other earth-engaging tool. Then hand pull any weeds that are too close to a desirable plant to be hoed out. Finally, rake away the weed tops; compost them unless they already bear seeds. (Do not compost purslane, because it can bloom and set seeds even after it has been pulled or hoed out.)

Add mulch as needed. A dividend of mulching with clippings, shredded leaves, or old hay is that they will biodegrade and so do not need to be removed. Simply plow the remains under at the end of the season.

Perennial weeds are worse problems in vegetable gardens than annual types because of their long-lasting root networks. Horse-nettle (*Solanum carolinense*) in particular is a serious pest because its far-ranging roots are never destroyed by tillage and remain to send up the viciously prickly tops in your pumpkin patch and similar havens late in the season, where they are likely to bloom and set seed unobserved. The berries enclosing the seeds are poisonous if ingested. Should you find horsenettle plants well separated from desirable crops, spray them with glyphosate (Roundup or Kleenup); its systemic action reaches through the root network. Other perennial weeds such as field bindweed (*Convolvulus arvensis*) and sandvine (*Cynanchum laeve*) can also be controlled this way, taking care to protect desirable vegetation from any of the glyphosate spray.

HERBS AS PART OF THE WHOLE

It is strange that so many gardeners are afraid to grow herbs, as if this were a daunting task. Also it is odd that so many think herbs must be in a garden by themselves. The truth is that many of the plants in this hard-to-define category will literally grow themselves in sites of their own choosing. For example, consider the catnip we find growing not only in the Heartland but also in the rest of the country—it was brought from Eurasia to this region by settlers many generations ago.

Culinary herbs—used for flavor— may as well be grown in vegetable gardens where they are handy for gathering along with the vegetables. Those that are annuals can be seeded into the spring garden along with the cucumbers and beans. Dill and summer savory will return year after year from self-sown seeds, so the first time you plant them may also be the last, unless in future gardens you somehow cultivate or mulch the volunteers out of

existence. It is handy to have home-grown "dill weed" (meaning the whole plant) ready at the same time you gather pickling cucumbers. Self-sown dill often obliges to provide this. Once started, summer savory also comes up by itself; sprigs will be available to flavor your first green beans, and continue to do so from then on. Basils are special for flavoring tomato dishes, so a few seeds or prestarted plantlets scattered among the tomato plants should provide convenient shoots at the same time you gather tomatoes. Sweet marjoram, florence fennel, borage, and parsley are other annual herbs or are handled as such, usually seeded in place each year. An end of a row or an edge of the garden would be convenient locations to have these herbs, as you are unlikely to need large quantities.

Perennial herbs that can go for years undisturbed deserve their own little bed at an edge of the garden or near the kitchen door. Or they can be incorporated into flower beds, as they are quite ornamental. They include these long-lived useful culinary plants: chives, oregano (*Origanum vulgare*), spearmint (planted in a bottomless tub to keep it from overrunning the others), thyme (*Thymus vulgaris*), and sage (*Salvia officinalis*). Contrary to popular impression, these herbs need no special soil or conditions except sunshine and a well-drained area.

EXTENDING THE SEASONS AND TAMING TEMPERATURES

By using cloches and cold frames, we can lengthen our fall and spring sea-

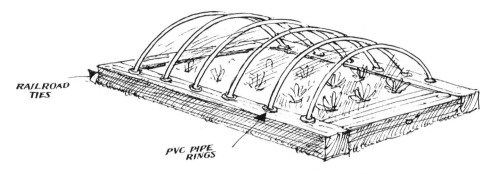

RAILROAD
TIES

PVC PIPE
RINGS

In a special lettuce frame, PVC pipe rings are sized to accept ends of smaller poly-pipe "ribs." This framework is then covered with clear polyethylene sheeting anchored at the sides and ends with tie-downs. Sow lettuce in January.

sons considerably and expand the list of plants we can grow. Hardware is available commercially both pre-assembled or for do-it-yourself construction. Modern technology gives us much to work with, such as clear plastic sheeting for covering temporary greenhouses and growing frames and PVC pipe or tubing for frameworks.

For example, a home gardener in a Kansas City suburb has made a special raised and covered lettuce bed where early each year he starts seeding a succession of gourmet lettuce varieties—long before they could be trusted to the out-of-doors. The raised bed is a rectangle of old railroad ties, with holes drilled at regular intervals to accept PVC pipe rings sized so the ends of arches of smaller diameter PVC pipe will fit into them. When all are in place, a sheet of clear polyethylene is drawn over them, forming a tunnel. Sheeting is anchored at each end with

tie-downs. Winds have rocked this cloche but have never blown it away.

Inside, his January sowings of fancy lettuces and a few other choice salad ingredients such as arugula come up quickly in the sun warmth caught by the poly covering. Growing fast in the lengthening spring days, they reach harvest by about the time outdoor plantings can begin. The "weather" under the cloche is steady and serene compared to the stop-and-go elements outdoors, with nightly freezes, heaving from thaws, washouts and shredding from rains, sleet and hail. In November the same bed is put to work covering sowings of spinach and ornamental kale being grown for holiday salads or decorating.

In Heartland latitudes, such growing frames are sure to be helpful in extending the growing season at both beginning and end, with almost year-round production.

SEEDING AND SPACING POINTERS FOR THIRTY-FOUR ANNUAL VEGETABLES

BEANS, LIMA. Sow a week after last frost date, 1½" deep, 4–5" apart, in rows 30" apart.

BEANS, POLE. Sow a week after last frost date, 1½" deep, 4–5" apart, in rows 36–48" apart. Needs trellis.

BEANS, SNAP (BUSH). Sow after last frost date, 1½" deep, 3" apart, in rows 24–30" apart.

BEETS. Sow three weeks before last frost date, ½" deep, 1" apart (thin to 3" apart), in rows 18–24" apart.

BROCCOLI. Sow seeds in cold frame or greenhouse six weeks before planting-out time. Cover seeds ¼". Transplant to garden three weeks before last frost date, 15–18" apart, in rows 30" apart.

BRUSSELS SPROUTS. Handle like broccoli.

CABBAGE. Handle like broccoli. Rows can go as close as 24".

CARROTS. Sow two weeks before last frost date, ½" deep, ¼" apart (thin to 1" apart), in rows as close as 18". Use fresh seed.

CAULIFLOWER. Handle like broccoli.

CELERY. Sow indoors twelve weeks before last frost date, ½" deep; set out in garden two weeks before last frost date, 6" apart, in rows 30" apart.

CORN. Sow seed on or after last frost date, 1½" deep, 3–4" apart (thin to 12" apart), in rows 30–36" apart.

CUCUMBERS. Sow a week after last frost date, ¾" deep, 8–10 seeds in a hill (planting circle), or if in row, 4–5" apart. Space rows 4–5' apart or allow 3' between hills.

EGGPLANT. Sow indoors eight weeks before planting-out time; transplant outdoors one week after last frost date, 30" apart, in rows 36" apart.

KOHLRABI. Sow three weeks before last frost date, ¼" deep, 2" apart (thin

to 6" apart), in rows 18–24" apart.

LETTUCE, HEAD. Sow ¼" deep in cold frame four weeks before planting-out time; transplant outdoors two to three weeks before last frost date, 8–12" apart, in rows 20–24" apart.

LETTUCE, LEAF. Sow seed four to six weeks before last frost date, ¼" deep, ½" apart (thin to 2" apart). If in row system, space rows 16" apart. May also be grown broadcast in raised beds and thinned to 4–6" apart.

MELONS (CANTALOUPES AND MUSKMELONS). Sow one week after last frost date, 1" deep, 6–12" apart, in hills spaced 5' apart each way.

OKRA. Sow on or after last frost date, 1" deep, 2" apart, in rows 36" apart. Thin plants to stand 15" apart.

ONION (SEEDS). Sow two to four weeks before last frost date, ½" deep, ½" apart (thin to 3" apart), in rows 18–24" apart. Use only fresh seed.

ONION (SETS). Set in outdoor garden four to six weeks before last frost date, 1½–2" deep, spaced 3–4" apart, in rows 18–24" apart (or can be set checkerboard style in raised beds).

PARSLEY. Sow four weeks before last frost date, ¼" deep, ½" apart (thin to 2" apart), in rows 18–24" apart. Use only fresh seed.

PARSNIP. Sow four to six weeks before last frost date, ½" deep, ½" apart (thin to 3" apart), in rows 18–24" apart. Use only fresh seed.

PEA. Sow outdoors four to six weeks before last frost date, 1" deep, 2" apart, in rows 30" apart.

POTATO, IRISH. Plant four to six weeks before last frost date. Plant seed potatoes (sets) 4" deep, 10" apart, in rows 3' apart. Use ½ peck of seed potatoes to plant 100' of row.

Potato, sweet. Set out prestarted plants one week after last frost date, 12" apart in rows 35" apart.

Pumpkin. Sow on or after last frost date, 1" deep, 6" apart (thin to 24" apart), in hills 7–8' apart.

Radish. Sow four weeks before last frost date, ½" deep, ½" apart, in rows 12" apart; or plant broadcast style and thin to 2" apart.

Spinach. Sow four weeks before last frost date, ½" deep, ½" apart (thin to 2" apart), in rows 18–24" apart.

Squash, bush. Sow after last frost date in warm soil, 1" deep, 6" apart (thin to 24" apart), in hills 4–5' apart.

Squash, vining. Sow after last frost date in warm soil, 1" deep, 6" apart (thin to 24" apart), in hills 6–8' apart.

Swiss chard. Sow two to four weeks before last frost date, ½" deep, 1½" apart (thin to 4" apart), in rows 18–24" apart.

Tomato. Sow indoors six weeks before planting-out date (a week after last frost date). If unstaked, set plants 4' apart in rows 4' apart. If staked, plants can go 18–30" apart in rows 3 to 4' apart.

Turnips. Sow four to six weeks before last frost date, ½" deep, ¾" apart (thin to 3" apart). For fall crop, sow in late July or early August.

Watermelon. Sow one week after last frost date, 1" deep, 6" apart (thin to 3 plants), in hills 5' apart.

Edible Landscapes
Gardeners everywhere without space for full-fledged vegetable gardens are simply raising edibles in combination with their ornamental plants. In the Heartland we can succeed with this idea in spectacular style. The only word of caution is to avoid combining edible plants with ornamentals such as roses that have to be regularly sprayed with pesticides. Here are sixteen of our best possibilities:

Asparagus. Ferny foliage from early summer on is a good fine-textured green screen or background for flowers. A perennial, it comes back every spring and never needs to be replanted.

Basils. Ornamental varieties, easy from seed, are 'Spicy Globe' (low, ball-shaped, and fine-foliaged; great for neat hedges and edges) and 'Purple Ruffles' and 'Dark Opal' (taller than 'Spicy Globe' with deep purple leaves; tasty). All are annuals.

Beans, climbing or pole. 'Blue Lake' and 'Kentucky Wonder' are two varieties that form dense vines 4 to 5 feet high or more. They make good garden backdrops when draped on fences or trellises. Purple-tinged varieties are also available. Use the beans like snap beans. Sow seed where you want plants to grow. They are annuals.

Chives (*Allium schoenoprasum*). This well-behaved, showy clump blooms in spring with purple-pink ball-shaped flower clusters. A hardy perennial, it grows 12 to 20 inches high.

Eggplant. This gray-green annual forms a stately 2-foot (or higher) plant that blends well with flowers. The purple (sometimes pink or white) shining fruits are always admired. Set out prestarted plants after frosts are over.

KALE (ORNAMENTAL TYPES). The lace-leafed, dense cabbagelike heads are 8 to 15 inches high and 12 inches across; they have green outer leaves around contrasting white, cream, purple, or red centers. Grow this annual in fall to add color to the Christmas season and beyond.

KOHLRABI. A cabbage family vegetable with a curious habit—its leaves extend from a ball-shaped root crown (the part you eat) at soil level. A handsome purple form, 'Purple Vienna,' is available; it remains showy over a long season. This annual grows 10 to 12 inches high. Sow seeds where you want plants to grow.

LETTUCES. For early spring any kind makes pretty, edible edging along walks, in gardens, and around shrubs. Sow seeds where you want plants to grow. This annual comes in leaf or butterhead types. Red-leaf forms (for example, 'Ruby') add color interest.

MINTS. Most of the many varieties are ornamental and make pleasing, edible ground covers in shaded areas. These perennials are spreaders.

OKRA. This annual provides a fast-growing background of green or red-tinted foliage with showy cream-colored flowers in summer and green or purple pods ('Burgundy') that are tasty in stews and skillet dishes or as a cooked vegetable. Sow seeds in warm soil where you want plants to grow. It grows 4 to 7 feet high.

PARSLEY. This plant has fernlike deep-green foliage that makes attractive ground cover, edging, or filler in flagstone crevices. Sow seed where you want plants to grow. Grows as an annual, although it is actually biennial if it survives winter.

PEPPERS (ORNAMENTAL). Compact, low deep-green plants of special vari-

Things Nobody Ever Tells You

● The perennial herb rosemary is not winter hardy outdoors anywhere in the Heartland. To enjoy this fragrant, tasty, and beautiful herb you must keep it in a sizable pot and bring it indoors to a sunny window for winter, or put it in a greenhouse or deep cold frame. Don't neglect watering or you will lose it.

● The baby cucumbers (gherkins or cornichons) that are pictured as the size of your little finger when they are ready for pickling whole grow too well in the Heartland's exuberant summers. After the cucumbers reach bearing age, prepare to harvest them at least *once a day*, preferably twice, to catch the little

fruits at the size and tender quality you want. Weekend gardeners, take note!

● "Determinate" applied to a variety of tomato means that it is a bush type and does not need to be staked or tied up to keep it neat and controlled in the garden.

● Add a few radish seeds to your early spring sowings of beets, lettuce, spinach, and parsley. The precocious radishes will break through first, marking the row and softening crusted soil for the slower kinds. When they are big enough, pull the radishes to eat, leaving the other vegetables beneficially spaced.

eties ('Holiday Cheer' or 'Fiesta') are covered in autumn with vivid yellow, red, orange, or purple fruits of round or long shapes that are edible but hot. They are suitable for drying, but use them sparingly. Start them annually from seeds.

RHUBARB. These bold-foliaged clumps rising early in spring and lasting through summer are attractive additions to ornamental gardens and need little attention. They are hardy perennials.

SAGE (*Salvia officinalis*). This plant

Vegetable Planting Sequence Spring through Summer

(See the maps in Chapter One for last/first frost dates)

Four to six weeks before last frost date

SOW SEEDS	SET OUT PLANTS
Leaf lettuce	Onions (also sets)
Leeks	
Parsnip	
Peas	
Potatoes (pieces)	
Spinach	
Turnips	

Two to four weeks before last frost date

SOW SEEDS	SET OUT PLANTS
Beets	Broccoli
Carrots	Brussels sprouts
Kohlrabi	Cabbage
Mustard	Cauliflower
Onions (seeds)	Head lettuce
Swiss chard	

At least one week after last frost date

SOW SEEDS	SET OUT PLANTS
Beans	Peppers
(lima, snap, pole)	Tomatoes
Sweet corn	Sweet potatoes
Cucumbers	

Two weeks after last frost (in warm soil)

SOW SEEDS
Melons (cantaloupe, muskmelon, and watermelon)
Okra
Pumpkins
Squash

Three months before first fall frost

SOW SEEDS
Beets (fall planting)
Broccoli
Chinese cabbage
Kohlrabi
Summer squash
Turnips (fall crop)

Two months before first fall frost

SOW SEEDS
Lettuces
Radishes
Spinach

comes in a silver-green leaf form and a cream-gold variegated form; it has a semi-woody base and blooms in spring with small blue-violet flowers in showy panicles. Use the leaves fresh or dried to flavor stuffings and meats. It is winter hardy throughout the Heartland and looks good with other perennials in the foreground in full sun.

STRAWBERRY. Any variety of this hardy perennial is good for ground cover or edging. The alpine or French strawberries are runnerless and easier to manage as edging. Use prestarted plants.

THYME. The two main types, *Thymus vulgaris* (woody upright subshrub) and *Thymus serpyllum* (creeping), are both winter-hardy perennials throughout the Heartland, and are useful for seasoning meats and soups. They make pretty edging for paths or beds; in early summer they bloom with purplish (or other) flower spikelets. Set out prestarted plants. Although harsh Zone 4 winters may kill it out, thyme regrows readily from seeds.

Several woody fruit plants also make attractive, edible landscapes: blueberries (if the soil is acidified); bush cherry; currants (best in partial shade); gooseberries; grape vines; and hazelnuts.

CHAPTER SIX

Fruit Gardens in the Heartland

Fruits have always been part of Heartland gardens. When pioneers from "back East" arrived here, fruits were the first trees planted. Native Americans before them had nurtured stands of wild plums, grapes, and hazelnuts around their villages and spread them from place to place. They enjoyed harvests of native black walnuts, pecans, and hickories and undoubtedly spread those, too.

Early settlers considered apples and pears the essential tree fruits and grapes the essential vine. Planting stock was available from fruit tree nurseries that seemingly were among the earliest business establishments in many communities. Tree fruits—especially apples—still take planting priority as they need several years to bear. Next will be grapes, then bush and bramble fruits, and finally strawberries.

Although having fresh fruits to eat is enough reason to plant them, most fruit plants offer beauty too, a point to note if you want an "edible landscape." Fruits can be the backbone of it. In laying plans, review the harvest sequence of the various kinds. Try to arrange fruits to follow each other through the season instead of coming all at once.

The best fruit planting time in the Heartland is early spring. If you are planting bare-root stock, early spring is the *only* practical time. If your nurs-

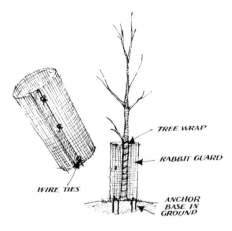

TREE WRAP

RABBIT GUARD

WIRE TIES

ANCHOR BASE IN GROUND

In grassy areas, protect young fruit trees from rabbits and mice by surrounding the trunks with collars of ¼-inch mesh galvanized screening.

ery supplies plants growing in containers or balled and burlapped, you have more leeway, but spring is still the best because the entire growing season lies ahead for establishing them. Planning and preparation can well begin the previous fall if circumstances permit. Deeply till or plow the area where fruit trees will go, incorporating leaf mold or any other organic matter available. It is a good opportunity also to till fertilizer into the future root zone. Even the planting holes can be dug in fall, filled with leaves or hay, and covered, ready for the spring arrival of plants. Doing such digging is far more pleasant in autumn than in blustery March.

Make planting holes of generous size and depth to accommodate roots without cramping. While opinions differ about the value of adding improvements—compost or peat—in the planting holes for fruit trees, most favor the idea. This is your only oppor-

Sequence of Ripe Fruit Harvests

MAY	Strawberries, gooseberries
JUNE	Cherries, raspberries
JULY	Blackberries, early cooking apples ('Lodi'), blueberries, apricots, early peaches
AUGUST	Elderberries, midseason peaches, plums
SEPTEMBER	Midseason apples, grapes, pears
OCTOBER	Pears, late apples, nuts (walnuts, pecans, and hazelnuts)

tunity. Position the tree at the same height it grew in the nursery. With dwarfed trees, the graft union should be just above ground level; otherwise the upper "normal" part may form its own roots and eventually neutralize the dwarfing effect given by the grafted rootstock. Put tree wrap or protector on the lower trunk as a guard against various perils, especially sunscald. In rural areas, a further necessity is a cylinder of screen wire around each base to keep gnawing mice and rabbits from girdling trees in winter.

APPLES

Our hardiest fruit tree is apple. It comes in three basic growth sizes from nurseries, which graft the named varieties on special interstems and/or rootstocks. In this way they tailor the tree to suit different situations and conditions.

Standard apple trees ultimately reach the full genetic size for the kind, averaging 18 feet or more in crown diameter and height. *Semidwarf* apples are slightly smaller than standard forms. *Dwarf* forms grow to only half the ultimate standard size or even less. Be sure you buy the size you intend; otherwise the mature tree may not suit the space you allowed for it.

Dwarf apple trees are favored today because they fit into small urban yards better than standard-size trees, letting you grow more varieties if desired and making their care easier without climbing ladders. Fruits are regular size. The dwarfs start bearing younger, usually within three or four years, whereas with a standard tree you may have to wait six or seven years. A special caution, however, on *dwarf* apple forms for the Heartland is that they need permanent bracing unless they are in wind-protected places. They have small root systems that cannot anchor the tree well against our winds. Unless you observe this precaution, you may find trees literally blown out of the ground after a summer rain and wind storm, a sickening loss. If you go in for espalier tree training for a formal garden effect, dwarf apples are our region's best subjects, at least among fruit plants.

SPACING THE APPLE TREES. Standard forms should be planted 22 to 28 feet apart; semidwarf forms, 15 to 18 feet apart; and dwarf forms, 12 feet apart.

POLLINATION. Most apple trees need pollen from a different variety to set fruit. In city gardens, apple trees elsewhere in the neighborhood may do this job, as bees will carry pollen a block or two. In country gardens, far from other apples, you'll need to plant two different kinds. 'Lodi' and 'Golden Delicious' are both good pollinators.

SITE. Essentials for apple trees are full sun and a well drained spot. A slight slope is excellent. As for soil—apple trees are fairly tolerant, doing better in heavy soils than in light, sandy ones. Organic material in the soil is definitely helpful.

PLANTING TIPS. It is good practice in this region to tilt the tree slightly to the southwest and plant it with the lowest side branch pointing in that direction. By creating a shade pattern, this strategy helps prevent sunscald (frost-cracking), a serious problem with young apples. If the plant is a single whip, head it back to about 3 feet, cutting just beyond a growth bud. If branched, select three well-spaced branches to keep and prune out the others. Head back halfway those branches you keep.

STAKING AND BRACING. At planting time, place a durable, well- anchored stake near the southwest side and guy the tree to it at midheight with wire threaded through a protective section of rubber hose. This stake should last two or three years; by then, standard or semidwarf forms should have rooted well enough to do without staking. In the case of dwarf apple trees, by the time they begin bearing they will need permanent bracing to prevent being upset by our summer rain and wind storms. A good way is to install three permanent equidistant ground anchors 4 feet out from the trunk and run brace wires from each 3 to 4 feet up around the main trunk. Cushion the wires with rubber-hose "sleeves" where they circle the trunk; inspect the wires yearly to see that they are not girdling the trunk.

The Heartland's Longtime Favorite Apples

LODI. This early-summer yellow cooking apple is hardy and a consistent producer; it is an improved, blight-resistant form of 'Yellow Transparent.'

JONATHAN. This crisp all-purpose apple ripens in September and keeps well all winter.

RED DELICIOUS. A late ripener, this apple keeps well and is good eaten fresh.

GOLDEN DELICIOUS. This yellow apple ripens in October. Although good eaten fresh, it is not particularly good for cooking except in sauces. It stores well.

WINESAP. This long-keeping apple ripens in October. It makes delicious salads, jellies, cider, and apple pies. It is not useful as a pollinator.

CORTLAND. This red all-purpose apple is crisp and spicy. It ripens in mid-fall.

Others may do well also. Newer varieties are worth investigating, especially disease-resistant kinds such as 'Liberty' and 'Prima' that need little if any spraying for disease.

SPECIAL CARE. Yearly pruning is usually a job for late winter to correct branching defects, thin branches to let in light, and help the tree bear its fruits. Occasionally, you may also need to water the soil, thin the fruits, and place spreaders between narrow-angled branches to train them outward. If fertilizing is warranted, do it in early spring using a basic 10-10-10 or similar fertilizer, 1 pound per tree distributed within the drip line but staying 1 foot out from the trunk.

To get perfect apples requires a season-long spray routine for diseases and insects, unless you try to control them biologically. Apple tree diseases are mainly scab, powdery mildew, cedar apple rust, and fire blight. Insect enemies include codling moth and aphids. The codling moth causes wormy apples. To control these problems, most growers use a commercial fruit tree spray containing fungicides (for diseases) as well as insecticides (for insects). Ask your garden supplier for a general fruit tree spray and follow package directions to mix and apply it. University extension offices recommend a spray schedule calling for at least eight sprayings through the growing season. Environmental concerns, especially in urban surroundings, may well make you hesitate to put on chemical sprays. Apple trees can survive without spraying, and fruits will develop, but many will be blemished or wormy. A current trend is toward using naturally disease-resistant apple varieties (a few do exist—for example, 'Liberty' and 'Prima') and biological controls for keeping down the worst of the apple insects. (See Chapter Eleven for information on biological insect controls.)

One important spraying you can do with no environmental qualms is the dormant oil spray of early spring, the most essential of the entire schedule. It rids trees of scale insects, mites, and insect eggs. Called "dormant" because it must be applied before buds swell to avoid damaging plants, it consists of a highly refined mineral oil carried in water that makes a spray coating which smothers the target insects.

CHERRIES, TART AND SWEET

The tart, or sour, cherries are our easiest tree fruit. Hardy and adaptable throughout the Heartland, they are a delight in gardens. The cloud of white bloom in spring is a rapturous sight. The bright-red cherries that follow are a feast for the eye and the palate.

The Heartland's Best Tart Cherries

MONTMORENCY. The large bright-red slightly sweet fruits ripen from mid-June to early July. This variety is hardy throughout the Heartland. Space the trees 15 to 18 feet apart.

METEOR. These notably winter-hardy semidwarf trees grow to about 10 feet high, with moderately spreading branches and large fruits that ripen in mid-June. Space the trees 8 to 10 feet apart.

NORTH STAR. This very cold-hardy variety is considered a genetic dwarf—it grows to a height of only about 8 feet. It is vase-shaped, and the fruits ripen in early June. Space the trees 8 to 10 feet apart.

The Heartland's Best Sweet Cherries

Recommended only for Zone 6 and the southernmost parts of Zone 5; trees should be spaced 20 to 24 feet apart.

KANSAS SWEET. This tree is one of the hardiest and best adapted of this type, although its red fruits are really only semi-sweet. 'Montmorency' will pollinate it.

YELLOW GLASS. Considered the hardiest of sweet cherries, this tree bears large yellow fruits. It needs a pollinator.

STELLA. This tree has dark red fruit. Self-pollinating, it can be used alone or to pollinate others. It is hardy only through Zone 6.

Although not as long-lived as apples, tart cherries start producing sooner, within three or four years. They are self-pollinating, so there is no need to plant two kinds. The neat little trees, only about 12 to 14 feet high, will fit in even a small yard. Seldom do they need any spraying or insect control. Pruning is needed merely to thin out branch tangles or remove dead wood. Tart cherries are the classic type for pies and pastries.

Sweet cherries are more for eating fresh as a dessert fruit, although they can be used in pastries as well. Other parts of the country can grow sweet cherries more reliably than the Heartland, for although the trees may endure our winters, the bloom buds often do not survive our mercurial springs. Sweet cherry buds are more cold sensitive than tart cherry ones. Also, fruits of some varieties may split as they ripen in our steamy spring weather. Sweet cherry trees generally grow larger than tart cherry types, reaching 20 feet high and wide, so they need more space. Also, since most are not self-pollinating, two varieties are needed.

Give both types well-drained soil and an elevated site where cold air does not collect. Because of their frost tenderness, sweet cherries do better in our urban areas where buildings protect them and where a microclimate softens late killing frosts.

CARE. Cherries have few disease or insect problems and most owners never spray them. In case of scale infestation, spray with dormant oil in early spring as described for apples. Birds may steal cherries as they ripen. Protect the fruit with bird netting thrown over the trees. Netting is sold at garden stores.

PEACHES, NECTARINES, AND APRICOTS

Certain areas of Zone 6 in the Heartland grow excellent peaches, but in much of Zone 5 within our region they are a borderline crop. Northward in Zone 4 they are out of the question. Trees themselves survive most winters in Zone 5b, but in many years the flower buds, expanding too soon, are killed by late freezes. Selection of site is very important—well-drained, loamy soil on a gentle slope (north- or east-facing is preferred) with good air circulation. Sometimes in an area where peaches regularly fail in open country, they succeed in nearby microclimates such as city or even small-town gardens where buildings afford protection. They might succeed in areas near major rivers or lakes, because of the tempering influence of water. The same is true with nectarines, the "fuzzless peaches." Look around in your community to see how peach trees fare before you invest in either peaches or nectarines.

Neither the peach nor the nectarine is considered long lived. Count on about ten years. Standard-size trees live longer than dwarfs. Both begin to bear the third or fourth year after planting. Dwarf forms of most peach and several nectarine varieties are available. These grow to about 10 feet high and wide. Standard-size trees reach 12 to 15 feet.

Also, several miniature or genetic dwarf forms of peaches and nectarines exist, growing as shrubs only 4 to 6 feet high. These extreme dwarfs have landscape possibilities—plant them around foundations, in tubs on patios, or elsewhere in protected corners. Their fruit is normal size and quality. If peaches have always failed where you garden, these miniatures deserve consideration. Grown in tubs, they could be overwintered in some unheated but sheltered area.

POLLINATION AND SPACE. Practically all peach and nectarine varieties are self-pollinating; a single tree will bear without another variety nearby. Space standard-size trees about 20 feet apart, and dwarf forms about 10 feet apart. The miniatures or genetic dwarfs can go as close as 5 feet.

CARE. Peaches and nectarines bear on young wood of the previous season. Prune to keep an open vase shape, heading back older branches to encourage new growth, which you selec-

Peach Varieties Recommended for the Heartland

Hardy in Zone 5b and south.

HARKEN. This is one of the hardiest varieties. A yellow freestone type, it ripens in July.

MADISON. Its yellow freestone fruits ripen in August.

BELLE OF GEORGIA. This high quality white freestone variety ripens in late August.

REDHAVEN. Its yellow freestone fruits ripen in July.

RELIANCE. This is also one of the hardiest, a yellow freestone variety ripening in August.

tively thin out. Sometimes trees set so much fruit they cannot support it. When that happens, thin fruits early, to about 6 inches apart, so those remaining will develop normally.

TREATING PROBLEMS. Peach leaf curl, a fungus disease that causes leaves to turn reddish and curl grotesquely in midspring, is preventable if trees are treated with a dormant late-winter spray of lime sulfur before the buds swell. Bordeaux mixture and a proprietary product containing chlorothalonil are also labeled for this as a dormant season spray. Peach tree borers, which tunnel under bark and can kill the tree, are indicated by masses of gum formed on bark near the ground. Scrape away the soil at the base of the trunk and inspect it. With a knife, clean off the gummy substance. If you find borers working beneath the bark, prick them out with the knife and destroy them. Do such work in mid-September; don't wait until spring. Another way to control peach borers is with pdb crystals (moth crystals). Remove surface soil from around the tree base to 1 foot out. Spread the crystals in a ring 2 inches away from the trunk. Then cover with several shovelsful of soil and tread it down. The crystals emit a gas that kills the borers. After five weeks, remove the soil mound and any remaining crystals and smooth the soil back to its former level. Use about 1 teaspoon of pdb per 1 inch of trunk diameter.

APRICOTS

Many Heartland gardeners plant and enjoy these trees merely as ornamentals, taking the rare years when they fruit as a dividend. Apricots never fail to bloom, with a cloud of delicate pink-tinged white flowers, usually giving the first real tree color of spring. The trees are quite cold hardy and long lived, but as with peaches, the precocious blooms are almost invariably nipped by freezes, so fruit seldom develops in our region. Protected sites make a difference if you live in a borderline area. A place to the north or east of a building, shaded in winter and early spring, may hold back bloom buds long enough to give them a chance with the weather.

Space apricots about 20 feet apart, as they live longer than peaches and make fairly large trees. They are more ornamental, with triangular shining leaves growing in an upright spreading form and reddish stems. They are pleasant trees to have, and in those years when they produce a crop, they create excitement. The hardiest variety is 'Goldcot,' which ripens in July, and is rated Zone 5. Nurseries have dwarf sizes available in most varieties, which mature at only 10 feet, about half the size of standard apricots. All are self-pollinating.

PLUMS

Relatives of peaches, cherries and apricots, plums come in such variety of types and origins as to be confusing. The two principal types are European (sweet, oval, and blue skin, known as prune-plums) and Japanese (round, red-purple skin with red or yellow flesh; used more for eating fresh). The European types are self-fruitful (need no cross-pollinator). Japanese types need cross-pollination by another Japanese

type. In addition, there are hybrids created by crossing Japanese types with native plums for hardiness; these are increasingly being used in northern areas—for example, 'Pipestone,' from the Minnesota Fruit Breeding Farm. These hybrids need cross-pollinating from another, similar hybrid. For winter hardiness and success in our region, the European plums have the advan-

Plum Varieties Recommended for the Heartland

European types

Sweet; good for eating fresh or for drying, canning, and preserves.

BLUFRE. This early freestone variety has blue skin and green-yellow flesh. It does best when planted with another variety for pollen. The fruits ripen in September.

DAMSON. The small blue-skinned, amber-fleshed fruits of this prolific variety ripen in September. They are used often in jams and jellies. The small upright tree needs little pruning.

STANLEY. This variety has oval blue-purple freestone fruits with yellow flesh; they ripen in early September.

Japanese types

Juicy, good for eating fresh or canning and preserves.

METHLEY. The fruit of this variety has red-purple skin and yellow flesh.

OZARK PREMIER. This semi-freestone variety has red skin and amber flesh; fruits ripen in August.

REDHEART. The fruits of this variety have dark-red skins and red flesh; they ripen in August. It is a good pollinator.

tage over Japanese types, as they bloom late enough usually to escape frosts. Japanese plums open blooms early and frequently are caught by freezes that kill the crop for that year.

Plums adapt to most soils. The trees fit well in edible landscapes as attractive backgrounds and screens covered with white flowers in spring. Japanese types have glossy foliage. Both types of plums come in standard and dwarf sizes. The standards grow to perhaps 20 feet; the dwarfs to 10 to 15 feet. Space standard-size trees 20 feet apart, and dwarf ones 15 feet apart. Expect yields 4 to 5 years after planting for standard-size plums; and a year sooner for dwarfs. Standard types are generally longer lived than dwarf forms. Disease and insect control are the same as for peaches. In late winter the dormant oil spray (mixed in water per package directions) is recommended for control of scale insects. Your general goal in pruning Japanese plums is to form an open, light-admitting vase shape much as for peaches. Prune so lowest limbs are about 3 feet above the ground, with four or five side branches forming the vase-shaped scaffold. European plums are less spreading and can be pruned more like apples. On the High Plains, it is better to leave branches low on the trunk, 12 to 20 inches from the ground, for winter shading against sunscald.

PEARS

Pears are hardier than peaches but not quite so hardy as apples, although they are as long lived. Many varieties are hardy in Zone 5. They all need cross-pollination with another variety, so

plant two kinds unless other pears grow nearby. (The ornamental Callery pears such as 'Bradford' will serve for pollination.) Pears are adaptable to a wide range of soils and are generally drought tolerant. The worst worry in growing them in the Heartland is fire blight, a summertime bacterial disease that attacks one branch at a time, darkening leaves as if they were burned. Some varieties are resistant (but not immune) to fire blight and thus are preferred. 'Bartlett,' the old-time favorite, is so blight prone in this region it is no longer recommended. Although the disease cannot be cured, it can be controlled to some extent by timely pruning off of affected branches well below the fired part. Dispose of prunings by burning. Disinfect pruning tools between cuts by dipping them in alcohol or chlorine bleach solution.

Space standard-size trees 25 feet apart, and dwarfs 15 feet apart. Plant and care for pear trees much the same as for apple trees, except pears need less staking and pruning. Pruning of pears is a bit different because of their strong vertical habit. When trees are young, aim for good spacing of the main limbs and cut away smallish shoots. To encourage outward growth, you may need to insert "spreaders" (2-foot-long laths with V-shaped notches at each end) to widen branch angles. Expect fruiting to begin five to six years after planting—earlier for dwarf forms. Avoid spring fertilizing of pear trees as part of a general strategy to discourage succulent growth associated with fire blight. Dormant oil spray in late winter, as recommended for apples, is good insurance against scale, mites, and other insects.

Pear Varieties Recommended for the Heartland

All are fire blight resistant.

DUCHESS. This self-fruitful variety is a good pollinator. Its fruits are yellow-green and tinged pink; they ripen in October.

KIEFFER. This is one of the cold hardiest (Zone 4) varieties. Its fruits ripen in October. Pick them while they are hard and store them indoors until they ripen. They can be used for canning.

LUSCIOUS. This variety was developed in South Dakota for the Great Plains; it is hardy to Zone 4. Its medium-size yellow fruits are dessert (not cooking) quality; they ripen in early October.

MAGNESS. The fruits of this variety are medium size, greenish, russeted, and thick skinned with smooth, sweet, juicy flesh. They store well.

MAXINE (also known as 'Starking Delicious'). This variety has medium-large yellow fruits of good quality for eating fresh or cooking; they ripen in mid-to-late September. The tree is vigorous, hardy, and upright.

MOONGLOW. This is a good pollinator for other varieties. Pick the fruits while they are yellow green and store them until they ripen (ten days). Pick them in mid-August to September 1.

SECKEL. This variety has small tan fruits that are spicy and sweet—ideal for cooking and jams. They ripen in September.

GRAPES

Grapes are the perfect "edible ornamental" trained over a fence, doorway, vine house, or arbor. If you want them primarily for berries rather than beauty, the traditional way is to grow them on wire trellises. The Heartland has all the natural requirements for grapes—any moderately good, well-drained soil that grows vegetables; abundant sunshine; warmth in summer; good air circulation; and winters matching the hardiness of the kind being grown. There are varieties suitably hardy for anywhere in our region.

In planning for grapes, decide first what you will use them for. Wine or juice? A fresh fruit dessert? For processing, you'll probably want to harvest all at the same time. But for table fruit, grapes should ripen a few at a time over a long period. In Missouri, the Heartland's leading state for grapes, growers count on yields of 15 pounds per healthy mature vine. Plan to space plants 8 to 10 feet apart along the trellis. Space trellises 10 feet apart. The trellises need not be erected until the second year. The autumn before planting, prepare soil with deep plowing or tilling and incorporation of compost or other organic material.

Set out plants as early in spring as possible to allow the full season for establishment. Dig a spacious hole, set the plant as deep as it stood in the nursery, spread its roots (removing any broken ones), refill the soil part way, water it well, finish refilling the soil, and water again thoroughly. Keep the ground cultivated out from the base 2 feet each way, or keep it mulched. Wood chips are good for this. Prune the vine back to the main stem and cut that down to four buds. The trellis can be built like a wire fence, with the end posts braced and two or three wires (use No. 9 clothesline wire) spaced upward 18 inches apart.

Pruning, the most time-consuming part of growing grapes, seems complex but becomes simpler with experience. Keep this objective always in mind: to limit the fruit-bearing shoots to what the plant can properly ripen. A second-ary objective is to provide parent canes for the following year. Grapes bear on current-year growth, which rises from last year's wood. Allowing a vine to overbear may weaken it and reduce future production. The best time for pruning is late winter before the buds swell. Equip yourself with hand pruners and loppers. On a new planting, give plants their first proper pruning on an above-freezing day the February after you planted them. Although experts describe several pruning systems,

Grape Varieties Recommended for the Heartland

CANADICE. The red, seedless, disease-resistant, multipurpose fruits of this variety ripen early. It is considered the hardiest of the seedless grapes.

RELIANCE. The red, seedless, disease-resistant fruits of this table variety ripen at midseason. Reliable.

MARS. The fruits of this table variety are blue, seedless, and highly disease resistant; they also ripen early. This grape is reliable and productive.

NIAGARA. The multipurpose fruits of this variety are white and have seeds; they ripen early. This grape is considered as hardy as 'Concord.'

CONCORD. The fruits of this table variety are blue and have seeds; they are used for juice and jelly. Considered the standard for all blue grapes, Concords are hardy and widely grown in the Heartland. They ripen late in the season; if they ripen unevenly, thin out fruits.

BETA. The fruits of this variety are small and blue and have seeds; they are used for juice and wine. This grape ripens early, and with its vigorous vine, is among the hardiest of all grapes.

CATAWBA. The fruits of this variety are red and have seeds; they are used many purposes. The late-ripening fruits grow on a vigorous vine.

BUFFALO. The fruits of this variety are blue, have seeds, ripen early, are disease resistant and multipurpose. They have a sweet flavor and are vigorous and reliable.

VENUS. The fruits of this table grape are blue-black and seedless; they ripen early. This moderately hardy variety has large berries on a vigorous vine.

FRENCH-AMERICAN HYBRIDS

AURORE. The fruits of this variety are white, have seeds, ripen at midseason, and are mildew resistant; this grape is suitable for the table or for wine. It is hardy, tasty, and productive.

BACO NOIR. The fruits of this variety are blue, have seeds, ripen at midseason, and make excellent red wine. It is vigorous and does best in the southern part of the region.

in a home garden it is not necessary to follow any one rigidly. Varieties differ in how they grow; you cannot always hold them to your will.

A favorite pattern, called the "Kniffin," consists of selecting one vertical cane led upward on a twine to the top wire where it is cut off and encouraged to grow side branches. All other base canes are removed. Two side shoots—one left, one right—are selected near the lower (or middle) wire junction and two more at the upper wire. All other side canes are removed. In the subsequent (second) spring, these side canes are pruned back to four or five buds each (total of about twenty buds if you have four side canes). Tying the vine to wires with cloth or plastic ribbon is necessary at first, but it soon anchors its new shoots with tendrils. In future years, bearing canes of the previous year are cut off and fresh parent canes are selected near the trunk at each location as replacements, always holding the number of new (fruit-bearing) buds to only four or five on each cane.

With less vigorous vines or in harsh conditions, a simpler alternative is to lead one main trunk up to the first wire, at which point a "fan" of three or four canes is selected and encouraged to ascend to the next cross wire; all other canes are removed. Handle the remaining canes the same as the "arms" under the Kniffin system.

Even grapes grown solely for ornament require annual pruning to keep them healthy and in bounds. Aim generally to remove at least one-third of the previous year's growth, as well as any dead wood. On windy sites it is best to train grapes low, under 4 feet, to reduce resistance and breakage. Also, form the habit of tying them to the trellis from the windward side.

Drip irrigation systems are espe-

LEFT: *The "Kniffin" system for training grapes to trellis after pruning. It takes about three years to bring a new vine to this approximate stage, which can be maintained from then on.* RIGHT: *The fan system is a simple alternative, especially in harsh conditions or for grapes grown partly as an ornamental. The plant will look like this by its third season after spring pruning.*

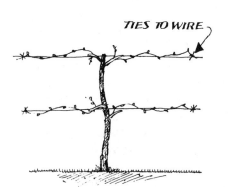

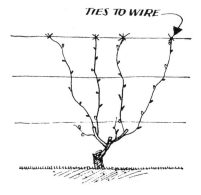

cially suited to grapes. Arrange and fasten the tubes along the lowest wire of each trellis, with an emitter above each plant; the drip system will be out of the way of weeding or cultivating activities. This mode of watering is a step ahead of overhead irrigation in reducing the potential for leaf disease problems.

Mildew and black rot are two fungus diseases common on grapes. Several insects also attack them, the most damaging being the larvae of the grape berry moth. Commercial fruit tree sprays will control these when applied according to package directions. If you prefer not to use chemical sprays, stick with disease-resistant varieties such as 'Mars.' As grapes must ripen on the vine to their ultimate sweetness, they are prone to mishaps such as being pecked or stolen by birds or damaged by rain. In a home planting, it is practical to protect each bunch with a paper bag tied on with string, or to protect the entire trellis with netting or lightweight row cover spread over the vines.

HARDY KIWI

Not yet widely tested as a fruit for the Heartland, this much-publicized Asiatic vine (*Actinidia arguta*) has raised high hopes with those who admire the fuzzy fruit of the subtropical kiwi sold in markets. As a fruit, this hardy kiwi (rated Zone 4) cannot compare with the subtropical form, but it has equal ornamental qualities. In fact, it has been grown here for years, although not commonly, as a landscape plant going by the name "bower vine" or "tara vine." It is a vigorous, twining, leafy vine and needs a strong trellis. Keeping it in bounds entails much pruning. The 1-inch-long fruits (actually berries) are greenish yellow, smooth skinned, and sweet; they ripen in September. These plants have male and female flowers on separate vines, so for fruit you need both the female and a male nearby to pollinate. Nurseries make both sexes available. Recently a few nurseries have offered a self-pollinating form, 'Issai,' from Japan that overcomes the need to plant two. It is reported to be slightly less vigorous and hardy. The main cultural need of hardy kiwi is a well-drained soil. It can grow in partial shade.

BRAMBLE AND BUSH FRUITS

In this group are some easily grown favorites, adaptable to small spaces and in several cases, ornamental besides. You won't have to wait long after planting (only a little over a year with most) before being rewarded with harvests of delicious berries that are definitely a luxury. Spring is the best time to plant them.

RASPBERRIES. Two main types, in four fruit colors, make up this group. Nurseries sell dormant plants in spring. With attention, all will grow throughout the Heartland. A good site is one in humusy, well-drained soil, that has sun most of the day. For red raspberries, whose fruits sometimes sunscald in hot locations in the south and west of our region, afternoon shade is helpful. In dry areas and drought years, watering may be necessary during the fruit-setting season (May and early June), so access to a water supply is a boon. A mulch of leaves or old hay helps. Many gardeners install post and wire trellises for raspberries, especially the black and purple types, to control the canes; but trellises are not essential to success. A 30-foot row of any kind would be enough for a family of five during fruiting season, with some left for jam, jelly, and the birds.

BLACK AND PURPLE RASPBERRIES. Purples are hybrids of red and black, but they grow like blacks. Space both kinds 2½ feet apart, in rows 7 feet apart. As they produce long arching canes in summer and fall, trellises (low posts with crossarms to which wires are fastened on each side) help a lot in keeping the plants neat and accessible. Set plants with the crowns 2 inches deep. Young canes soon emerge and grow upward. As they reach 30 inches, pinch out the soft tips to stimulate the rise of side branches called "laterals." This process increases yields, as side branches will bear the crop the following spring. In late winter go through and prune side branches back to about 10 inches. In their second year, after they mature their berries, these canes will die, and new canes will rise to replace them. Cut out the old canes at the ground and remove them to keep the planting disease free. Do this right after harvest, in July or August. Black and purple raspberries bear once a year over a three-to-four-week season in June–July. They spread from tip-layers where canes arch to the ground; resulting plantlets may be transplanted to expand your planting. Here are some recommended varieties: black— 'Bristol,' 'Allen,' 'Cumberland,'

'Blackhawk'; purple—'Royalty' and 'Brandywine.'

RED, YELLOW, AND EVER-BEARING RASPBERRIES. Most in this group are red; the few yellow or amber varieties, such as 'Fallgold,' are handled like the reds. Space them 30 inches apart, in rows 7 feet apart. They grow stiffly erect, unlike the black and purple kinds, and increase by traveling roots, sending up new plants well away from the parent. Keep aisles cultivated between rows or along sides to confine plants to a band about 30 inches wide, leaving room for access. Pruning consists mostly of removing old plants after they have fruited. Kinds like 'Latham' that bear only in June may be cleaned up in late July; but ever-bearing varieties like 'Heritage,' which start ripening in July and continue into autumn, are not cleaned of their old canes until late fall or the next spring. This sort of pruning can be done with a grubbing hoe to remove all of the old plant. In working over the patch, also hoe out weaklings so only the huskiest crowns are left, separated from each other about 12 inches. Some recommended varieties are 'Heritage' and 'Titan' (ever-bearing red), 'Latham' (red), and 'Fallgold' (fall-bearing yellow).

Keep black and purple raspberry plantings well separated from red raspberries to prevent their exchanging anthracnose organisms, one of the worst disease pests of either kind. For the same reason, avoid planting raspberries of any sort close to blackberries. A planting of either type of raspberry can be expected to last about ten years before it needs replacement, probably in a new location.

BLACKBERRIES

Blackberries look like black raspberries, but when you pick them, the core comes too. The fruits are larger than raspberries, 1 inch long and thimble shaped, with a distinctive, pleasing taste; they ripen in late June through July. Even though wild blackberries thrive throughout much of the Heartland, the cultivated varieties do not fare as well. Among the many different kinds in commerce are numerous hybrids derived from more tender species. Least hardy are the trailing types (boysenberries and dewberries); these are also the most disease prone and hard to handle and so are not recommended for our region. Our most suc-

After spring pruning, raspberry plants should look something like this.

cessful kinds are the upright growers that spread by root suckers. 'Darrow' is among the hardiest of this group. Among the thornless varieties, which are generally not so hardy as the thorny kinds, 'Chester' is recommended. Anyone who has encountered the efficient thorns of blackberries can understand why thornless forms have been sought out.

Start a new patch by setting plants 4 feet apart and allowing them to form clumps for convenience in tending. A trellis as described for black raspberries helps in controlling them in a row. Fruits form on canes of the previous year. The first year as these rise, pinch back the tips to 3 to 4 feet, to induce branching, which increases the subsequent crop. The second year, after those canes have fruited, cut them out at the base, as they will die anyway. During spring pruning, thin out plants, saving the strongest. For the best ber-

RASPBERRIES

RED

BLACK

ries, plants need steady moisture through the spring bloom season until fruits are fully colored. They are picked dead ripe, when they part easily from the stem.

A problem in growing blackberries in the Heartland is that blooms are often killed by late freezes. In selecting a site, therefore, favor a north or east slope, or possibly one shaded by a building in spring, to delay blooming to a safe date. Soil type is not of great importance, as blackberries seem tolerant—but it helps if the soil lends itself to frequent shallow cultivation to control the excess of plantlets that arise from root suckers far from the parent row.

GOOSEBERRIES

Nature bestowed on the Heartland a wealth of wild gooseberries, but the cultivated varieties such as 'Pixwell' are great improvements in the size of fruits and productivity. The tailoring and good behavior of the plants make them suitable for landscape uses in a small garden, as they form compact clumps about 3 feet across and 30 inches high, ideal for a low, maintenance-free hedge. Two or three plants are enough to supply all the gooseberries most families would want—not because enthusiasm is lacking for the fruits but because they take so much preparation time in the kitchen. Each berry must be "stemmed and sterned"—pedicels removed on one end and calyx remnants on the other.

Gooseberries are a northern plant and so do better in the north than in the south, but any place in our region can grow them with no trouble. In the hottest and driest areas, give them afternoon shade. A clay or heavy loam soil is suitable for these plants because such soils stay cool. A summer mulch is good, too, for insulation and to keep down weeds.

Set out plants in spring, at least 3 feet apart. Hardly any pruning is needed the first few years, but since the best fruiting comes on younger canes, a process of renewal should be followed eventually, by which two or three of the oldest canes are removed at the crown each spring before leafing.

For some obscure reason, perhaps impatience, many people pick their gooseberries while they are still hard and green. Lots of sugar must be added to make them edible. They are better for you and just as tasty if you let them ripen on the plant to a rosy hue. They become sweeter, softer, prettier, and also more perishable, but at any stage gooseberries are readily preserved by freezing, with no blanching or other preparation needed.

One recommended variety is 'Pixwell,' because the berries hang conveniently below the thorns and because it resists powdery mildew, a disease that plagues most others.

CURRANTS

'Red Lake,' the prevailing variety of this fruit, is so good there is little need for another. Close relatives of gooseberries, currants came from northern Europe. They have more problems with heat than with cold and therefore do better in the north of the Heartland than in our warmer zones. Yet they grow nearly throughout. The small ruby-red berries, in grapelike clusters, have found a place in gourmet restaurants, garnishing beverages, fruit salads, and meat dishes. Two generations ago they were gathered by the peck and made into marvelous-tasting, brilliantly colored jellies and jams.

A single plant is enough for average home use if having fruit is the only motive. But currants make agreeable landscape shrubs as well—dark-green foliage on neat rounded bushes 3 to 5 feet high. Plant them in spring 1 inch deeper than they stood in the nursery. In southern areas, choose heat-protected sites—a spot shaded on summer afternoons, possibly near a downspout for extra moisture. Currants thrive in heavy, cool soil. Mulching with grass clippings or bark chips helps to keep roots cool. Avoid cultivating, as roots are shallow. Leave about 5 feet between plants; in southern areas where they do not grow as large, leave 4 feet.

BLUEBERRIES

The only parts of the Heartland where blueberries grow naturally (under such folk names as "huckleberry") are in the Ozark Mountains. It takes effort to grow them almost anywhere in the Heartland, but many gardeners succeed, even commercially in southern Missouri and southeastern Kansas. Complete soil modification is essential to make and keep it acidic. This consists first of excavating a 3-by-3-foot hole 18 inches deep. Remove two-thirds of the soil completely. Mix equal amounts of peat and sand into the remaining soil up to ground level. Add

sulfur to lower the pH to 4.5 (test it to be sure). In spring, set plants in the prepared hole. Some settling is allowable to catch rainwater. Aluminum sulfate, ½ cup per plant per season, is often used in this region to maintain the acidity of the soil, but if this is overdone it leads to toxicity problems. Two blueberry varieties are needed for cross pollination. Successful varieties in southeastern parts of the Heartland with Zone 5 or 6 winters are 'Earliblue,' 'Bluecrop,' and 'Blueray.' Expect them to grow about 5 feet high in rounded, upright form.

With shining leaves, creamy-white spring flowers, and red autumn foliage adding to the appeal of the sweet, blue fruits in summer, blueberries rank among the top edible ornamentals. No wonder we all want to grow them.

ELDERBERRIES

American elder, *Sambucus canadensis*, grows wild all across the Heartland. Birds and people of earlier ages made good use of these late-summer purple-black berries. Arriving settlers harvested them eagerly for pies, wine, and jelly. Improved varieties have been introduced with larger berries and better behavior in gardens. With broad white panicles of tiny flowers in June and shining summer foliage on 10-foot plants, these qualify as edible ornamentals and are especially appropriate in wildlife gardens. They revert to coarse "bare bones" in winter with no screening effect. The plants naturally spread underground by suckers reaching out from the parent. Although cultivated varieties are less prone to this, they will still do it, so plant them where stray shoots will be no concern. Space plants 8 feet apart. Partial shade in summer and a low spot where runoff gives extra moisture will help them. Plant two varieties for cross-pollination, unless there are wild stands nearby that will serve. New plants should bear their second year.

'York' has the largest berries; 'Nova' has a high-yield record; and 'Johns' is noted for large berries that ripen early. All are recommended throughout our region.

STRAWBERRIES

Strawberries have put many Heartland youngsters through college, proof that these popular fruits succeed here if handled well. The two main production types are the June-bearing and the ever-bearing. June-bearers give a great crop in late spring and then are over for the year. Ever-bearers give a good set in spring and then continue at a reduced rate into autumn. When production volume is the objective, June-bearers are the choice. For home gardens where a modest but continuing supply of fresh berries is the goal, ever-bearers are chosen. Of either, be sure to get certified virus-free stock. Be careful in selecting varieties. Ask your area extension agent or nearby commercial growers what kinds are grown successfully. Local conditions make dramatic differences in the performance of a variety.

Choose a site that is sunny and has well-drained, humusy soil, preferably

The correct planting depth of a strawberry plant. The crown should be at ground level—not too high, not too low.

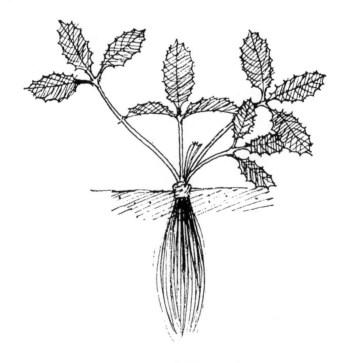

loamy or sandy. A slight elevation is good to avoid late frosts. A source of water for irrigation is the final essential. If the place is in grass, prepare it a year ahead and keep it cultivated so that perennial weeds will expire. Plant as early in spring as the soil can be worked. Mix in fertilizer, 1 pound per 100 square feet of a formulation such as 10-10-10. Plants will probably be dormant and bare root. Keep them shaded and damp while planting. Set each plant so the crown (thickened zone where leaves emerge) is exactly at ground level.

The two basic systems for arranging strawberries are the *matted row*, for June-bearers and *hills* for ever-bearers, which make fewer runners. For June-bearers in matted rows, space plants 18 inches apart in rows 42 inches apart; let plants runner out and root undisturbed for the first summer. The result should be mats about 18 inches wide separated by a clear aisle and ready for good production the next spring. *Keep blossoms picked off the first summer* to strengthen

plants for a big yield the following spring.

For ever-bearers arranged in hills, set plants 12 inches apart in rows 12 inches apart, but leave every third or fourth row vacant for a path. *Keep all runners cut off all season* and *any blooms pinched off* that develop before July. Then let them bloom. The first berries will ripen in August.

For both types, watering will be needed, as strawberries are shallowly rooted. If rains fail through the growth season, provide water, 1 inch per week. Drip systems are ideal for watering strawberries. In fall spread seed-free straw among young plants for mulch; after a few hard frosts, add more mulch for winter protection, to a total of three inches. Draw back the mulch in spring as growth begins, but leave it over the ground to cushion fruits.

Continue these methods in the second and subsequent seasons, watering when rains fail, fertilizing, and mulching. When late spring frost threatens a patch in bloom, cover it with blankets

Things Nobody Ever Tells You

🐦 Tart cherries have to be pitted before you can put them in a pie or cobbler. A perfect pitting tool is a wire paperclip. Push one end of the clip into the dimple where the stem was, and lift the seed out. Before paperclips, our grandmothers used wire hairpins.

🐦 How do you know when grapes are ripe aside from tasting them? Look at the stem and seeds. Both turn brownish when the fruit is ripe. The color of the berries is not a good guide, as

grapes acquire their final color well ahead of peak flavor. Unlike many fruits, grapes do no further ripening after they part from the vine.

🐦 Pick strawberries early in the day before heat hits. Leave on the green caps; the berries will last longer. Refrigerate them at once if you must hold them more than a day or two. Do not wash berries until just before you are ready to eat them.

or row covers. Early morning is the best time to pick ripe berries.

After three or four years, plantings become so crowded they need renovation. After harvest, run a tiller or hoe through each row, leaving a 10-inch-wide strip undisturbed but destroying the rest. Go through the undestroyed part and hoe out any weak plants, leaving survivors about 6 inches apart. Resume care as before.

Some recommended June-bearing varieties are 'Earliglow,' 'Surecrop,' 'Redchief,' and 'Guardian.' Two recommended ever-bearing varieties are 'Ogallala' and 'Ozark Beauty.'

Ornamental Strawberries

No strawberries are entirely care free, but alpines, the non-running, small-fruited type grown ornamentally, do come close. They make attractive low edgings around shrubbery borders, walks, and terraces; through summer they usually offer pleasing nibbles of flavorful, fragrant fruits. Space them 12 inches apart and handle as you would any perennial flower. Or grow them in containers. These strawberries are hardy in our region and will last for years. Alpine strawberries are easily grown from seeds available from many catalogs.

Nut Trees

Gardeners who plant nut trees are doing something for posterity. This ultimate "edible ornamental" is a long-term project. No harvests may be had for many years. The planter is repaid quickly, however, with other dividends such as cool shade, beauty, wind pro-

tection, and nesting sites and shelter for birds and squirrels. Most nut trees require spacious grounds. The chart on page 87 gives approximate space requirements for kinds practical in the Heartland. Study the site and climate needs of nut trees before making decisions, or look about you to see what kinds succeed in your area. Nut trees do not need much pruning or spraying. If deer are in your area, it is wise to put a guard around young trees or protect them with deer repellent to prevent antler damage, which can be severe.

Black walnuts are native throughout most of the Heartland and thus are considered hardy; but they may not fruit every year if they are in frost pockets that catch late frosts or freezes. Upland sites are best. Remember that the roots of black walnuts exude a toxin that cripples or kills many garden plants within their reach—tomatoes, potatoes, blackberries, apples, azaleas—so avoid planting black walnuts near gardens. On the other hand, walnuts and lawns get along perfectly. Favorite black walnut varieties for our region are 'Sparrow' and 'Ohio.' Carpathian (or Persian) walnuts apparently do not contain the toxin; the hardiest varieties are 'Colby' and 'Hansen.' Carpathian walnuts are about as cold hardy as black walnuts. Both black and Persian walnuts are susceptible to bark cracking by winter frosts while young. In this region young plants should be kept wrapped up to their lower branches until their bark thickens.

Pecans are native to southern Missouri and southeastern Kansas and quite a way northward up the major river valleys. They will not thrive in dry hill country or in thin soils. Southern pecan varieties will probably not survive our winters. The northern areas should grow the early-ripening (mid-September) varieties such as 'Colby,' 'Peruque,' 'Posey,' and 'Major.'

Chestnuts, Chinese and American, are both rated hardy in Zones 4 to 9. Early in the 1900s a blight hit American chestnuts and it has brought them to near extinction. Therefore, the Chinese chestnuts, which are resistant, have largely replaced the American species. Recently, however, blight-resistant hybrids between the American and Chinese species have been developed and introduced as Dunstan hybrids. With nuts and upright habit resembling American chestnuts, these hybrids are expected to grow over the same wide area as the individual species. American chestnuts were not native this far west, but they were planted and grew here. A group of mature fruiting American chestnuts grows today at Arbor Lodge in Nebraska City, Nebraska. Chestnuts of both types do best on uplands or hilltops, where air circulates and frost does not settle.

Hazelnuts (filberts), rated hardy in Zones 5 to 8, are the best-adapted nut plant for small gardens. Under good conditions, they form large spreading shrubs up to 10 feet high that make excellent screens or backgrounds in landscapes. Only rarely do they fail to produce a crop in the Heartland. Hybrids with European filberts (*Corylus*) vary in hardiness. American hazelnuts (*Corylus americana*) are native to much of the Heartland except for the drier western parts.

Nut Trees Recommended for the Heartland

KIND	DISTANCE FROM OTHER TREES (IN FEET)	YEARS TO BEAR	NEED FOR TWO VARIETIES TO POLLINATE?	HARDINESS ZONES
Black walnut	50	8–12	No	4
Persian walnut	40	6–10	No	5
American chestnut	40	7	Yes	4
Chinese chestnut	40	7	Yes	South edge of 4
Hazelnut	10	3	Yes	5
Pecan	40	8–10	Yes	South edge of 5

Annuals–A Short Life but a Flowery One

Of all the inventions of nature, the seed is among the cleverest. Seeds are what our annual garden flowers are really about. Nature's objective undoubtedly was survival of the species. But the scenario called for colorful, attractive flowers that would lure insects to complete the pollination so that fertile seeds would form. Then when winter freezes destroyed the plant, the seed would remain to provide a new beginning the next year. Those enticing flowers, so quick to develop, are favorites of our gardens.

Kinds like petunias, marigolds, nasturtiums, and portulaca certainly brighten a Heartland summer. Gardeners are content with the delusion that this lavish display of color is put on just for them.

New gardens particularly depend on annual flowers for a send-off. Notice how many newlyweds, in their first home, plant petunias along the walk. Pansies blink from little pockets by their door, and marigolds soon line their driveway. The lively color of the annual flowers makes a raw new place look lived in the very first summer.

Annuals appeal to beginning gardeners because they are so quick and easy. They are ideal for children's projects, as success is assured. The bedding-plant growers make scores of annuals widely available every spring, well started and growing in convenient potlets. All you have to do is plug them into the prepared ground and water them. The investment is small, the rewards great.

Annuals also are especially suited to short-term plantings in hanging baskets, barrels, and window boxes. For a shaded location, we have numerous adapted kinds, like impatiens, that will perform well there. For a hot and sunny location, we have many heat- and drought-tolerant kinds that offer possibilities.

Those who like to keep fresh flower bouquets in their homes have a list of favorite annuals that furnish the basics for arrangements from spring to fall, starting with pansies in April. What would we do in summer without cosmos, celosias in all shapes and sizes, lisianthus, zinnias, and the foliage of coleus? Then there is the roster of kinds that when dried furnish arrangements through winter—such as globe amaranth and strawflower.

Some of the annuals excel as bedders for massed effects. Designers use them to color the landscape as an artist paints from a palette. Sweeps of petunias, dusty millers, and nicotianas are planted into broad designs that can be seen from blocks away.

There are also annual kinds that are simply "good company" in gardens of mixed perennials, kinds that reseed themselves and return each year with practically no effort by the gardener. They contribute color, each in its season, and earn their keep. Kinds such as poppies, cornflowers, bells of Ireland, and cleome are of this sort. Gardeners discover their own favorites and welcome them into the perennial garden. They recognize the self-sown seedlings each spring and spare enough from the hoe to keep them going.

A free and pleasant education about the world of annual flowers is available from catalogs of the big retail seed companies widely advertised every winter. Merely answer their ads to receive their catalogs; usually there is no cost.

Gardeners with the right facilities—a sunny, warm window or fluorescent growing lights and shelves—can easily start their own plantlets from seed if they wish. To do so is both an interesting project and an economy. Directions for handling seeds either indoors or outdoors in the ground are found on seed packets.

Increasingly, however, many gardeners obtain their annuals as prestarted plants that begin to appear at nurseries or supermarket parking lots with the first warm days of March. Production of bedding plants has become a big industry. They are a convenience to the purchasers and undoubtedly encourage more people to beautify their grounds with annuals than ever would do so otherwise. If you obtain your plants as prestarts, observe the following guidelines that will heighten your success:

❧ Shop first at local greenhouses and established garden centers, as their plants will have had consistent professional care—not always true of the temporary sales yards in shopping centers and parking lots.

❧ Buy early while plants are fresh from the grower and have not had time to dry out or suffer other damage.

❧ Select vigorously growing plants that have not yet started to bloom. They will develop wider root systems and generally perform better longer in your garden than plants already blooming.

❧ Look at the label that usually accompanies each flat or pot to be sure of the color of plants not in bloom.

Planting these prestarted seedlings is simple. Just tap or push them out of their pots, reset them in the prepared soil of your garden bed, and water them in. For an extra boost use a little starter fertilizer mixed into the transplant water. As a finishing touch, mulch them. Dried grass clippings are good for this and usually available. See the chart on pages 100–103 for recommended spacings of most kinds and other details.

The Heartland's Most Important Annuals

CLEOME. Also called "spider flower," this tall, elegant plant blooms through the dog days of summer with an admirable blend of style and stamina. The interesting airy flowers form atop long stems that can be seen from afar. Usually they are rose or pink; a white form is also available. Cleome may be grown from seeds sown in place. If allowed to go to seed in the fall garden, it will volunteer the next spring to repeat the performance. Use it as an accent or background plant.

COCKSCOMB (Celosia). There are two types, crested and plumed (named for the shape of the flower's head), and several colors, although the main colors are red and scarlet. These are drought and heat tolerant and versatile. They give a vivid effect as bedding plants, and have many admirers as cut flowers. They also dry well for winter bouquets. To grow them, merely seed them in place in a sunny spot after the soil warms.

COSMOS. Showy daisy-shaped blooms on graceful long stems make these favorites for cut flowers as well as for season-long garden color. The two types, derived from different species, differ in plant height and colors. The Klondike types form early semi-double or single flowers in yellow, orange, or scarlet on low (2-to-3-foot) hedgelike plants. The Sensation types form large single blooms in lilac and rose tones and white on stately plants

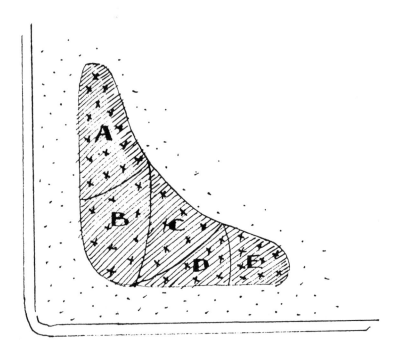

An accent bed of annuals at a driveway entrance (in full to half-day sun). A—mixture of blue ageratum and white sweet alyssum. B—lavender Vinca rosea (Catharanthus). C—purple Salvia farinacea 'Victoria.' D—nicotiana 'Nicki Rose.' E—mixture of blue ageratum and dusty miller.

4 feet or more in height; these are best in backgrounds. Both are easily seeded where they are to grow; be sure to plant them in a sunny spot.

IMPATIENS. For color in shade (white, lavender, and pinks to vivid red and coral) nothing surpasses impatiens. Shapely, mounded plants, they are handsome wherever you put them. They can take heat but not drought. Be prepared to water them through dry spells. The New Guinea impatiens, of recent discovery and development, is an outstanding container plant noted for nonstop flamboyant bloom and often for colorful foliage, some with cream or red variegations. You may see the New Guinea hybrids recommended for sunny places, but in the Heartland give them shade also, at least two-thirds of the day.

MARIGOLD. For bedding, edgings, and foreground plantings in sunny areas, the dwarf French-type marigolds are preferable. For cut flowers and backgrounds, the taller, larger "American" types are best; they come in an abundance of color tones, all in the yellow-gold-orange range. In our region marigolds are prone to the "aster yellows" disease that causes plants to stunt and turn yellow and distorted. The most practical remedy when you see this is to pull and discard the affected plant. There is no cure, but by

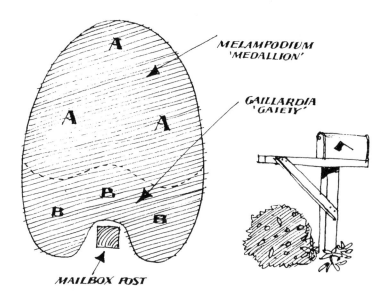

An accent planting at a mailbox (in full sun).

roguing you can slow the spread. Insects carry the virus from plant to plant; you may find other plants such as asters and zinnias affected also, and with them you should do the same—remove them.

NICOTIANA. Flowering tobacco, a relative of the petunia, is more tolerant of heat and drought than the petunia and seldom falls prey to insect or disease. Use it instead of petunias where you want a reliable, season-long show of colors—white, light green, rose, red. Breeders have tailored the plants to neat low mounds, crowned by the upright and orderly flower panicles. Give nicotianas full sun to partial shade.

PETUNIA. These come in several types, each with special qualifications. The most heat, drought and storm tolerant and thus most durable for bedding effect in our summers are the single floribundas and single multifloras. Both bloom prolifically; of these two types the floribundas (for example, the 'Madness' series) have the larger flowers. Grandifloras have the largest flowers of all and look especially good in urns, hanging baskets, and window boxes. Although double forms are available, they seldom make as great a show as the singles and are better for containers viewed from close range. Petunias now come in virtually every spectrum color except true sky blue. Many are bicolors with white zones, and some have attractive dark veining effects. But do not expect modern petunias to have much fragrance.

Annuals for Every Need

To overplant vacant spaces left by spring bulbs: Ageratum, alyssum, pansy, petunia, portulaca, verbena, *Vinca rosea* (periwinkle).

For tubs, hanging baskets, planters, and window boxes:
IN SUN: Ageratum, alyssum, dusty millers, geranium, nasturtium, petunia, portulaca, verbena, *Vinca rosea* (periwinkle).
IN SHADE: Begonia (fibrous), browallia, impatiens, *Lobelia erinus*, torenia.

For arranging: Bells of Ireland, China aster (*Callistephus*), cosmos (both types), gladiolus, lisianthus, marigolds (larger growers), scabiosa, snapdragon, statice (*Limonium sinuata*), tithonia, zinnia.

For accent edgings: Alyssum, begonia (fibrous), dahlberg daisy, dianthus (pinks), dusty millers, gazania, marigold (dwarf types), nierembergia, pansy, pepper (ornamental), petunia, phlox (Drummond), portulaca, *Salvia splendens*, verbena.

For hot, dry conditions: Cleome, Cape marigold (*Dimorphotheca*), dahlberg daisy (*Dyssodia tenuiloba*), gaillardia, gazania, gomphrena, *Melampodium*, portulaca, sunflowers, *Vinca rosea* (periwinkle).

For drying to make winter arrangements and wreaths: Celosia, cornflower, gomphrena, nigella, statice (*Limonium sinuata*), strawflower.

For foliage effect: Amaranthus, basils (ornamental types), coleus, dusty millers, ornamental kale, flowering cabbage, ornamental grasses.

For massed bedding-plant effect: Begonia (fibrous), celosia, dahlias (dwarf types from seed), heliotrope, lavatera (mallow), marigold, *Melampodium*, nicotiana, *Vinca rosea* (periwinkle), petunia, *Salvia splendens*, *Salvia farinacea* (blue bedder salvia), zinnia.

Annual vines for trellis or fence: Moonflower, morning glory, black-eyed Susan vine (*Thunbergia*), cypress vine (*Ipomoea quamoclit*), hyacinth bean (*Dolichos lablab*).

Annuals to seed directly where you want them to grow:
IN EARLY SPRING: Alyssum, bells of Ireland, California poppy (*Eschscholzia*), cornflower (*Centaurea*), cleome, gaillardia, hollyhock, larkspur, nigella (love-in-a-mist), portulaca, shirley poppy.
AFTER FROST'S END: Abelmoschus, amaranthus, celosia, cosmos, *Dimorphotheca*, gomphrena, marigold, nasturtium, nicotiana, sunflower, zinnia.

VINCA ROSEA OR PERIWINKLE (*Catharanthus*). This adaptable plant seems made to order for our region, and we have long used it. Recently developed forms eclipse the older ones, with larger flowers in pink, rose, white, and eye patterns and growth habits suited for ground-cover uses, borders, and featured containers, even hanging baskets. The glossy foliage is always presentable, seemingly immune to insect or disease. This is one of our most drought-tolerant annuals. Use it instead of impatiens in shady areas where you cannot water. Vinca can take either shade or sun.

ZINNIAS. These are flowers for full sun. Many types from low to tall and with flowers from tiny to saucer size are available for different uses. With zinnias, it is important to use mildew-resistant varieties such as the 'Zeniths' or 'Dreamlands' to avoid having plants disfigured by this common fungus disease of late summer. Or as an alternative, make a midsummer sowing so you will have young, vigorous, clean plants for the fall display. Our region grows very good zinnias. They make wonderfully colorful cut flowers.

FOUR POPULAR BIENNIALS

The plants in this small group, grown from seeds, differ from annuals in that they usually do not bloom until the second year after you plant them. They are often used among the other flowers of a perennial garden. Once started, they will reseed and maintain themselves for a long time. All are widely grown in our region.

CANTERBURY BELLS (*Campanula medium*), 2-inch-long pink, blue, or white bells ranged up a sturdy 30-inch spike bloom for several weeks starting in May. Give "cup and saucer" part shade, especially in southern areas of our region. Be prepared to water them through dry periods. Seeds are usually started in special beds in August, for transplanting the next spring.

FOXGLOVE (*Digitalis*) is usually seeded in August for bloom the following June. Some kinds ('Foxy') bloom sooner, the same summer from a spring sowing. Although foxgloves do best in cooler, moister climates, they often surprise us with a superb show of stately spires bearing white, yellow, or rose-tone bells, often spotted, above a rosette of neat foliage. Give them part shade, and be ready to water them through droughts.

MONEY PLANT (*Lunaria annua*) has purple summer blooms that are soon followed by the dollar-size papery

Some Favorite Combinations of Annuals

🌂 White alyssum seeded among flowering kale, for a frilly combination up to December.

🌂 Fibrous begonias in white or pink or impatiens of any hue edged with torenia or blue *Lobelia erinus*. This is a summer combination for shade.

🌂 Dwarf bedding dahlias, any color, fronted with white periwinkle (*Vinca rosea* or *Catharanthus*).

🌂 Blue salvia 'Victoria' (*Salvia farinacea*) edged with white or pink multiflora petunias or dwarf marigolds.

white seed pods prized for winter bouquets and craft work. Sow this outdoors in fall where you want it to bloom the next year. It is a tolerant, easy plant.

FORGET-ME-NOT (*Myosotis alpestris*), an April-May flower, needs semishaded, moist areas where it will reseed itself and come back year after year. Sweet sky-blue flowers, each with a small yellow or white eye, are on plants only 6 inches high, forming a ground cover. Sometimes it fades out in the heat of summer, but it returns in autumn. It is a favorite for planting among daffodils. In the Heartland, you can sow seeds in autumn where you

want them to bloom; mulch lightly over winter. Give this plant humusy soil.

SUMMER BULBS THAT ARE HANDLED AS ANNUALS

These are not all really bulbs, although that is what most gardeners call them. As they are tender and cannot survive our winters, they are planted in spring and taken up in fall to be stored in a frost free place until spring. These six kinds are widely used throughout our region.

CALADIUMS. For shaded beds under trees or along north sides of houses or other buildings and for container plantings in such areas, caladiums are good accents with bold and tropical heart-shaped leaves in striking green, cream, pink, and crimson combinations. They are usually prestarted indoors in spring by laying the tubers (roots down, growth points upward) partly submerged in damp peat and kept in a 70-degrees or warmer place to induce growth. As new leaves arise, transfer tubers to the garden bed or planter. Soil should be warm. Water-

*A garden of everlastings (for dried arrangements) fronting a fence or wall (in full sun). A—blue statice (*Limonium sinuata*). B—white globe amaranth (*Gomphrena*). C—yellow-bronze mixture of strawflowers (*Helichrysum*). D—green bells-of-Ireland (*Molucella*). E—red-crested cockscomb (*Celosia*) such as 'Red Velvet.' F—purple globe amaranth (*Gomphrena*). G—purple-white mixture of love-in-a-mist (*Nigella*).*

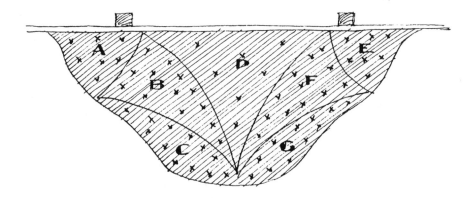

ing regularly and feeding caladiums monthly with a diluted nitrogen fertilizer (fish emulsion is good) keeps them growing. Caladium tubers will last from year to year and even increase if you lift them before frost, clean, and store them packed in dry peat or sawdust in a plastic bag at 60 degrees. Some gardeners growing them in pots store pot and all, undisturbed.

CANNAS. Cannas are traditional favorites across the Midwest because they grow so well in our summers. Both foliage and flowers have landscape impact—the foliage bold and tropical looking, the blooms in vivid showy clusters. We handle them as annuals, planting the rhizomes out in midspring, enjoying bloom from June to frost, and then lifting and storing the root clumps in a frost-free place over winter. Give cannas full sun. They excel as screens or backdrops or as centerpieces in tiered plantings with ornamental grasses and lower annuals such as marigolds or gloriosa daisies. Dwarf canna varieties are suited to large containers such as cut-down barrels.

Newly purchased canna rhizomes are likely to be small single divisions dry from prolonged storage. To give them a good start, soak them in tepid water for a day before planting to recharge their moisture and spur growth. Rhizomes you save and store from a previous year will take off faster; in spring divide last year's clumps into generous sections each with several growth buds, and they will soon make husky plants. For greatest landscape impact, mass many of the same variety together. Plant cannas in prepared ground after the soil warms, covering growth tips only lightly. Water them as necessary.

DAHLIAS FROM TUBERS (as differentiated from seeds). For at least a century, Heartland gardeners have grown champion dahlias. Soil and climate suitable for corn or potatoes will grow dahlias too. Dahlias bloom from midsummer to late fall. Fanciers recognize many different types based on distinct flower forms and sizes, some 1 foot across. They come in heights from low to towering. Properly conditioned, they make great cut flowers. Tall growers need staking against our boisterous winds, and in dry summers all need extra water to produce those gorgeous flowers. Dahlias are often adopted as a hobby, and they repay in full such attention as added organic matter in the soil, fertilizing, disbudding, added supports, shading against searing sun, and spraying or covering against insects. In planting, dig holes 5 inches deep, lay dahlia tubers horizontally or slightly tilted with the "eye" (growth bud on the stem portion) uppermost; cover lightly. Do this after spring frosts end and the soil is warm. If the variety will be tall and require staking, place the stake at planting time to avoid root disruption later. Refill the planting hole only partially, completing the job gradually as growth progresses.

Dahlia hobbyists keep their valuable tubers from year to year by digging and storing them each autumn after a killing frost. Cut down tops just above ground level, and with a digging fork carefully lift clumps and invert them to dry a few days. Brush off loose soil but allow any that clings to remain. Store clumps undivided in boxes in a frost-free place, adding sawdust or peat packing to prevent shriveling. In spring, just before replanting, divide and clean tubers. Cut them apart to single tubers, each with a stem portion that holds a bud for new growth. Without that bud, there will be no growth.

GLADIOLUS. Gardeners in the Heartland have long grown gladiolus for their spectacular value as cut flowers. They give gardens color, too. Clumps of them here and there in perennial beds make summery accents. They perform almost like clockwork in the number of days each variety takes from planting to flower. This figure usually is given in catalogs or on labels. If you plan a garden party for a certain date, you can select varieties, note their

"days to flower," count back on the calendar to plant, and rest assured of fresh blooms for your event. With all colors available except true blue, they can tie into almost any color scheme. Plant five or six of a kind together, spaced 5 inches apart, to give a strong stroke of design in the garden. For cut flowers, the corms are usually rowed out like vegetables and are often given a wire support for the whole row to keep stems straight. In autumn, lift the entire plants, remove the tops, and cure and store them as cleaned corms in a cool, dry place over winter. You'll probably notice an increase in quantity—a nice return on your investment. Cover gladiolus corms of normal size with 5 to 6 inches of soil to anchor the spears so they stand up against summer storms.

HYMENOCALLIS OR PERUVIAN DAFFO-DILS (*H. narcissiflora*). The Heartland's warm summers suit these South American amaryllis relatives perfectly. The white, sometimes cream-colored, lilylike flowers have fringes and narrow lancelike lobes with unusually exotic effect. The speed with which bulbs rush into bloom after planting is amazing, about three weeks being a depend-

---

A pink-, blue-, and white-flowered window box, 3 feet long, for a shaded location. A—Lobelia erinus 'Sapphire' (blue), three plants. B—Impatiens 'Super Elfin Pink' (six plants). C—sweet alyssum 'Carpet of Snow' (two plants).

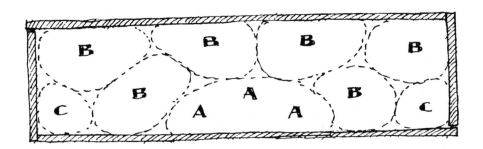

able interval. You can time their planting for garden events when you want something dramatic in bloom. The strappy green fountain of foliage that emerges while the blooms are maturing looks lush and tropical, even through the toasty days of August and September, lasting until the first freeze. The plants will grow in large containers. Some gardeners like to combine them in tubs with caladiums, using just one bulb at the center as a foliage accent for the caladiums around the outside. In autumn, move planted containers to storage in a basement, and do not disturb them until replanting time the next spring. Or store bulbs dug from the garden, tops removed, in paper bags or boxes where the temperature remains around 50 degrees. Do not let them chill or they may not bloom the following season. Only the largest bulbs will bloom, but others can be "rowed out" in a bed to enlarge and bloom some future year. Plant hymenocallis bulbs only 4 inches deep in sun or light shade.

TUBEROSES (*Polianthes tuberosa*). These are traditional cut-flower favorites that respond beautifully in warm summers. Do not let the common name mislead you to expect anything roselike. "Tuberose" derives from the tuberlike root clump. The spires with small waxen-white lilyshaped florets, often double, are usually heavily perfumed. The stately flower spikes arise from a basal mound of handsome grasslike leaves. Blooming in August or September, this plant contributes pristine flowers at a time when such are scarce, with fragrance scarcely matched by any other flower.

Handle them much as you would cannas. Newly purchased bulbs will probably be single divisions that may not bloom the first year unless they are of unusually generous size. Store those first-year clumps, dug up just before frost, and replant the next spring without dividing them—and you should then see blooms. In future years, large clumps can be divided into cup-sized clusters, but never reduce them to single divisions.

Things Nobody Ever Tells You

You can keep petunias looking young, vigorous, and flowering by cutting the long stems back halfway in midsummer. Do them one at a time, each day or two, to prevent the butchered look. Follow with a feeding of properly diluted liquid fertilizer. They will soon look leafy and flowery again.

Fibrous (wax leaf) begonias actually do best when crowded together; 5 inches is not too close. They grow into a canopy that shades and cools the soil, and retards evaporation, so the plants prosper.

Early morning is the best time to gather most kinds of cut flowers. Late evening is next best. Take a pail of water to the garden and sink each stem into it immediately after cutting. Stand the collection in a quiet shaded area for ten hours or so before arranging. As you assemble the bouquet, recut stems under water as an extra life-prolonging measure.

Easy Annuals for the Heartland

(Arranged alphabetically by commonest common name)

NAME / SUN OR SHADE (CODE: *FULL SUN; #PART SHADE; @SHADE)	USES / SPACING DISTANCE
African daisy (*Dimorphotheca aurantiaca*)*	Edging, container, cutting, bedding; 8"
Ageratum (*A. houstonianum*)*#	Edging, container, bedding; 10"
Alyssum, sweet (*Lobularia maritima*)*#	Edging, container, fragrance, bedding; 6–8"
Amaranth (*Amaranthus tricolor*)*	Background, bedding; 15"
Aster, China (*Callistephus chinensis*)*	Container, cutting, bedding; 10–12"
Begonia, fibrous (*B. semperflorens*)*#@	Edging, container, bedding; 8"
Bells of Ireland (*Molucella laevis*)*#	Cutting; 10"
Black-eyed Susan vine (*Thunbergia alata*)*#	Background; 12"
Browallia (*B. speciosa*)*@	Container, hanging basket, bedding; 9–12"
Cabbage, ornamental (*Brassica oleracea*)*	Edging, container, bedding; 12"
Calendula (*C. officinalis*)*	Cutting, bedding; 9"
Canterbury bells (*Campanula medium*)*#	Border; 12"
Cockscomb (*Celosia cristata*)*	Background, cutting, bedding, drying; 9"
Cleome (*C. spinosa*)*	Background, border, bedding; 10"
Coleus (*C. hybridus*)*#@	Background, container, bedding; 12"
Cornflower (*Centaurea cyanus*)*	Background, cutting, bedding; 8"
Cosmos (*C. sulphureus* and *C. bipinnatus*)*	Background, cutting, bedding; 10"
Dahlia (dwarf forms from seed) (*D. coccinea* and *D. pinnata* hybrids)*	Background, container, cutting, bedding; 12–24"
Dahlberg daisy (*Dyssodia tenuiloba*)*	Edging, container; 5"
Dusty miller (*Chrysanthemum* or *Senecio* spp.)*#	Edging, container, cutting; 7"
Flowering tobacco (*Nicotiana alata*)*#	Edging, container, bedding; 9"
Four o'clock (*Mirabilis jalapa*)*	Background, bedding; 12"
Gaillardia (*G. picta*)*	Cutting, bedding; 10"
Gazania (*G. pinnata*)*	Edging, bedding; 10"
Geranium (*Pelargonium* x *hortorum*)*#	Container, cutting, bedding; 12"
Globe amaranth (*Gomphrena globosa*)*	Edging, container, cutting, drying, bedding; 10"
Gloriosa daisy (*Rudbeckia hirta*)*#	Background, cutting, bedding; 12"
Heliotrope (*Heliotropium arborescens*)*	Background, cutting, fragrance, bedding; 12"
Hollyhock (*Alcea rosea*)*	Background; 12"
Impatiens (*I. wallerana*)*@	Edging, container, bedding; 15"
Kale, ornamental (*Brassica oleracea acephala*)*	Edging, container, bedding; 15"
Larkspur (*Consolida ambigua*)*	Background, cutting, border; 6"
Lavatera (mallow) (*L. trimestris*)*	Background, bedding; 8"
Lisianthus (*Eustoma grandiflorum*)*	Cutting; 12"
Lobelia, edging (*L. erinus*)@	Edging, container; 6"
Love-in-a-mist (*Nigella damascena*)*#	Cutting, bedding, drying; 8"
Marigold (*Tagetes* spp.)*	Background, edging, container, bedding; 6–12"
Melampodium (*M. paludosum*)*	Container, bedding, border; 12"
Nasturtium (*Tropaeolum minus*)*	Edging, container, cutting, fragrance, bedding; 6"

SEASON / COMMENTS

Summer/fall. Cream, yellow, or apricot combinations.

Summer/fall. Best for blue effect.

Summer/fall. White, rose, or purple; 4" high; self-sows.

Summer/fall. Accent plant with vivid-red foliage.

Summer/fall. White, pink, rose, or purple.

Summer/fall. Red, pink, or white; Foliage often bronzy.

Summer/fall. Green bells on spire; often self-sows.

Summer. Small climber; round orange blooms.

Summer/fall. Starry blue-purple flowers.

Fall. Rose, pink, or cream centers in ruffled green heads.

Spring. Needs coolness; start early; yellow marigoldlike flowers.

Early summer. White, pink, or lavender; biennial.

Summer/fall. Plumed or crested; red or pastels; some with reddish foliage.

Summer/fall. Tall accent; white, pink, or rose; self-sows.

All season. Colorful foliage—purple or yellow, bronze, or rose tones.

Spring/summer. Blue, white, pink, or rose; self-sows.

Summer/fall. Two distinct groups: yellow-orange and white-pink-lavender.

Summer/fall. All colors but blue.

Summer. Tiny yellow daisies.

All season. Silvery, low, lacy foliage.

Summer/fall. Pink, rose, white, red, or greenish; some are fragrant.

Summer. Red, yellow, or white flowers that open in late afternoon.

Summer/fall. Red, rose, yellow, or maroon wheel-shaped blooms.

Summer/fall. Low, wide rosettes; red-yellow daisies that close at night.

Summer/fall. Indispensable accent; red, white, pink, or coral.

Summer/fall. White, pink, lavender, or red.

Summer/fall. Large gold-tone daisies; some double; live several years.

Summer/fall. Dark-blue flower heads; textured foliage.

Spring/summer. Spires of cream, pink, red, or purple; some live several years.

Summer/fall. Best flower for shade; white, pink, rose, salmon, or violet.

Fall. More frilled than ornamental cabbage; rose tones with white; green foliage effect.

Spring/early summer. Self-sows; sow in fall for spring bloom; pink, purple, or white.

Summer. Dramatic large pink or white blooms; not for cutting.

Summer. Long-lasting white, pink, or purple cupped blooms; some double.

Summer/fall. Trailing, low, with small vivid-blue flowers.

Summer/fall. White, blue, or rose; self-sows.

Summer/fall. Low to tall and several flower forms; most in gold-yellow tones.

Summer/fall. Starry gold daisies on durable rounded green plant; heat tolerant.

Spring to fall. Gold, orange, or mahogany; edible.

Easy Annuals for the Heartland continued

NAME / SUN OR SHADE (CODE: *FULL SUN; #PART SHADE; @SHADE)	USES / SPACING DISTANCE
Pansy (*Viola x wittrockiana*)*#	Edging, container, cutting, bedding; 6"
Peppers, ornamental (*Capsicum annuum*)*	Edging, container, bedding; 12–15"
Petunia (*P. x hybrida*)*	Edging, container, cutting, bedding; 8"
Phlox (*P. drummondii*)*	Edging, container, bedding; 6"
Pinks (*Dianthus* spp.)*#	Edging, container, cutting, bedding; 7"
Poppies, California (*Eschscholzia californica*)*	Bedding, meadows; 8"
Poppies, shirley (*Papaver rhoeas*)*	Bedding, filler among perennials; 8"
Portulaca (moss rose) (*P. grandiflora*)*	Edging, container, bedding; 6"
Salvia (scarlet sage) (*S. splendens*)*#	Edging, container, bedding; 10"
Salvia, blue (*S. farinacea*)*#	Background, cutting, bedding; 10"
Sanvitalia (creeping zinnia) (*S. procumbens*)*	Edging, ground cover, container; 6"
Snapdragon (*Antirrhinum majus*)*#	Edging, container, cutting, bedding; 6"
Statice (*Limonium sinuata*)*	Cutting, bedding, drying; 12"
Strawflower (*Helichrysum bracteatum*)*	Cutting, drying, bedding; 10"
Sunflower (*Helianthus annuus*)*	Background, bedding, cutting; 10"
Sweet pea (*Lathyrus odoratus*)*#	Cutting, fragrance, border (bush types); 5"
Sweet william (*Dianthus barbatus*)*	Edging, cutting, bedding; 7–10"
Tithonia (Mexican sunflower) (*T. rotundifolia*)*	Background, cutting, bedding; 15"
Torenia (wishbone flower) (*T. fournieri*)#@	Edging, container, bedding in shade; 6"
Verbena (*V. x hybrida*)*	Edging, container, bedding; 8"
Vinca rosea (periwinkle) (*Catharanthus roseus*)*#	Edging, container, bedding, border; 8"
Zinnia (*Z. elegans*)*	Background, edging, container, cutting, bedding, border; 8–10"

SEASON / COMMENTS

Spring. Every color; some with faces, some without.

Summer/fall. Round or long, slender pods in red, yellow, or purple hues.

Summer/fall. Multiflora (small flower types) succeed best; every color but true blue.

Spring/summer. Red, pink, blue, or white; all under 20" high.

Spring to fall. White, pink, or red flowers with fringes; fragrance.

Spring/summer. Yellow-gold cups; silver foliage.

Spring/summer. Many colors; many doubles; self-sows.

Summer/fall. Bright colors; flowers close in evening; self-sows.

Summer/fall. Favorite for scarlet accent.

Summer/fall. Blue and white; may live over mild winter.

Summer/fall. Tiny orange blooms, like miniature sunflowers.

Spring to fall. All colors but blue; dwarf to tall forms.

Summer. Everlasting; rose, blue, or white.

Summer. For dried bouquets; crimson, pink, gold, or white.

Summer. Dwarf forms for bedding; blooms face sun.

Spring. Vine types need trellis; plant early to beat the heat.

Spring/summer. Biennial; white to crimson and combinations.

Summer/fall. Vivid scarlet-orange blooms; dense plants.

Summer/fall. Blue-lavender blooms on neat, low plants.

Summer/fall. Low and spreading; all colors but yellow.

Summer/fall; low, mounded, and spreading; white, pink, red, or lavender; eye zones.

Summer/fall. Wide range of heights; all colors but blue-purple.

CHAPTER EIGHT

Perennials – Through the Years

A garden perennial, in the strict sense,
is a flowering nonwoody plant that will live
at least three years. This separates the group
from biennials, which normally expire
after they bloom the second summer, and
from annuals. The distinction is
not always definite.

Our region is rich with possibilities in perennial flowers. Many of those offered in catalogs and nurseries had ancestors native to the Heartland. Although we may not grow the same delicate beauties found, for example, in gardens of the mild South or the cool Northwest, we have more than enough of our own of equal beauty and admirable stamina. In our region, you can have a garden with plants that offer a steady succession of color at least nine or ten months of the year.

A perennial garden is more than just a collection of perennials. It involves many decisions about colors, heights, textures, and placements for good effect and performance. Learning about perennials is a plant-by-plant process. Nobody can tell you as much about them as you yourself will observe in your own garden. The sooner you start, the better. It is no happenstance that so many of the best perennial gardeners are senior citizens.

List A: Basic Heartland Perennials for Shade/Partial Shade

Ajuga reptans (carpet bugle)
Aquilegia x *hybrida* (columbine)
Arum italicum (Italian arum)
Astilbe x *arendsii* (astilbe)
Bergenia cordifolia (bergenia)
Cimicifuga racemosa (bugbane)
Convallaria majalis (lily-of-the-valley)
Dicentra spectabilis (bleeding-heart)
Ferns
Helleborus orientalis (Lenten rose)
Hosta (plantain-lily)
Iris cristata (crested iris)
Iris tectorum (roof iris)
Lilium (lilies, especially Oriental hybrids)
Liriope muscari (lily-turf)
Mertensia virginica (Virginia bluebell)
Phlox divaricata (wood phlox)
Polygonatum biflorum and *P. odoratum* (Solomon's-seal)
Thalictrum (meadow-rue)
Tricyrtis formosana (toad-lily)

WHERE TO PUT PERENNIALS AND HOW TO USE THEM

Organizing a garden creates questions: Do you want one big border with color from spring to fall? Or should you divide garden areas into seasonal plots, for spring, summer, and fall? Or do you want a "theme" garden, where you strive for one special effect in your planting, such as a gold garden, a white garden, and so on? Or do you want to relate your design to the house style, such as a pioneer cottage garden with historic plants or a Victorian reminder? Part of the creativity is deciding these questions. Remember that mistakes can be corrected. As a garden is a living thing, it can change as it goes along.

Perennials need not be formally arrayed. Little groups beside a step, along a fence, at junctions of paths or corners of buildings, in shaded alcoves—all are ways you may see them used. The classic and most lavish use of perennials is in the broad "herbaceous borders" associated with European and English tradition. We can and do have perennial borders nearly as splendid. But we must match plants to Heartland conditions.

Where levels change and you have

retaining walls separating upper elevations from lower ones, you have a perfect place for ribbons of perennials along both or all levels. If the area is shaded, you should choose shade-suited perennials (see List A on page 106); if the area is sunny, choose from the more numerous sun-suited kinds (see List B below). Probably sunny spots can have more color, although shade gardens have many possibilities for pleasing bloom and foliage—as in the world of *Hosta* varieties. Some retainers, such as stone dry walls, present pockets for roots of rock-garden perennials that do well there and are seen better than at ground level (see List C on page 108).

A north-facing wall obviously is cooler most of the year than a south-facing one. Thus it offers places for ferns, bleeding hearts, and bergenias. A north-south fence or wall offers great east and west exposures befitting a broad range of plants. A wall or fence fronting south is for sun-loving and heat-tolerant kinds such as rudbeckias, eryngiums, sunflowers and gay-

---

List B: Basic Heartland Perennials for Sun

Achillea filipendulina (fern-leaf yarrow)
Achillea millefolium (milfoil)
Artemisia ('Silver Mound' and others)
Asclepias tuberosa (butterfly milkweed)
Aster novae-angliae and *A. novi-belgii* (Michaelmas daisy)
Baptisia australis (blue false indigo)
Ceratostigma plumbaginoides (blue leadwort)
Chrysanthemum coccineum (painted daisy)
Chrysanthemum morifolium (garden chrysanthemum)
Chrysanthemum x *superbum* (Shasta daisy)
Coreopsis verticillata (thread-leaf coreopsis)
Echinacea purpurea (purple coneflower)
Euphorbia polychroma (cushion spurge)
Gaillardia x *grandiflora* (blanketflower)
Geranium sanguineum (bloody cranesbill)
Gypsophila paniculata (baby's-breath)
Hemerocallis x *hybrida* (hybrid daylily)

Heuchera x *brizoides* or *H. sanguinea* (coralbells)
Hibiscus moscheutos hybrids (hardy hibiscus)
Iberis sempervirens (candytuft)
Iris (bearded types, dwarf, intermediate, and tall)
Iris sibirica (Siberian iris)
Lilium (lilies: Asiatic, Aurelian, and Oriental hybrids)
Limonium latifolium (statice)
Lythrum salicaria (loosestrife)
Monarda didyma (beebalm)
Nepeta mussinii (catmint)
Oenothera speciosa (evening-primrose)
Papaver orientale (Oriental poppy)
Phlox paniculata (summer phlox)
Platycodon grandiflorum (balloon-flower)
Salvia x *superba* (meadow sage)
Scabiosa caucasica (pincushion flower)
Tradescantia virginiana (spiderwort)
Verbascum chaixii (mullein)
Veronica latifolia (speedwell)

feathers, gaillardia, artemisias, and ornamental grasses.

Besides putting perennials in borders, you can put them in "islands" of any size or shape you please. Islands are usually irregular in outline and surrounded by a sea or moat of green lawn. They might be bordered with gravel or pavers of some type. These beds are openly and primarily showcases for plants.

SIX MAJOR PERENNIALS

Six major kinds of plants can form the framework of a Heartland perennial garden: peonies, daylilies, irises, hardy hibiscus, hostas, and Asiatic and Oriental hybrid lilies. Grouped together, these plants will provide color from spring to fall.

PEONIES. Peonies, a contribution from China, can be part of a mixed garden or planted alone. The dark, glossy foliage is handsome all summer, even after the flowers of May and June are gone. Use peonies as a background, as edging for drives or walks, or along foundations, walls, or fence lines. Peonies of herbaceous type (the most familiar kind) die down with frost. The red emerging shoots are one of the thrills of early spring.

For longest bloom, plant several kinds or varieties that flower in succession. The little fern-leafed *Paeonia tenuifolia* and the old-fashioned red *P. officinalis* are earliest, along with tree peonies (these are handled like shrubs; see Chapter Ten). The singles and Japanese kinds and the hybrids like 'Red Charm' will be next, soon followed by the whole procession of doubles—favorites for Memorial Day. The latter type are rated as early, midseason, and late, their total season extending over three or four weeks in May and June. Hot windy weather may shorten their spans.

Plant peonies away from tree roots and where they can get good drainage and sun at least half the day. The best planting time is midautumn, as early as you can obtain the roots. This is also the best time for digging and dividing your older peonies. Set them so the "eyes," or growth buds (little pink nubs near the root crowns), are no more than 1½ inches below soil surface. Each root should have three to five eyes or more. Before planting, spade up the area and work in organic material such as peat and a handful of balanced fertilizer well below the root zone. Fill and settle the soil around

List C: Perennials for Rock Gardens and Edgings

Ajuga reptans (carpet bugle)
Armeria maritima (sea pink)
Aurinia saxatilis (basket-of-gold)
Cerastium tomentosum (snow-in-summer)
Coreopsis auriculata nana
Dianthus (pink)
Geranium sanguineum (bloody cranesbill)
Phlox subulata (creeping phlox)
Prunella (self-heal)
Sedum spurium (stonecrop)
Stachys byzantina (lamb's-ear)
Teucrium chamaedrys (germander)
Thymus (thyme)
Veronica incana (woolly speedwell)

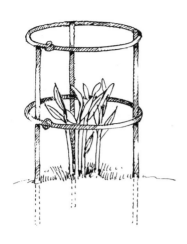

Put the peony ring in place early, while new stems are growing. It keeps bloom stems off the ground.

and over the roots and water well.

Some gardeners install metal supports ("peony rings") in early spring to hold up the heavy plants at bloom time. The big double varieties are especially prone to going down in storms. Another remedy for "flopping" is to remove some of the side buds so each stem has fewer blooms to support. You will note that some varieties are more upright than others. Singles and Japanese varieties, for example, need no help in holding up their flowers. Disbudding also increases the size of individual blooms—a point to remember in case you ever want especially nice ones to show.

A fungus blight called "botrytis" may attack peonies, causing foliage to brown and flower buds to dry up without opening. Sanitation—the complete removal of plant tops down to ground level each autumn—largely controls this. Dispose of infected tops

by burning or burying them, so that the organisms cannot return. In early spring, just as new shoots emerge, apply a fungicide spray such as Bordeaux mixture to eradicate any overwintering spores.

Sometimes peonies mysteriously refuse to bloom. The reason is usually found to be one or more of these causes: tree shade has overtaken them; roots are planted too deep or soil has accumulated over them; or nearby trees or shrubs are making undue competition.

DAYLILIES (*Hemerocallis*). Daylilies have been the flowers of the twentieth century all across North America. In the Heartland, they are surely the backbone of garden color in June and July, some continuing to autumn. It is hard to imagine what our summer gardens were like before modern daylilies. Early settlers knew the *Hemerocallis fulva*, the tawny daylily, with modest flowers of rusty orange. It "went wild" in old farmyards and ditches, spreading by underground rhizomes. It does not set seeds. Over the last several decades, many hybridizers have bred *Hemerocallis* into a wealth of sizes and colors and extended the blooms not only to more hours of the day but more days of summer. Some rebloom late into autumn, but the main color is over by August.

Not really lilies, although related, daylilies form mounds of straplike foliage that send up scapes bearing dozens of buds that open one by one, each lasting but a day (hence, *day*lily). Modern varieties remain in well-behaved clumps. Colors include red, wine, pink, apricot, lavender, even purple, and an infinity of cream-yellow-gold tones—along with multicolor effects in eye zones of contrasting hues. Some have ruffled, fluted petals or other adornments. Some are fragrant. A bloom lasts throughout a day whether in water or not. A number of different blooms merely laid on a plate make an easy and pretty centerpiece.

Although a clump of modern daylilies will gradually enlarge, it can remain several years before it outgrows allotted space and needs dividing. This trait alone places it among the more care-free perennials. But further, the daylily is seldom attacked by insects or disease and needs no staking. It performs whether in full sun or part shade and in a wide range of soil types and conditions. It is among the most drought tolerant of perennials, although of course it grows better when it gets a modicum of moisture.

The ideal site is a well-drained, sunny place in loamy soil. Space new plants 2½ feet apart. You can set them out in spring, summer (even in bloom), or fall. Position the plant so the junction of green tops with flaring roots is just at soil surface. Tall growers look best toward the back of a border; small growers farther forward. Many miniature varieties suited for edging are now available. Daylilies do well among peonies in a planting. From the color standpoint, those with yellow, gold, cream, or melon hues are easiest to combine with other perennials. Globe thistle (*Echinops*), lythrums, coralbells, and hardy hibiscus are a few of the perennials that look well with daylilies. The hardest colors to handle are the toasty orange-reds. Put them in a special planting by themselves where you want a little excitement.

IRISES. The pale blue and yellow small-flowered "flags" still found in old cemeteries and farmyards are relics of pioneer days. Forerunners of today's tall bearded irises, they gave little hint of the rainbow of brilliant colors that would emerge. Like daylilies, tall bearded irises (*Iris* x *germanica*) have become a hobbyist's flower; they lend themselves to collecting. One of the favorite and best ways to use them is in specialty gardens of just bearded irises. Among them are all colors except true red. They have sturdy substance, size, and poise; their petals wear fancy trims of lace, fluting, or crimping; the scapes produce blooms far beyond the number of old ones. Elegant bicolor contrasts may be found and even vivid beard effects.

Tall bearded irises are the best known because they are impossible to ignore at bloom time in May; but they are by no means the only worthy irises. There are bearded irises in smaller sizes as well—intermediate, or border, irises down to dwarf and miniature varieties for the very edge of the garden. Generally, the smaller they are, the earlier they bloom, with those miniatures opening almost as early as crocuses. All are hardy and grow well in the Heartland. These irises accept almost any soil found in our area, provided it is well drained. Even a tight clay soil provides the needed drainage if you form a low ridge on which to place the plants.

Give tall bearded irises full sun and allow 18 inches between neighboring plants or between clumps. These irises need dividing every three years, a task done soon after bloom time. Lift the clump and pull it apart into single rhizomes, retaining only one or two of them to plant back.

In planting these irises, open a shallow hole in the prepared soil and draw up a low mound at the center on which to rest the fleshy rhizome, spreading the roots out and down. The rhizome grows from the foliage fan end, so in planting, direct those ends outward away from others to avoid early crowding. Fill the hole with soil, barely covering the rhizome. Aside from the need for frequent dividing, care of these irises is very simple. Strive to keep them free of weeds. They tolerate drought well, without watering. They are hardy in Heartland winters. Newly set plants benefit from a light hay or leaf mulch to prevent thaws from uprooting them the first winter.

Siberian irises, of beardless type, are enjoying renewed popularity. Although individually the white, blue-violet, or purple flowers are smaller than those of tall bearded irises, they make a good show, as there are many of them. Blooming just after the peonies and bearded irises, Siberian irises have superior garden qualities in that they maintain themselves for many years with little attention. Seldom in need of dividing, not affected by insects or disease, and adaptable to most soils, they can grow in sun or semi-shade. Not quite as drought tolerant as bearded irises, Siberian irises need spring moisture to promote good bloom. Their erect, slender, 30-inch stems make them graceful in bouquets and the flowers last well. Their slender leaves have much finer texture than the foliage of bearded irises; in autumn these leaves turn yellow.

Other types of irises well suited to the Heartland include the roof iris (*I. tectorum*), spuria or butterfly iris (*I. spuria*), crested iris (*I. cristata*), and the hybrid Louisiana irises bred from species native to the South but proven hardy farther north.

HARDY HIBISCUS. The hardy hibiscus, or "rose mallow" (*Hibiscus moscheutos*) hybrids, are destined for increasing importance in many Heartland gardens, at least those of Zone 5 and farther south. They are taking the role in summer landscapes that peonies play in spring ones.

Hybrids such as 'Southern Belle' and 'Lord Baltimore' were derived from hibiscus species native to the United States and even our own area. Thus, although they vary, they survive Zone 5 winters and flourish in our summers. Their blooms are the largest of any perennial—opening in July and continuing into fall if seed pods are removed as they form. Shrublike, these hybrids range in height. The lowest are the 'Disco Belles,' at about 2½ feet. Others may reach 5 feet. Foliage is dark green and durable, making them good backgrounds for a border or for hedgelike effects along walls, steps, or drives. They perform successfully in large containers if they're kept watered regularly. Colors are white, pink, and rose tones to red, many with contrasting eye zones.

Note that these flowers are not for cutting, as they soon fold. Old blooms fall off voluntarily; new ones open daily.

These hardy perennials are often grown as annuals, since the seeds sprout quickly in warm, moist soil and plants bloom soon. Seedlings are readily transplanted. As the plant ages, the crown and root system grow so extensive that transplanting becomes a major task. They are often slow risers in spring, so mark their place to avoid damaging the new growth. They are not bothered by heat but benefit from occasional watering through dry summers. Clean away the old season's stems each fall or early spring, cutting at ground level. In our region, no major pests seem to plague these striking flowers.

Give a clump of hardy hibiscus generous space, at least 2 feet from neighboring plants, where there is sunshine most of the day. Plant the root so the growth point is just below soil surface, in a well-chosen, well-prepared spot, where it can remain undisturbed.

HOSTAS. Shade has overtaken many Heartland gardens that started out sunny but became overhung with trees. A wonderful influx of hosta (plantain-lily) varieties and species has come along to make shade gardening more colorful and interesting. Up until about midcentury, only a few types of hostas were widely available. Gardeners of that generation knew the Funkia, or August-lily (*H. plantaginea*), with its fragrant white flowers and pillow of light green foliage. They also had the smaller lance-leafed hosta, *H. lancifolia*, with its narrow pointed leaves and late-summer display of small lilac-colored trumpet flowers. It is still used today for edging drives and paths all across the Midwest. In the 1960s many hybrids began to appear, spurred by a national society of hosta enthusiasts. Most of these have more striking foliage variegations or coloring. Hostas are especially admired in the Midwest, where both summer and winter conditions suit them well.

They now range from dainty green-gold miniatures less than 1 foot across to bold crinkly blue-green giants with foliage mounds 4 feet wide. The flowers, usually secondary to the foliage, nevertheless add much late-summer interest. Flower colors run from white through lavender to strong purple.

Although tolerant, hostas do best in loamy, humusy, moderately moist soil. Our winters are no problem, for these plants from Asia have built-in hardiness. Summer heat and humidity may bring out a few pests to watch out for. For example, slugs eat holes in the leaves (and sometimes consume them entirely). Various traps and baits are commercially available. Also, some gardeners put out saucers of beer, which slugs will crawl into and drown themselves. Hot winds may brown the leaf edges of some hostas, especially those with much white, cream, or yellow variegation. A great deal depends on knowing what to expect of the variety you plant so you can place it in an appropriate spot. The all-green-foliage kinds are generally more vigorous than the variegated. Some kinds showing variegated leaves in spring will turn all green in summer and fall. Dappled shade as provided by trees is ideal for all.

Mulching benefits hostas in summer. Removal of spent flower stalks in late summer improves the autumn appearance. Many hostas turn gold with fall frosts, bolstering color in the late garden. Long lived, they go for years with little attention. When plantings begin to crowd, division is in order. Lift clumps in early spring, as soon as growth tips show, and pry them apart into single plants or cup-sized sections, each with roots, to replant.

LILIES. Real lilies, members of genus *Lilium*, are often confused with other so-called lilies such as daylilies, blackberry-lilies, and the like. But real lilies are a group apart, true aristocrats. The Asiatic and Oriental hybrid lilies created in the twentieth century have been a boon to gardens everywhere.

These manmade hybrids, most of which originated in the United States since World War II, combine the qualities and adaptability of their various Asiatic ancestors. They perform as well in the Heartland as anywhere, and that means well indeed. With an array of colors (all but blue), heights (up to 6 feet or more), bloom forms (reflexed, bowl-, trumpet-, or cup-shaped, facing up, out, or down)—they provide a tremendous summer lift among perennials. They span a long bloom season from May to late July or August.

In addition to Asiatic hybrid lilies, we in the Heartland can grow the Oriental hybrids such as the 'Imperial,' with its exotic wide, flat blooms, the trumpet or aurelian lily hybrids such as 'Black Dragon,' and many others. These lilies serve primarily as garden accents of supreme quality, but they last so well as cut flowers that some are added to cutting gardens to use just for bouquets. An advantage of the newer hybrid lilies is their disease resistance. Most lilies carry a virus impossible to eradicate, but the modern hybrids are vigorous enough to withstand it. The hybrids generally are stronger and easier growers than the individual lily species.

Lilies grow from bulbs. They are best purchased and planted in fall, when specialty dealers sell and ship them and when the best garden centers stock them. Sometimes to prolong the sales season the dealers and garden centers put bulbs in plastic bags or pots and offer them in spring, but freshly dug bulbs planted in autumn or even early winter are to be preferred. Protect bulbs from drying as if they were living plants.

Lilies combine well with other perennials. In a border, place them about halfway back (regardless of their height), not all the way. They do not obscure what is behind them, and you will want them close enough for viewers to appreciate them.

Give them a site that is in sun or afternoon shade and well drained—for example, on a slight slope or in a bed slightly raised. Around the base, plant shallow-rooted perennials like veronicas or thymes that cover and shade the ground. Or mulch them with leaf mold or shredded bark. These lilies root from the stem as well as the bulb; cultivating them closely may damage their roots. Snap off seed pods as they develop, leaving the rest of the plant to mature naturally, as it rebuilds energy in the bulb for the next year.

Lilies are worth extra pains with ground preparation. Dig deeply and mix in abundant compost or damp peat and a half bucket of sand for each clump. Incorporate a balanced (10-10-10 or equivalent) fertilizer in the bottom of the planting hole. For the best show, plant at least three of a kind to a clump. Rest the bulbs on an unfertilized layer 5 to 6 inches below ground level. Fill over bulbs to ground surface with mellow soil and mark the planting well so you will not disturb it the next spring while stems are emerging. Staking of the taller growers is advised to brace stems against our winds. A botrytis disease occasionally affects lilies, causing leaves to brown or tips to die back. A fungicide spray containing benomyl such as is used on roses will control this problem.

Many other kinds of lilies will grow in our region as well. An oldtime favorite is the Madonna, *Lilium candidum*. Its spire of chaste white blooms rises from a leafy rosette that emerges in fall and overwinters. Plant this one in August and set bulbs shallow, covered only 1 inch deep.

ORGANIZING PERENNIALS FOR SEASON-LONG COLOR
In today's average-size house lot and with the amount of caretaking time you are likely to have, the usual ap-

proach is to start with one border planted with kinds providing a succession of bloom from early spring to late fall. See the backbone lists for spring (p. 116), summer (p. 118), and fall (p. 120) color for some planting ideas. Acquire

Twenty-Five Heartland Native Perennial Wildflowers Suitable in Gardens

Amsonia tabernaemontana (blue star)
Aquilegia canadensis (wild columbine)
Arisaema triphyllum (jack-in-the-pulpit)
Asclepias tuberosa (butterfly milkweed)
Callirhoe alcaeoides (light poppy mallow)
Coreopsis grandiflora (bigflower coreopsis)
Echinacea angustifolia (purple coneflower)
Geranium maculatum (cranesbill)
Helenium autumnale (sneezeweed)
Helianthus maximiliani (Maximilian sunflower)
Hydrophyllum virginianum (Virginia waterleaf)
Liatris aspera (button blazing star)
Lobelia cardinalis (cardinal flower)
Monarda fistulosa (beebalm)
Oenothera macrocarpa (Missouri evening-primrose)
Penstemon cobaea (cobea beardtongue)
Petalostemum purpureum (purple prairie clover)
Phlox divaricata (wood phlox)
Ratibida pinnata (gray-head coneflower)
Ruellia humilis (wild petunia)
Senecio plattensis (prairie groundsel)
Silene stellata (starry campion)
Solidago speciosa (showy goldenrod)
Tradescantia ohiensis (spiderwort)
Verbena canadensis (rose verbena)

some catalogs to study. Go on from there, taking into account heights, shade-sun needs, and colors and bloom times.

A plan on paper is essential. Make it to scale, with a grid indicating dimensions. Then over it tape a transparent overlay (available at art stores) on which, with erasable markers, you can block out planting places for your choices of spring, summer, and fall color plants. By putting overlays together and changing as needed, you can eventually come up with a workable plan. Consider plant heights and habits as you compose this scheme. It need not be planted all at once. Changes will occur as time and experience lend guidance. Essentially, your first plan gives a framework for future reference and a degree of sensible arrangement. The most important early placements are the permanent plants such as peonies, baby's-breath, dictamnus, baptisia, lilies, hardy hibiscus, and hostas—as these are lifetime plants and some are difficult to move. Other kinds such as irises, coralbells, sedums, yarrows, columbines, and daylilies are easily moved around. If you plan to include spring blooming bulbs (tulips and daffodils), plant them at the beginning for the early reward of color they give.

An example of a perennial garden planned for a long season of interest might include:

EARLY SPRING: crocus, daffodil, hellebore, basket-of-gold, creeping phlox, candytuft, bluebell, dwarf irises.

MIDSPRING: snow-in-summer, columbine, tall bearded iris, coralbell, peony, dictamnus, Oriental poppy.

EARLY SUMMER: Shasta daisy, baptisia, geranium (true species types), lythrum, globe thistle, balloon-flower (*Platycodon*), penstemon.

MIDSUMMER: lily, daylily, allium, yarrow, coreopsis, sea holly (*Eryngium*), hardy hibiscus, coneflower, summer phlox, sea lavender, blackberry-lily.

LATE SUMMER: hardy aster, hosta, lycoris, monarda, liatris, feverfew, *Sedum spectabile*, leadwort, perovskia, goldenrod, ornamental grasses, *Rudbeckia fulgida*.

AUTUMN: liriope, colchicum, chrysanthemum, late liatris (blazing star), Japanese-type hybrid anemones, artemisia, *Tricyrtis* (toad-lily), lobelia, Maximilian sunflower.

USING NATIVE PLANTS

Heartland gardeners currently are rediscovering their native perennials, perhaps surprised that our region was the homeland of so many perennials seen in catalogs and nurseries. You could create a long-lasting and colorful garden just of Heartland natives.

Many of these are becoming available at nurseries and in catalogs. Nurseries are learning how to handle and propagate them. Such plants should never be lifted from the wild. Nursery-grown plants, potted and established, are far more likely to survive the move to your garden than anything dug from a roadside, not to mention the environmental, legal, and ethical objections.

If you have the knack of growing from seeds, you can start many native plants that way. Wildflower or native plant societies usually include seed exchanges among their activities. This is an excellent source of strains you can be sure are climatically suited to our region. Such societies also offer learning opportunities. Here are the addresses of these societies in the Heartland: Kansas Wildflower Society, Mulvane Art Center, Washburn University, Topeka 66621; Missouri Native Plant Society, P.O. Box 6612, Jefferson City 65102; and Nebraska Wildflower Society, RR2, Box 1135, Madison 68748.

Backbone Perennials for Spring Color

Ajuga reptans (carpet bugle)
Amsonia tabernaemontana (blue star)
Aquilegia x *hybrida* (columbine)
Aurinia saxatilis (basket-of-gold)
Brunnera macrophylla (Siberian bugloss)
Cerastium tomentosum (snow-in-summer)
Chrysanthemum coccineum (painted daisy)
Chrysanthemum x *superbum* (Shasta daisy)
Dictamnus albus (gasplant)
Euphorbia cyparissias (cypress spurge)
Helleborus orientalis (Lenten rose)
Heuchera x *brizoides* or *H. sanguinea* (coralbells)
Iberis sempervirens (candytuft)
Iris (bearded types, dwarf, intermediate, and tall)
Iris sibirica (Siberian iris)
Mertensia virginica (Virginia bluebell)
Paeonia lactiflora (peony)
Papaver orientale (Oriental poppy)
Phlox subulata (creeping phlox)
Polemonium caeruleum (Jacob's-ladder)
Viola odorata (garden violet)

WATER GARDENS

Some type of water garden may have a place in your plans. Many gardeners become fascinated with the idea of pools and the extra dimensions they add—the movement and color from fish, possibly sound from a fountain, reflections, and aquatic plants such as water-lilies. Once built and under way, water gardens pretty much take care of themselves, without adding to your work load. Heartlanders' enthusiasm for water gardens is justified, since from the climatic viewpoint we can do very well with them and the cooling presence of water is welcome in our summers. Construction of pools is easier and more economical than before (using the plastic liner approach)—now most people can afford them and do-it-yourselfers can build them. Given that construction, planting, and maintaining of water gardens are the same here as elsewhere and that there are many good books on the subject, I will delve no further into it except to commend the idea.

FERNS FOR SHADE

Despite their fragile appearance, some ferns have surprising staying power. They are among our most useful plants for sunless areas under tree shade or by north-facing walls. In addition to shade, they need an organic soil and moisture in spring while they are making rapid growth. Once established, they need little care. They have no serious insect or disease pests. It is good practice to add leaf mold over the crowns in winter to provide for the growth to come.

OSTRICH FERN (*Matteuccia pensylvanica*). This tall (2 or more feet in height), bold plant, with plumelike fronds that arch gracefully, is good for accent beside a shaded step or porch. It spreads by underground runners, making a good cover. In late spring it sends up brown spore-producing stems.

JAPANESE PAINTED FERN (*Athyrium goeringianum* 'Pictum'). This tolerant plant makes a neat 6-inch mound of silver and green fronds touched with red on midribs and stems; it increases slowly by crownlike offsets. It would provide an interesting accent to a small shade planting.

HAY-SCENTED FERN (*Dennstaedtia punctilobula*). The restrained size (only 10 to 12 inches high) and fine texture of the sword-shaped fronds make this a good slowly increasing ground cover. It can grow in moderate shade, as under trees.

CINNAMON FERN (*Osmunda cinnamomea*). The cluster of cinnamon colored, spore-bearing stems rising at the center of crowns in summer is unique to this tropical-looking light-green fern. New growth in spring has red-brown hairs. Vigorous, the plant may reach 30 inches in a good Heartland site.

CHRISTMAS FERN (*Polystichum acrostichoides*). Evergreen, this fern gives winter color; its deep-green shining fronds are distinctive. It is native to the Missouri Ozarks, where it inhabits rocky woods on northeastern slopes. Fronds may reach 2 feet and are more spreading than ascending. Give it a cool, wind-protected site. Water it through drought.

SENSITIVE FERN (*Onoclea sensibilis*). Found in the wild in many parts of the Heartland, this hardy, tolerant fern is useful in the right circumstances. It serves best as a ground cover around high shrubs or small trees in backgrounds where its traveling habits (it creeps from underground rhizomes) will not crowd out delicate neighbors. In wet places it can take full sun, but it tolerates short-term drought if shaded. With the first frost, it browns and recedes for winter. This fern is not clump-forming; its fronds rise individually to about 2 feet.

ORNAMENTAL GRASSES

The number of grasses used ornamentally has expanded dramatically. The old Southern favorite pampas grass (*Cortaderia selloana*) is not reliably winter hardy anywhere in the Heartland, although sometimes it survives mild winters. Some gardeners handle it as an annual, replanting each year. A substitute across the southern parts of our area is plume grass (*Erianthus ravennae*), rated Zone 6, whose fountainlike foliage is surmounted late in summer with purple-silver flower spires.

For a hardier bold, tall grass that keeps its decorative quality into winter, we can hardly do better than the Eulalia, or maiden, grass (*Miscanthus sinensis* 'Gracillimus') rated hardy through Zone 4 (to 25 degrees below zero). Its winter plumes are prized for arrangements. Several other varieties of this same species have come along, most equally hardy, offering different patterns of variegation, foliage color, or style of seed plumes. *Miscanthus* grows large, so allow plenty of space—3 feet from nearby perennials. As these clumps rise vertically to 5 feet, they are visible from afar, year-round except in early spring after you have sheared away the previous year's growth. In the Heartland, we use them successfully in foundation plantings and as accents for island gardens or regular flower borders, combined with other perennials.

Eulalia, or maiden, grass is beautiful all winter.

Of more modest size is fountain grass (*Pennisetum alopecuroides*), a slightly less hardy plant rated for Zone 5 winters. This plant has been a standby of park departments all over the region for bordering formal summer beds combining cannas and various annuals. Fountain grass is well named—its stems arch over gracefully,

Backbone Perennials for Summer Color

Achillea filipendulina (fern-leaf yarrow)
Artemisia ('Silver Mound' and others) (mugwort)
Asclepias tuberosa (butterfly milkweed)
Baptisia australis (blue false indigo)
Chrysanthemum parthenium (feverfew)
Chrysanthemum rubellum ('Clara Curtis')
Clematis integrifolia (solitary clematis)
Coreopsis verticillata (thread-leaf coreopsis)
Delphinium x *belladonna* (Chinese delphinium)
Echinacea purpurea (purple coneflower)
Echinops ritro (globe thistle)
Eryngium maritimum (sea holly)
Gaillardia x *grandiflora* (blanketflower)
Geranium sanguineum (bloody cranesbill)
Heliopsis helianthoides (false sunflower)
Hemerocallis x *hybrida* (hybrid daylily)
Iris, Louisiana (the entire group)
Liatris spicata (spike gayfeather)

Lilium (lilies: Asiatic, Aurelian, and Oriental hybrids)
Limonium latifolium (statice)
Lythrum salicaria (loosestrife)
Monarda didyma (beebalm)
Nepeta mussinii (catmint)
Oenothera speciosa (showy primrose)
Perovskia atriplicifolia (Russian sage)
Phlox paniculata (summer phlox)
Physostegia virginiana (false dragonhead)
Platycodon grandiflorus (balloon-flower)
Polygonatum biflorum and *P. odoratum* (Solomon's-seal)
Rosa (roses: garden types such as 'The Fairy')
Rudbeckia fulgida (perennial black-eyed Susan)
Scabiosa caucasica (pincushion flower)
Stachys byzantina (lamb's-ear)
Thalictrum rochebrunianum (meadowrue)
Veronica longifolia (speedwell)
Yucca filamentosa (yucca)

with the seed heads picking up light in a magical way. Easy to grow from seeds, it makes a fairly good show the same summer and fall. A single clump of it in a well-chosen planter makes a pleasing picture.

All of the ornamental grasses do best in full sun; they are drought-tolerant clump grasses that gradually expand in diameter. You can divide clumps if desired; do this in spring before growth starts.

CARING FOR PERENNIALS

PLANTING. Make an effort to plant perennials well. Spade deeply and dig in peat or compost. Scatter a balanced fertilizer such as 10-10-10, 1 cup per 10 square feet, and dig this in too. Allow plants their needed space, and mark the location with stakes to prevent trampling or disturbance. Water them well and lay a light mulch around and over the crown for shade. Place a label beside it. Unless rains arrive miraculously on schedule, water faithfully until the plants are safely established.

Keep weeds out. Hand pulling is the best way, particularly around shallow-rooted kinds like irises, phlox, or lilies that might be damaged by cultivation. A compost mulch spread over a perennial bed once a year, preferably in spring, is a great help both in controlling early weeds and in shading soil to keep it cool while summer heat is on. The granular weed preventers containing Dacthal and Treflan work well against annual weeds. Read the label carefully and follow it. Some perennials are confronted by special weed situations. For example, tree seedlings (elm, oak, and mulberry) and perennial grasses (bluegrass and bromegrass) come up often in perennial clumps such as creeping phlox. So do dandelions. They can overwhelm it if permitted. First try pulling the invaders after a rain has softened the soil. The grassy weeds are hard to remove entirely and soon regrow. The only final remedy is to lift the plant, turn it over for full view, and extract every strand of the weedy invader; then replant. Dandelions prosper in clumpy plants like monarda and lilies. A V-pronged dandelion digger can pry them out without undue damage to the host. Tree seedlings, if small, can usually be pulled; but those too big will have to be lopped down to a stump, which should be carefully painted with a stump-killer chemical obtainable from garden stores. Read and follow the directions on the label. Cover treated stumps with foil or plastic wrap to keep rain from washing the substance into the roots of the desirable plant, possibly damaging it, too.

REMOVING SPENT FLOWERS. "Deadheading" is the blunt term for this operation. The reason for it is to keep plants looking good, growing, and producing further blooms after the first round. Kinds such as peonies, daylilies, and irises do not usually rebloom, but they often set seeds. Unless you intend hybridizing or saving the seeds, the best practice is to cut spent flowers from peonies, pull out the spent scapes from daylilies, snap out spent bloom stalks from the base of irises, and break off lily seed pods where they join the pedicel. Spreading plants such as veronicas, dianthus, creeping phlox, basket-of-gold, and true geraniums can be sheared. Use shears made for hedges.

STAKING. Delphiniums, lilies, foxgloves, baptisia, globe thistles, and sometimes monardas and tall yarrows are among the upright-growing perennials that may need staking against rain and winds. Since stakes do not improve appearance, you want them as inconspicuous as possible. The commercial green-stained bamboo stakes are probably as good as anything, although you may have your own supply of saplings from a woodlot. It is far easier to install stakes early in the season while you can move around without trampling plants. Commercial ties, colored to blend with foliage, are available, or you may improvise with strips from hosiery or baler twine—whatever works!

FERTILIZING. Scatter a balanced granular fertilizer over the garden in early spring after first cleanup to be worked in gently as you cultivate or do spring transplanting. This one feeding might suffice, but a mild fertilizing in August is also a good idea. September often brings rains to our region, washing the fertilizer down to roots where it can be absorbed to strengthen the plant for the next year. Foliar feeding, using one of the soluble balanced fertilizers, is another technique for early summer. Lily growers especially commend this idea. Just mix it with water, usually 1 tablespoon to 1 gallon, and spray it on.

DIVIDING AND MULTIPLYING. In early spring look over perennials for those that have outgrown their space and need dividing. Some that need to be divided frequently are hardy asters, chrysanthemums (most need it every year), snow-in-summer, coreopsis, heuchera, creeping phlox and summer phlox, *Physostegia*, sedums of several types, and the mat-forming veronicas. Just lift the old clump (use a digging fork to save roots), pull it apart to the needed size, and plant back one portion. Water it in with a transplant solution of water lightly laced with high-phosphorus liquid fertilizer.

Some perennials hardly ever need dividing—*Brunnera* (forget-me-not), *Clematis integrifolia*, bleeding-heart, baby's-breath, liatris, candytuft, Sibe-

Backbone Perennials for Fall Color

Artemisia ('Silver Mound' and others) (mugwort)
Aster x *frikartii* (frikarti aster)
Aster novae-angliae and *A. novi-belgii* (Michaelmas daisy)
Ceratostigma plumbaginoides (blue leadwort)
Chrysanthemum x *morifolium* (garden chrysanthemum)
Festuca ovina glauca (blue fescue grass)
Helenium autumnale (sneezeweed)
Heliopsis helianthoides (false sunflower)
Lavandula angustifolia (lavender)
Liatris spicata (spike gay-feather)
Lobelia cardinalis (cardinal-flower)
Miscanthus sinensis gracillimus (Eulalia grass)
Perovskia atriplicifolia (Russian sage)
Sedum spectabile (live-forever)
Solidago (goldenrod)

ABOVE: *Pools with plants (here, water-lilies and lotus) make hot days feel cooler in the Heartland. Firms selling water plants are good sources for technical assistance on pool building and planting.*

RIGHT: *Ageratum at front and mixed colors of vinca (periwinkle) behind make up a simple, pleasing planting of annuals that will last the summer until frost.*

Flowering crab apples are the Heartland's most dependable and adapted spring-flowering trees. Here, variety 'Snowdrift' displays its spring colors, to be followed in fall by small orange-red fruits.

Flowering dogwood grows wild in Missouri, but in the north and west it soon exceeds its limits. The precocious, profuse variety 'Cloud Nine' here lights up a small garden in Kansas City in April.

High summer in a Heartland perennial garden is a lively, joyous experience of colors, textures, fragrances, and interests. Daylilies, summer phlox, roses, clematis, and Russian sage are some of the players in this July scene.

Peas, onions, and lettuce will soon be gathered from this tiny city vegetable garden. Low wire supports keep the pea vines in order.

Garden aristocrats, true lily hybrids (Lilium)
developed in recent decades perform well in
Heartland perennial gardens. Shown is one of
the summer-blooming Oriental hybrids.

*Dutch hybrid crocuses arise on this grassy bank
every March, cheering passersby. The owner post-
pones mowing the lawn until the foliage ripens,
assuring a repeat performance the next year.*

ABOVE, LEFT: *The hardy, widely adapted wintercreeper euonymus* (Euonymus fortunei *'Vegetus') responds to creativity. Here the gardener trains it over a framework and clips it to create an open screen around the terrace. Although not green all winter, the vine renews its foliage early each spring.*

ABOVE, RIGHT: *A scrap of space between driveway and fence holds shrubs, dwarf lilac* (Syringa meyeri), *and variegated dogwood* (Cornus alba) *underplanted with coral-bells* (Heuchera).

OVERLEAF: *Hardy hibiscus have become Heartland favorites for bolstering garden color in summer. The showy flowers continue to open over a long period.*

ABOVE: *Throughout the Heartland are many public rose gardens where home gardeners can observe how different varieties perform and how professionals care for the plants. Shown is E. F. A. Reinisch Rose Garden in Topeka, Kansas.*

RIGHT: Clematis integrifolia *(foreground), a seldom-seen bush form of clematis, blends its nodding flowers with the rose-pink spires of Lythrum (loosestrife) behind it.*

ABOVE: *Herb garden consisting mainly of fragrant kinds includes old-fashioned pinks* (Dianthus), *catmint (blue with grayish foliage), and thymes allowed to creep over the bricks of paths.*

LEFT: *Raspberries of black, red, gold, and purple varieties, including everbearers, are good backyard fruits for the Heartland. Here a clutch of big 'Royalty' raspberries ripens atop a plant trained to a fence.*

ABOVE: *Among azaleas in the Heartland, the most climate-tolerant kinds are those of Exbury, Knaphill, and Mollis hybrid descriptions, all of similar ancestry but widely varied in bloom color and size of plant or flower. Blooming before leaves open, they make a brilliant show.*

LEFT: *The native yellowwood* (Cladrastis lutea) *of southern Missouri and elsewhere in the southeastern United States makes a hardy and tolerant small shade tree over much of the Heartland. In early summer its fragrant trailing flowers add extra pleasure.*

ABOVE: *Functional concrete steps are softened into the landscape by the collections of daylilies along each side. Daylilies* (Hemerocallis) *are excellent bank holders all year.*

LEFT: *Yellow daylilies and purple coneflowers* (Echinacea) *bloom together in July to highlight a Heartland garden.*

ABOVE: *Trumpet honeysuckle vine* (Lonicera sempervirens) *lends summer color over a long period and attracts hummingbirds.*

RIGHT: *Throughout the Heartland,* Colchicum autumnale *(autumn "crocus") arises on bare scapes every September and October to add to autumn's colors.*

PREVIOUS PAGES: *Count on tulips for a rousing show of spring colors. The Heartland grows practically every kind. Here, 'Apeldoorn,' a classic Darwin type, glows against the dark foliage of 'Crimson Pygmy' barberry.*

ABOVE: *This gardener gave a large yard area over to a naturalized planting of daffodils for a great spring show. As most daffodils are long lived and require little help once planted, this display repeats each year, provided foliage is allowed to ripen after bloom time.*

LEFT: *Sultanas* (Impatiens) *have no equal in the Heartland for giving summer color in shade, both in containers and in ground beds. Regular watering is a key to success with these annuals.*

ABOVE: *A sweeping view inspired this Nebraska garden, which encircles the house. Plants are matched to each exposure; on this sunny east side, penstemons play a prominent role.*

LEFT: *Tall bearded irises are the Midwest's favorite perennials for color in May and June. Never failing, they show all colors but true red, and hundreds of combinations.*

ABOVE, LEFT: *Among the penstemons are a few Heartland natives with good garden potential.* Penstemon grandiflorus *(shell leaf penstemon, shown) blooms in mid spring in many tones of pink, plum, and lavender, as well as white.*

ABOVE, RIGHT: *Take advantage of vertical space if your garden is small. Young cucumbers (foreground) start their climb, and tomatoes already tower behind them.*

For sure season-long color in containers, consider coleus. Easy to grow from seeds or cuttings, this foliage plant comes in countless colors and variations from chartreuse to rosy tones to near purple. Accepting partial shade, it thrives in hot weather.

ABOVE: *Epimediums (barrenworts) have possibilities as ground covers. Not only are they hardy, they are also nonaggressive, refined, and semi-evergreen. Delicate flowers appear in spring. Chrysanthemums set at the front of this bed will use the epimediums as a backdrop for their autumn flowers.*

RIGHT: *Monarda 'Cambridge Scarlet' combined with gloriosa daisies here make a vivid effect. Both are descended from North American native plants of our region.*

ABOVE: *Columbines, hostas, and other shade-loving plants flourish on the north side of a sun-swept house, where shade prevails after midday.*

LEFT: *Large-flowered clematis are dramatic vines for fences and trellises. Available in many hues, they are hardy and adapted in the Heart-land, beginning to bloom in early summer.*

PREVIOUS PAGES: *Bleeding-heart is an old-fashioned favorite perennial for shade, usually seen with red-pink flowers. This is the rare white form, 'Alba.'*

ABOVE: *The herb bed near the kitchen is handy for the cook. This one is raised for drainage and convenience in tending. Berry boxes were placed temporarily over newly set transplants to shade them from hot sun.*

LEFT: *"Surprise lily,"* Lycoris squamigera, *shoots up bare bloom scapes in late July and early August. By then, its spring foliage has disappeared. Here, blue leadwort* (Ceratostigma) *and lamb's ear* (Stachys) *were used as ground cover over the bulbs.*

ABOVE: *American holly, native to the extreme southeastern part of the Heartland, makes a tall evergreen tree where conditions suit it, as on this lawn in Carthage, Missouri. Where soils are drier or more alkaline, or where winters are more severe, this holly becomes impractical. New hybrid hollies, however, now offer possibilities for extending holly boundaries.*

RIGHT: *Most hostas, which are hardy through-out our region, are dual-purpose perennials, prized both for foliage and for flowers.* Hosta tardiflora, *seen here, has especially long-lasting trumpet-shaped flowers in autumn. Give them a moist, shaded place.*

ABOVE: *Nicotiana (flowering tobacco) has been developed into an admirable annual bedding plant suited for borders and edgings like this one and in a range of blending colors. With few pests and diseases, this plant performs long and well in the Heartland's summers.*

RIGHT: *Verbenas are well adapted to basket growing, as their low trailing habit is just what we want in this sort of container. Their drought tolerance also suits them well to this purpose.*

ABOVE: *Strawberries serve admirably as ornamental ground cover along this driveway. The gardener chose an ever-bearing variety to give a long season of bloom and fruiting.*

RIGHT: *The glorious spectacle of flowering trees and shrubs makes spring a magic time in the Heartland's many beautiful communities where effort has gone into such plantings. Forsythia and flowering crab apples make a striking combination in early April.*

Place labels always in the same position so you can find them easily.

rian irises, limonium (statice), Oriental poppies, lythrum, *Platycodon* (balloon-flower), and hardy hibiscus.

If the perennial is some shallow-rooted kind like blue plumbago (lead plant) that has spread beyond its intended dimensions, you can merely dig away excess from the sides until the clump is back to size.

You are always left with a harvest of extra plants. Potted up, these are welcome at community or garden club plant sales or as gifts to friends.

LABELING. Put markers beside plants to identify them. In addition to the name, include the date of planting. The source of the plant is also useful information. Form the habit of placing labels always in the same position near the plant, whether left, right, or center, so you can readily find it. The perfect label has not yet been invented and may never be. Plastic markers turn brittle, and wood rots. Metal markers are the longest lasting provided you use really permanent ink on them. The paint pens, available at craft stores, are the most permanent and easy to read markers. For insurance, write the plant name on the back of the marker with a very soft lead pencil. Although faint,

the pencil remains after the paint wears off. It is wise to have a diagram of the garden showing positions of at least the main perennials expected to remain for many years. When labels have vanished and your memory fails, you will still know what's where.

WINTERIZING. Perennials selected for hardiness in your area need little preparation for winter. Newly planted ones or young plants that lack extensive roots will probably benefit from having an airy mulch laid over them to slow down the "heaving" from freezes and thaws. Kinds touchy about drainage—such as candytuft—gain from having an inch of dry sand poured over the crown.

Resist the impulse to clean up the garden in autumn. Aside from weed removal, such cleaning is not needed. The garden winters better without it. The standing stems help buffer scouring winds; their shadows steady soil temperatures; and they offer a "snow catch" to collect and hold whatever snow falls—often not much, in our open (windswept, sunny, and dry) winters. Snow is good insulation. Christmas tree boughs cut into convenient lengths and laid over the beds in January help shade the ground and keep it safely frozen through fickle February, until the northbound sun finally tells the garden to wake up.

HARDY BULBS FOR YOUR PERENNIAL GARDEN

The word "bulb" is used here to cover some (such as crocus) that technically are corms and some (such as windflowers) that are tubers. Tulips and daffodils are true bulbs. Regardless, they are all little bundles of storage cells that, when conditions are right, will stir into growth and bring forth flowers. All are planted and handled much alike.

October is the ideal bulb planting time and the earliest you can get bulbs. Choose sites where water never stands, such as gentle slopes or the edges of elevated beds, or where the soil is porous so water drains right through. Sunlight is needed by all plants for ripening their foliage. The earliest kinds, such as crocuses, that complete their growth cycle before trees leaf out can prosper in areas shaded by trees in summer. Later kinds such as tulips, daffodils, and alliums need at least half a day of sun.

Usually the best show comes when you group five or more of the same variety together. Improve the soil if necessary by incorporating compost or damp peat and sand. Excavate the planting hole wide enough for proper spacing (see the chart on pages 134–35 for distances of minor bulbs). Fork over soil at the bottom of the hole and dig in some high-phosphorus fertilizer or bone meal; then spread a layer of unfertilized soil or a layer of sand over it on which to rest the bulbs.

For tulips and daffodils, have the bottom of the planting hole 8 inches deep. For crocuses, have it about 4 inches deep. In very soft or sandy soil, bulbs can go deeper than these levels; in dense clay, they can go less deep. In the chart on page 124, planting depths suggested could be raised or lowered slightly depending on soil density.

Daffodils, tulips, crocuses, and hya-cinths are the four best-known perennial bulb flowers, but many others also perform well in Heartland gardens. Most but not all are flowers of spring. Every garden has places for them.

DAFFODILS (*Narcissus*). Combining well with perennial flowers, daffodils live indefinitely and keep their places. You can also "naturalize" them, randomly clumped or scattered through grassy areas, shrubs or woods as if nature had put them there. Expect blooms to appear about forsythia or lilac time. Although most are yellow, some are pure white, and a few have pink, greenish, or orange touches. If you start with the earliest little kinds (such as 'February Gold'), you can expect a daffodil season six weeks long. Many are fragrant; all are wonderful cut flowers. Another plus, they are relatively immune to pests. They are unlikely to be rooted out by moles or gophers, chewed by rabbits, or grazed off by deer. They can take seemingly ruinous freezes or late snows and still straighten up and revive. After extremely dry autumns and winters, such as our region experienced in 1988/89, some kinds may not bloom well or at all. At such times, one good watering in November before freeze-up would correct the problem. Allow spring foliage to ripen naturally. Space bulbs 4 to 6 inches apart.

TULIPS. By far the most colorful of spring bulbs, tulips span the entire color spectrum and a considerable bloom season. They start as soon as the ground thaws with the low-standing cream and red *T. kaufmanniana*, go on to the blazing 'Red Emperor' and its

kin, and then into the main host of Tri-
umphs, Darwins, and Lily-flowered,
and finally the late doubles about five
weeks later when the 'Van Houtte' spiraea blooms. In perennial gardens, tulips are best handled by planting them
in groups, each of one variety, near the
front of the bed. Special plantings of
them along walks or drives or fronting
shrubbery are dramatic. In planning,
remember that the foliage dies away
and disappears by mid-June. To fill
these spaces, you will need to set in annual flowers such as petunias or sweet
alyssum to color and cover the voids.
Let tulips mature their foliage naturally; snap off any seed pods that form.
The foliage stage is over by mid-June.
Space bulbs 6 to 8 inches apart.

CROCUSES. Appearing in late winter
when any sign of spring is a thrill, crocuses are indispensable. They succeed
nearly everywhere, producing cups of
gold, lavender, purple, or white in glorious defiance of the elements. Tuck
these low, clump-forming plants into
nooks, or scatter them among low
ground-covering plants —even lawns.
The large Dutch hybrids, which reach
5 inches high at their apex, make a
good show among pachysandra or
Vinca minor ground covers. If naturalized in lawns, they make the best display when scattered lavishly across
slight slopes to be viewed from a lower
level. A common method of making
such plantings is to fling out the corms
and then follow with a trowel or bulb
planter, burying each one 3 to 4 inches
deep where it fell. Their need to ripen

Things Nobody Ever Tells You

Peony shoots in spring seem to be
equipped with antifreeze. Gardeners
often waste work and worry trying to
cover the young growth against spring
frosts when the plants would do better
left alone. It is later, after plants are
well up and buds have formed, that late
sharp freezes might do damage. Fortunately, this seldom happens. Many
modern peonies, having been developed in our region or in Minnesota,
have built-in Midwest stamina.

Single or Japanese-type peonies are
good choices for low-maintenance
gardens, as they hold up their blooms
unassisted, and when spent petals finally fall, there is no noticeable litter
to clean away.

Some of the ornamental alliums, or
flowering onions, may become pests if
they are allowed to shed seed in the
garden. Two examples are the garlic-
chive (*A. tuberosum*) and the drumstick
allium (*A. sphaerocephalum*). Allium
seeds falling into nearby clumps of perennials may germinate and prosper
there, threatening the well-being of
the plant they invaded; they are hard to
root out without damaging the host.
Attend promptly to deadheading such
plants before seeds fall.

Avoid planting garden chrysanthemums under streetlights or security
lights that burn all night. These plants
respond to "day" length, and the artifi-
cial light interferes with bud set and
bloom.

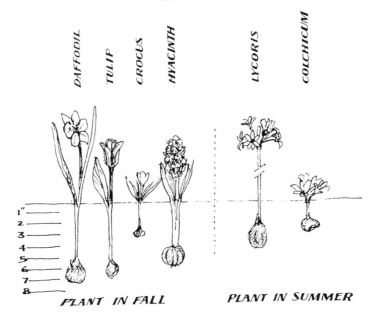

DAFFODIL TULIP CROCUS HYACINTH LYCORIS COLCHICUM

1"
2
3
4
5
6
7
8

PLANT IN FALL   **PLANT IN SUMMER**

Depth guide for planting bulbs.

their grasslike leaves may conflict with your desire to mow the lawn, but let the mowing wait until crocus foliage yellows, showing maturity. Soon the expanding lawn conceals all traces of this plant.

Some species crocuses such as *C. tomasinianus* are too small and delicate to compete with ground covers, although you could naturalize them in lawns. They do better in crannies of rock gardens, along bases of walls or posts, or between flagstones where you are sure to see them.

A few of the fall-blooming species crocuses are reliable in the Heartland. *C. speciosus* (lavender) and *C. sativus* (purple with scarlet anthers—the true saffron crocus) are two that do well. These send up foliage in fall ahead of blooms. They are so small that they are easily overlooked or buried under other plant foliage if used among perennials. So place them in areas not likely to be cultivated or overgrown. Tree shade is no problem, as in autumn the tree leaves are falling off at the very time the crocus foliage rises into the newfound sunshine. Space bulbs 4 to 6 inches apart.

HYACINTHS. These spring bulb flowers are securely popular if for no other reason than their fragrance. The formal effect of their erect flower spikes calls for using them differently from most spring bulbs. They do well accenting architectural elements: fronting walls, lining walks, brightening doorsteps or entryways. They do not blend well in mixed perennial gardens or lend themselves to naturalizing. Where you want to mass them in beds or carry out designs, take care to plant all at the same depth to get an even stand. Also, see that all in the planting are equally well watered in late fall to foster root growth. Otherwise, there may be thin places in the spring ranks. In the Heartland, winter drought is more of a threat to hyacinths than cold. Space bulbs 8 inches apart.

Two Hardy Bulbs That Bloom in Summer/Fall

Surprise-lily. Magic-lily, resurrection-lily, naked lady, and hardy amaryllis are all other common names for *Lycoris squamigera*, a long-lived addition to late summer gardens. The names refer to the disappearing habit of the spring foliage and the reappearing of the summer flowers on bare scapes. The fragrant lilac-pink, lilylike flowers clustered at the tops of 2-foot stems come at the end of July or in early August, when other color is scarce. Long lasting when cut and pleasing in the garden, they give our August landscapes a needed boost.

Combined with other perennials, they look best set back midway in the border where neighboring plants supply greenery for what *Lycoris*'s bare stems lack. The best time to plant or transplant these bulbs is the dormant interval, mid-May through June after foliage has died down. Another possible time comes in early autumn after blooms fade. Mark the planting place so you won't accidentally dig into it. Set bulbs so the tops of the long necks are 1 to 2 inches below soil surface. This *Lycoris* is hardy throughout our region. Other *Lycoris* common in the South, such as *L. radiata*, do not usually survive the Heartland's winters except in protected circumstances or in our most southerly extremes. Space bulbs 6 inches apart.

Colchicum autumnale. Often mistakenly called the "autumn crocus" (it is not related to the crocus), *Colchicum autumnale* follows the same growth pattern as *Lycoris*—vigorous spring foliage that dies down by summer and then blooms that come from the corms in September and October. Regardless of weather, the large lilac or pink (rarely white) flowers emerge nestling against the ground, looking fresh and beautiful. They make a picture if planted with a ground-hugging sedum such as 'Dragon's Blood,' or beside a clump of late-blooming blue leadwort (*Ceratostigma plumbaginoides*). The best planting or transplanting time is during the summer dormancy. Set corms about 3 inches deep. *Colchicum* will endure indefinitely in Heartland gardens. Space bulbs 4 to 6 inches apart.

The Minor Hardy Bulbs

The term "minor" refers to size and not importance. These little bulb flowers are among the most welcome of spring. Dealers sell them in fall, which is when you should plant them. Choose foreground places where they will show, since most are small plants. As with other spring bulbs, their foliage must ripen undisturbed, and the corms or bulbs underground should be kept from harm during their long dormancy. The chart on pages 134–135 gives details on thirteen kinds widely grown in our region. A world of others exists for those willing to experiment and take chances with occasional losses. The best advice about kinds of uncertain hardiness is to provide them with porous soil in a well-drained site.

Eighty-Four Perennials to Grow in the Heartland[a]

NAME / SUN OR SHADE (CODE: *FULL SUN; #PART SHADE; @SHADE) / HARDINESS ZONE	HEIGHT AND SPREAD / BLOOM OR COLOR SEASON
Achillea filipendulina 'Coronation Gold' (fern-leaf yarrow)*(4)	3½ × 2'; June–August
Achillea tomentosa (woolly yarrow)*(4)	10 × 10"; June–September
Achillea millefolium (milfoil)*(4)	2 × 1½'; June–September
Ajuga reptans (carpet bugle)#(4)	8 × 6"+; April, May
Amsonia tabernaemontana (blue star)*#(4)	2 × 3' May
Aquilegia (columbines)*#(4)	3 × 2'; May, June
Artemisia ('Silver Mound')*(4)	12 × 18" throughout growing season
Asarum europaeum and A. canadense (gingers)#@(5)	5–10" spreading; #throughout growing season
Asclepias tuberosa (butterfly weed)*(4)	2 × 2'; June, July
Aster, hardy (Michaelmas daisies)*(4)	Up to 4' high; August–October
Aster x frikartii ('Wonder of Staffa')*#(5)	2 × 2'; June–Oct.
Aurinia saxatilis (basket-of-gold)*(4)	9 × 15"; April–May
Baptisia australis (blue false indigo)*#(4)	4 × 4'; May, June
Belamcanda chinensis (blackberry-lily)*(5)	30" (bloom stems); July, August
Bergenia cordifolia*#(4)	12" (bloom stems); April, May
Brunnera macrophylla (perennial forget-me-not)#(4)	12" mound; April–June
Campanula carpatica (bellflower)*#(4)	4", mounding; June–August
Campanula medium (Canterbury bell)*#(4)	2½' erect; June, July
Cerastium tomentosum (snow-in-summer)#(4)	6" mat-forming; April, May
Ceratostigma plumbaginoides (blue leadwort)*#(5)	6" spreading; August–October
Chrysanthemum coccineum (pyrethrum or painted daisy)*(4)	3' erect; May
Chrysanthemum morifolium (garden chrysanthemum)*(5)	2' average, mounded or upright; September–November
Chrysanthemum rubellum ('Clara Curtis')*(4)	12" spreading; July–September
Chrysanthemum parthenium (feverfew)*#(5)	20 × 14"; June–October
Chrysanthemum x superbum (Shasta daisy)*(4)	2 × 1'; May–July
Cimicifuga racemosa (bugbane)*#(4)	5'+ erect; July, August
Clematis integrifolia (solitary clematis)*#(4)	3 × 2'; June, July
Convallaria majalis (lily-of-the-valley)#@(4)	8" spreading; May
Coreopsis lanceolata*(4)	Up to 3' and mounded; June–September
Coreopsis verticillata (thread-leaf coreopsis)*(4)	Up to 2' and mounded; June–fall
Delphinium belladonna and D. grandiflorum (chinense) (Chinese delphinium)#(4)	4 × 2'; May, June

COLOR EFFECT / COMMENTS

Gold flower heads; ferny green foliage. Erect habit.

Creamy-yellow flowers over ferny gray foliage. Well behaved.

Pink, red, tangerine pastels; ferny green foliage; new hybrids preferred; spreads.

Lipped blue-purple flowers on spikes above spreading basal foliage; green, variegated, or bronzy.

Small starry sky-blue flowers above willowy foliage; turns yellow in fall.

Every color and combination. Foliage suffers in summer heat.

Silvery foliage, fine texture.

Dark-green foliage effect. *A. europaeum* is evergreen and smaller than *A. canadense*, which is deciduous.

Dense vivid-orange flower heads. Late emerging; drought tolerant.

Pink, ruby, purple, white, or lavender daisy flowers. Divide yearly.

2" lavender flowers. Water through droughts.

Yellow panicles above gray foliage. Shear halfway back after bloom.

Blue lupinelike flowers; durable soft-green foliage. Permanent background plant.

Red-dotted orange flowers, black seed clusters. Leaf fans look like irises.

Pink-to-white flower clusters; shiny leaves are semi-evergreen.

Small blue flowers over large heart-shaped leaves. Water in drought.

Lilac-blue or white, bell-shaped flowers on low plants. Use in rock gardens or as edging.

Large white, blue, pink, or rose flowers on upright stems.

White starry flowers over gray foliage. Divide every other year.

Deep blue ½" flowers amid glossy leaves; red in autumn.

Pink, red, or white daisies on long stems; ferny base foliage.

Yellow, gold, bronze, ruby, white, or purple tones in many forms. Divide clumps every spring; give good drainage.

Single rose-pink daisies with yellow centers. Notably durable; early bloomer, hardy.

Small white daisy flowers; divided foliage. Short lived but self-sowing.

Large white daisy flowers with long stems. Good cut flower; divide every other year.

Long fluffy white racemes on wiry stems above dark-green foliage.

Nodding dark-blue bells atop slender stems; silver seed heads follow. Best when staked.

Fragrant white bells above dark-green leaves. Best used as ground cover.

Round daisies with wide yellow ray flowers. Good cut flower.

Delicate yellow daisies over fine wiry foliage; erect clump.

Blue tones or white. Short lived but take our summers better than traditional types; give cool, calm location; mulch.

Eighty-Four Perennials to Grow in the Heartland continued

NAME / SUN OR SHADE (CODE: *FULL SUN; #PART SHADE; @SHADE) / HARDINESS ZONE	HEIGHT AND SPREAD / BLOOM OR COLOR SEASON
Dianthus deltoides (maiden pink)*#(3)	6" mat-forming; May, June
Dicentra eximia (fringed bleeding-heart)#(4)	12 × 15"; May–August
Dicentra spectabilis (bleeding-heart)#@(4)	2 × 3'; May, June
Dictamnus albus (gasplant)*(4)	3 × 2'; May, June
Echinacea purpurea (purple coneflower)*(4)	3 × 1½'; July–September
Echinops ritro (globe thistle)*(4)	3½ × 2'; June–September
Epimedium pinnatum (barrenwort)#@(4)	8 × 8"; May–fall
Eryngium maritimum (sea holly)*(5)	1½ × 1'; June, July
Gaillardia x grandiflora (blanketflower)*(4)	2 × 2'; June–September
Galium odoratum (sweet woodruff)#@(5)	6" spreading; May, June
Geranium (several species) (cranesbill)*#(4)	1½ × 1¼'; May–July
Gypsophila paniculata (baby's breath)*(4)	1½ × 2'; May–July
Heliopsis helianthoides (false sunflower)*(4)	3 × 2'; July–frost
Helleborus orientalis (Lenten rose)#(4)	14 × 12"; March–May
Heuchera sanguinea (coralbells)*#(4)	2' flower stem, 1' clump; May–June
Iberis sempervirens (candytuft)*(4)	8 × 20"; April, May
Iris sibirica (Siberian iris)*#(4)	30" erect; May, June
Lamiastrum galeobdolon variegatum (golden archangel)#(5)	8" spreading; June–August
Lavandula angustifolia (lavender)*(5)	1½ × 2'; June–September
Liatris spicata and *L. scariosa* (gayfeather)*(4)	30 × 20"; July–September
Limonium latifolium (statice)*#(4)	1½ × 1½'; June–September
Linum perenne (blue flax)*(5)	2 × 1'; May–July
Liriope spicata (lily-turf)*@(5)	10 × 18"; August–September
Lobelia cardinalis (cardinal flower)*#(4)	4' × 9"; July–September
Lythrum salicaria (loosestrife)*#@(4)	3' × 15"; June–September
Mertensia virginica (bluebell)#@(4)	1 × 1½'; April, May
Miscanthus sinensis 'Gracillimus' (Eulalia grass)*#(4)	5 × 4'; year-round
Monarda didyma (beebalm)*#(5)	30 × 20"; June–August
Nepeta mussinii (catmint)*(4)	8 × 20"; May–August
Oenothera fruticosa (sundrops)*#(5)	1 × 1'; May, June

COLOR EFFECT / COMMENTS

Single rose, pink, or white fringed flowers on slender stems; foliage evergreen. Use in rock gardens or as edging.

Smaller sprays of pink (or white) hearts over ferny grayish foliage. Keep moist to prolong bloom.

Racemes of drooping rose-white hearts. Soft foliage disappears in summer.

Spires of rose-pink or white blooms on upright lemon-scented plants. Drought tolerant; permanent.

Imposing cone-centered flowers on stiff stems; rose tones or white. Drought tolerant.

Blue globelike flowers atop prickly white and green foliage. Drought tolerant; use in background.

Foliage effect often bronzy; small yellow flowers in spring. Refined ground cover; spreads slowly.

Stiff blue-tinged spiny foliage topped with ½" thistlelike silvery heads. Drought tolerant.

3" red-yellow wheellike flowers on long stems. Good for borders and cutting.

Refined whorled dark-green foliage; white flowers in loose cymes. Useful ground cover.

Lavender with darker veins or pink or blue. Some form spreading mats; long lived.

Tiny white or pink flowers in airy billowing sprays. Good cut flower or blender among perennials.

Orange or yellow sunflower-shaped flowers for late-garden color or cutting.

Leaves evergreen and glossy. Nodding 2" green-purple-white-pink flowers. Long-lasting.

Dainty pink, rose, or red bells on slender stems above neat mound of foliage. Good drainage.

White flower clusters above shining, fine-textured evergreen foliage. Shear off first bloom for repeat.

Each slender scape bears 1 or 2 wide-petaled 3" flowers of purple, blue, white, or yellow. Long lasting.

Green-silver leaves, lipped yellow flowers in groups along spreading, rooting stems. Trim back after flowers have bloomed.

Gray-leafed plants bear small fragrant purplish flowers in clusters near stem tips.

Purple-pink or white fluffy florets cover erect spikes above linear green foliage. For cut flowers or as accent.

Tiny pink-violet florets covering branchy panicles above wide green base foliage. Long lasting.

Limber stems bear pale blue 1" flowers that close in the afternoon. Good in meadow gardens; self-sows.

Evergreen grasslike foliage, lavender or white flowers on low spikes in fall. Shear plants each spring.

Sturdy stems rising from green leafy base are topped with scarlet 5-lobed flowers. For wet places.

Rose, pink, or purple spires on willowy, erect stems; good vertical effect. 'Dropmore Purple' and 'Morden Pink' recommended varieties.

Pink-to-blue stages in clustered bells on soft leafy stems that die away in summer.

Green-white striped in summer, gold in fall, light catching in winter. Our best hardy ornamental grass.

Red, pink, violet, or white flower heads atop erect stems.

Small lipped blue flowers above billowy low silver foliage. Good as edging.

2" yellow flowers on stems rising from base leaves. Use in foreground.

Eighty-Four Perennials to Grow in the Heartland continued

NAME / SUN OR SHADE (CODE: *FULL SUN; #PART SHADE; @SHADE) / HARDINESS ZONE	HEIGHT AND SPREAD / BLOOM OR COLOR SEASON
Papaver orientale (oriental poppy)*#(4)	2 × 1'; May, June
Penstemon (beard tongue; species and hybrids)*#(5, 4)	2 × 1'; May, June
Phlox paniculata (summer phlox)*#(5)	3 × 1'; July–September
Phlox subulata (creeping phlox)*#(4)	6" spreading; March–May
Physostegia virginiana (false dragonhead)*#(4)	3' erect; July, August
Platycodon grandiflorum (balloon-flower)*#(4)	30 × 20"; July, August
Polymonium caeruleum (Jacob's-ladder)#(4)	12 × 15"; May, June
Polygonatum biflorum (Solomon's-seal)#@(4)	3' arching stems; May, June
Rudbeckia fulgida (perennial black-eyed Susan)*#(4)	2 × 2'; July–September
Rudbeckia hirta (gloriosa daisy)*#(4)	30 × 15"; June–August
Saponaria ocymoides (creeping soapwort)*(4)	6" spreading; May, June
Scabiosa caucasica (pincushion flower)*(4)	1½ × 2'; June–August
Sedum spectabile (live-forever)*#(4)	15 × 20"; August–November
Sempervivum tectorum (hen-and-chickens)*(5)	3" spreading clusters; year-round
Stachys byzantina (lamb's-ear)*#(4)	4" foliage in April–December; 10" flower stems in June
Thalictrum rochebrunianum (meadow-rue)#(5)	4' erect; July, August
Thymus serpyllum (thyme)*#(4)	4" spreading; May, June
Tricyrtus hirta (toad-lily)#@(5)	2½ × 2'; September–frost
Veronica spicata (spike speedwell)*#(4)	10" spreading; May, June
Veronica incana (woolly speedwell)*#(4)	8" spreading; May
Yucca filamentosa (Adam's needle)*(4)	5 × 3'; June, July

[a]See the text for others.

COLOR EFFECT / COMMENTS

Brilliant red, orange, or pink flowers over hairy foliage that disappears in summer. Needs good drainage.

Showy red, pink, white, or blue-lavender tube flowers on erect stems above base foliage. Many kinds; drought tolerant.

Showy red, pink, salmon, white, or blue-lavender flowers on erect stems. Needs staking, watering, and deadheading, but worth it.

Dense mats of needle foliage with early flowers in all hues but yellow. For banks, rock gardens, and edgings.

Rose, pink, or white flowers on tall spikes. Good cut flower; can be invasive.

Showy blue-violet, pink, or white bells. Good cut flower; provide good drainage.

Panicles of blue or white flowers amid ferny foliage. Afternoon shade best.

White bells in twos below green stem and leaves. Black autumn berries. Place at close view.

Dark-centered gold daisies spread by rhizomes. Drought tolerant.

Single types have 5"-wide gold flowers with bronze zones. Good cut flower; short lived; self-sows.

Small dark-pink flowers cover fine-textured foliage. Needs good drainage; for front of border.

Flat 3" blue corolla with center tuft of stamens. Good cut flower; mulch in summer.

Pink flower heads darken with autumn until finally coppery rust; succulent foliage. Indestructible; 'Autumn Joy' a favorite.

Pink-red flowers on short stalks emerge from mature plants in summer. Best for walls or rock gardens.

Woolly silver-white leaves in spreading clumps; purple rings of florets on erect bloom spikes.

Airy lavender flowers above fernlike foliage. Use as background; mulch.

Dark fine wiry foliage topped with purple spikelets. For edging and crevices.

Soft green arching stems bear odd-shaped white-purple-speckled flowers. Mulch; keep watered.

Tapering spikes of blue-lavender, rose, or white flowers; green foliage.

Lavender-blue spikes, usually nodding, above silvery foliage mat that retains color all summer.

2" creamy-white bells up and down a tall, erect panicle; stiff evergreen leaf spears. Striking accent.

Ground Covers—Alternatives to Grass

NAME / SUN OR SHADE (CODE: *FULL SUN;
#PART SHADE; @SHADE) / HEIGHT   HARDINESS

Aegopodium podagraria 'Variegatum' (goutweed)#@ 8"	Hardy throughout
Ajuga reptans (carpet bugle)*#@ 6"	Hardy throughout
Cerastium tomentosum (snow-in-summer)* 6"	Hardy throughout
Ceratostigma plumbaginoides (blue leadwort)*@ 6"	Through Zone 5 (-20 degrees), but mulch in north
Convallaria majalis (lily-of-the-valley)#@ 8"	Hardy throughout
Coronilla varia (crown vetch)*# 12"	Hardy throughout
Cotoneaster horizontalis 'Perpusillus' (rockspray cotoneaster)*# 2'	Hardy only to about -10 degrees
Epimedium grandiflorum and *E. pinnatum* (barrenwort)#@ 8"	Hardy throughout, but not drought tolerant
Euonymus fortunei 'Coloratus' (winter creeper)*#@ 6"	Hardy to -20 degrees or colder if under snow
Festuca ovina 'Glauca' (blue fescue)*# 10"	Hardy throughout; fairly drought tolerant
Galium odoratum (sweet woodruff)#@ 6"	Hardy throughout, but not drought tolerant
Geranium sanguineum (cranesbill)*#10"	Hardy throughout
Hedera helix (English ivy; also Baltic or Bulgarian)#@ 6"	Hardy throughout if snow covers
Hemerocallis fulva (tawny daylily)*#@ 30" scapes	Hardy throughout; drought/heat tolerant
Hosta lancifolia (narrow-leafed plantain-lily)#@ 10" foliage and 20" flower stems	Hardy throughout; drought/heat tolerant
Juniperus horizontalis (creeping juniper, 'Bar Harbor,' 'Wilton,' 'Blue Rug,' and others)*# 6–10"	Hardy throughout
Lamium maculatum (dead-nettle)@# 12"	Hardy throughout; tolerant
Lamiastrum galeobdolon (golden archangel)@# 8"	Hardy throughout; tolerant
Liriope muscari (lily-turf)@# 10"	Hardy through Zone 5 (-20 degrees)
Lonicera japonica 'Halliana' (honeysuckle)*#@ 12"	Through Zone 5 (-20 degrees)
Lysimachia nummularia (moneywort)@# 4"	Hardy throughout
Pachysandra terminalis (Japanese spurge)@# 8"	Hardy except in windy, open winters; not drought tolerant
Phlox subulata (creeping phlox)*# 6"	Hardy throughout
Potentilla tabernaemontani (*P. verna*) (spring cinquefoil)* 3–6"	Hardy throughout; not drought tolerant

COLOR EFFECT / COMMENTS

Soft green-white foliage spring to fall; white flowers like Queen Anne's lace in spring. Plants may be invasive.

Spreading mat in summer; blue flowers on low spikes in spring. Variegated or bronzy forms available.

Grayish mat through growing season; white starry flowers in late spring. Spreading habit.

Green in summer, turns reddish in fall, and bare in winter; blue flowers in late summer. Spreads underground; give good drainage.

Dark-green foliage spring to frost; white bell flowers in spring. Divide occasionally.

Dark-green mounded compound leaves; dense foliage; pink flowers in early summer. Drought tolerant; tends to spread.

Semi-evergreen shrub whose small glossy leaves turn red in fall; pink flowers in spring. Use on banks. The most prostrate variety.

Refined green divided leaves; small odd-shaped yellow or reddish flowers in spring. Establishes slowly; shear in late winter.

Leaves green with purple undersides; all turn purplish in winter. Shear twice through summer for best ground-cover appearance; climbs if permitted; woody plant.

Erect silvery-blue clump grass. Gives color touch in limited area; shear off bloom stems; dies back in winter.

Neat whorls of slender green leaves through summer; small fragrant white flowers in spring. Needs rich organic soil.

Sprawling mound of rounded incised leaves; pink or rose-purple round flowers spring through summer if old blooms are sheared off.

Dark glossy evergreen leaves on rooting stems. Takes 2–3 years to establish; use on north of buildings or under trees; climbs if permitted.

Greens in spring, blooms in June, browns with freezing. Spreads by rhizomes; controls erosion on banks; blooms are sterile; no seeds.

Shining pointed dark-green leaves; lilac flowers in late summer. Rhizomes spread slowly, making solid stand.

Needle evergreens, various leaf hues—green, bluish, or purplish; prostrate branches spread out several feet from crown. View plants at nursery to aid in choosing.

Green-white heart-shaped leaves; a semi-evergreen; pink-white flowers.

Variegated green and white; yellow flowers at leaf axils. Plants spread by runners; shear after bloom to improve form.

Grasslike mounds; nearly evergreen; spikes of small purple flowers in September. Shear off old foliage each spring.

Green foliage most of winter; creamy blooms spring through summer. Clambers; woody; may climb trees; best on difficult banks in need of dense, lasting cover. Spreads.

Small round leaves on creeping stems, flat against ground; small yellow flowers in spring.

An evergreen; shining foliage on erect stems. Spreads slowly by underground stems; needs organic soil and consistent moisture.

Needlelike spreading mounds, flower-covered in spring. Good on rocky, sunny banks.

Glossy green leaves through growing season; small yellow flowers in summer. Forms mat by rooting branches.

Ground Covers—Alternatives to Grass continued

NAME / SUN OR SHADE (CODE: *FULL SUN; #PART SHADE; @SHADE) / HEIGHT	HARDINESS
Rosa wichuraiana (memorial rose)# 10–20"	Hardy to -10 degrees
Sedum spurium 'Dragon's Blood'*# 3"	Hardy throughout; drought tolerant
Symphoricarpos orbiculatus (buckbrush)*#@ 2½–3'	Hardy throughout; heat/drought tolerant
Thymus serpyllum (creeping thyme)* 4"	Hardy into Zone 5 (-15 degrees)
Vinca minor (periwinkle or myrtle)*#@ 6"	Hardy throughout; in north, needs snow cover

Minor Hardy Bulbs to Plant in Fall for Bloom in Spring and Summer

NAME / PLANTING DEPTH / SPACE APART	BLOOM TIME / HEIGHT / COLOR(s)
Allium christophii (flowering onion) 4" 12"	May, June; 18"; pink-violet
Allium moly (flowering onion) 3" 4"	May; 10"; yellow
Allium sphaerocephalum (flowering onion or drumsticks) 3" 5"	June; 2½'; red-purple
Allium caeruleum (flowering onion) 3" 6"	June, July; 20"; lavender
Anemone blanda (windflower) 2" 3"	April; 5"; white, pink, or lavender
Chionodoxa (glory-of-the-snow) 3" 3"	March; 4"; bright blue
Eranthis (winter aconite) 2" 3"	March; 3"; gold-yellow
Galanthus (snowdrops) 3" 4"	March; 4"; white with green dots
Leucojum vernum (spring snowflake) 3" 5"	March–April; 6"; white with green tips
Muscari armeniacum (grape hyacinth) 3" 5"	Early to mid-April; 6"; blue-purple
Puschkinia scilloides (striped squill) 3" 4"	April; 5"; white-blue
Scilla campanulata (Endymion hispanicus) (wood hyacinth) 4" 6"	May; 10"; white, pink, or lavender
Scilla sibirica (Siberian squill) 3" 4"	March–April; 5"; true deep blue

COLOR EFFECT / COMMENTS

A semi-evergreen; shining foliage on clambering, prickly procumbent canes; has 2" white flowers in pyramidal clusters in May. Holds banks.

Dark red-green foliage forms mat, topped in summer with small crimson flowers. For small areas along walks and flagstones; spreads fast.

A shrub; soft green leaves on arching branches; small red berries in autumn. Spreads by rooting runners; can cover waste ground under high trees.

Almost evergreen; short spikes of purple flowers in spring; small leaves in low shrubby mats. Spreads by rooting stems; needs good drainage.

Shining evergreen leaves in neat, dense clumps; bright-blue or white flowers in spring. Does best in shade.

USES / COMMENTS

Round umbel 6" in diameter is striking accent. Long lasting when cut; dries well.

Good in rock gardens, as edging, or among ground covers. Foliage dies down in summer.

Good as border accent or cut flower. Bulbous flower umbels atop thin scapes.

Good as borders or cut flowers. Forms attractive clumps. NOTE: Many other alliums do well in the Heartland.

Good as borders, or along paths. Daisy-like flowers and deeply cut foliage; accepts part shade; soak tubers before planting.

Naturalize in grass, under shrubs, or in rock gardens.

Good along paths or naturalized under shrubs where not disturbed. Soak tubers before planting.

Naturalize or plant under shrubs or at base of rocks or walls.

Naturalize in ground cover, among ferns, or along edges. Fragrant nodding bells.

Good in rock gardens, along paths, or among tulips or daffodils. Increases fast; foliage usually comes up in autumn.

Good in rock gardens, as edging, or naturalized under shrubs.

Naturalize in English ivy or pachysandra ground cover. Tolerates moderate shade.

Naturalize in grassy areas, rock gardens, or among daffodils. Spreads; nodding bells.

Heartland Roses

*Many wonderful garden roses have
been grown in the Heartland over many years.
Fanciers have staged rose shows that were
national in scope—and the quality of the blooms
exhibited was the equal of those shown
anywhere. Yet, experienced growers would
be the first to suggest that this is not
the easiest place in the world for roses. In the
next breath they might add that it is not the
hardest place either. And that whatever it
takes, roses are worth the effort. Roses
need more care than many
other plants.*

In the huge world of roses are dozens of different classes; but the main ones we are concerned with are the hybrid teas, grandifloras, and floribundas, which bloom repeatedly through summer and autumn with individual or clustered flowers of supreme color, style, substance—call it "beauty." Most in these classes are descended from fairly tender ancestors. Our winters usually are cold enough, or erratic enough, to kill them unless they are protected. Hence, a major factor in growing roses here is protecting them over our winters. Take heart; we need not go to the ultimate measure they do in Minnesota, of burying the whole plant.

THE MOST TENDER TO THE HARDIEST

First, some basic definitions of the main types, going from the most tender to the hardiest.

HYBRID TEAS. This class is the one that comes to mind when you think of roses. Hybrids teas have slender pointed buds, satiny blooms of every rose color including dramatic blends and bicolors, and bushes that in this region generally stay under 4 feet high because the tops die back every winter and must be pruned down to living tissue. It is the classic rose for arranging and exhibiting, usually producing a single large bloom atop a long stem. The venerable 'Peace' rose is a good example.

GRANDIFLORAS. This class was created by the American Rose Society to accommodate new developments that did not fit under "hybrid tea" or "flori-

bunda," although in some respects these roses are similar to both. They bloom both singly and in clusters. Usually they grow strong and tall, with plants rising well above the hybrid teas and flowers usually not quite as large. They come in all rose colors, and as they bloom in sprays atop the upright canes, they make a good show. The pink 'Queen Elizabeth' is the best example of a grandiflora and was the original variety to be recognized in that class.

FLORIBUNDAS. The cluster-blooming floribundas are shrubbier, with lower stature and much smaller individual blooms than the hybrid teas, but they do produce more prolifically. 'Ivory Fashion' is a prime example. Floribundas are more likely to be planted for landscape effect than for cut flowers or exhibiting, although the bloom stems are certainly useful in bouquets.

MINIATURES. In the last few years, minatures have become immensely popular for several good reasons. They are generally hardier than hybrid tea roses—rated Zone 5—and their smallness makes them much easier than regular roses to protect for winter in case of need. Their petite size suits them perfectly for the smaller gardens prevailing today, and the abundance of new varieties makes them highly collectible. In many, the blooms are faithful small-scale copies of hybrid tea roses, with the high centers, reflexed and pointed petals, and smooth and long-lasting substance; they are ideal for small arrangements. Plants bloom repeatedly through summer. Every rose show now offers classes for miniatures. In a home garden you can grow them in special display beds, or use them as edgings or accents in small area plantings. Raised planters display them well, and a few with cascading habit, such as 'Red Cascade,' are wonderful in hanging baskets or rock gardens. They can be grown in pots of ample size if they are sheltered over winter in a cold frame. Many people are tempted to make house plants of them, growing them indoors in pots; but for long life and satisfaction miniatures really do best outdoors in the ground, as they are true roses and need the dormancy of winter as part of their cycle.

POLYANTHAS. Historically, polyanthas are among the ancestors of floribundas, only lower, bushier, and with finer foliage and individually smaller flowers in dense clusters. They bloom repeatedly from early in the season to Thanksgiving. Versatile, they find many landscape uses—as dooryard shrubs, low hedges, and mixed among perennial flowers to bolster color during slack times. They are cold hardy enough that they need no winter protection over at least the southern half of our region (Zone 5), something that cannot be said of the kinds previously described. 'The Fairy,' with its soft-pink blooms, exemplifies this class and is probably the best in it.

OTHER ROSES. This group includes climbers of several sorts (which must be trained to trellis or fence, as no rose can twine or cling), ramblers, "landscape roses," and a large and growing category of "shrub roses," old and new.

It is impossible to generalize about the hardiness of these roses. They differ from kind to kind. Likewise, the size and style of the plants vary. Before investing in these it is wise to study them at your nearest public rose garden that includes shrubs and climbers to see what has endured and what they look like.

A relatively new category of landscape roses has been developed under the trademarked name "Meidiland." These should find uses in future Heartland gardens if they live up to expectations—they are rated hardy to Zone 3. They are propagated on their own roots—not budded to different roots as most roses are—so even if the top is killed back in a bad winter, the roots will send up new growth identical to the previous ones. These roses are used for hedges, barriers, and background (some of them grow up to 4 feet high) and for coloring the landscape, as they bloom over a long season. Although they are promoted as low in maintenance, do not be surprised if you find it necessary to spray them for leafspot disease or for occasional insect outbreaks. This is true of practically all roses.

SELECTING YOUR ROSES

Whatever kinds of roses you choose, take care to purchase top grade, fresh plants, and be prepared to plant them without delay. Although roses are commonly sold in potted form at nurseries, you can also get dormant bare-root plants there early in spring, and these are preferred by rose specialists because with them you can see what you are getting. With the potted ones, you have to take it on faith that the nursery has not reduced the root system to get it into the pot. The only advantage of potted rose plants is that you can obtain and plant them any time through the growing season. Avoid those prepackaged bargain roses offered in spring at discount stores in sales yards set up in parking lots. Not only can you not see what you are getting but also you cannot know what abuse (drying out, freezing, or overheating) the plant has already received from store personnel or other handlers before them. Also, the prepackaged roses are lower grades—rejects from the top-rated group, with reduced chances of giving satisfaction.

Almost all roses commercially produced and sold in the United States come from areas with milder winters than ours—California, Arizona, or Texas. Some gardeners worry that from this circumstance the roses are predisposed to die in Heartland winters, but such is not the case. Cold hardiness is determined by heredity, not environment. Virtually all the roses shipped in for sale in our region have the genetic hardiness to survive our winters under the normal protection gardeners here give them.

For further information on selecting roses, see the annual "Handbook for Selecting Roses" published each year by the American Rose Society. It lists hundreds of currently available varieties, with their classification, colors, and performance ratings based on a survey of the membership. The booklet can be bought for $2.00 from American Rose Society, P.O. Box 30,000, Shreveport, LA 71130-0030.

SELECTING THE SITE AND PREPARING THE BED

Roses are usually given a bed by themselves rather than being mixed among other perennials. A special rose bed displays the plants well and is easier to care for than plants scattered about. Select a site that will be in sun—ideally, morning sun—at least half the day. It is a fine point, but our hot afternoon sun sometimes bleaches rose colors. To help with disease control, the place should have good air circulation but be protected from the full blast of hot southwestern winds. A slight slope, away from overhanging trees, is good. A clay-loam soil is ideal, but if enough organic material is mixed into the soil as you prepare it, even a sandy, silt loam will do. One final necessity is good drainage; it must not be a low place where water stands. In choosing the location, take availability of water into account. In the Heartland, there will be times when you need to water. Drip irrigation systems are perfect for rose gardens. Consider installing such a system as soon as the roses are planted or even before.

Many growers plan rose beds (hybrid teas, grandifloras, or floribundas) to be three roses wide—or about 6 feet—allowing 2 feet between plants and a margin around the sides. You can tend such a bed from either side without stepping into it.

Pliny the Elder told gardeners of two thousand years ago to "dig deep for roses." It is the same for us today in the

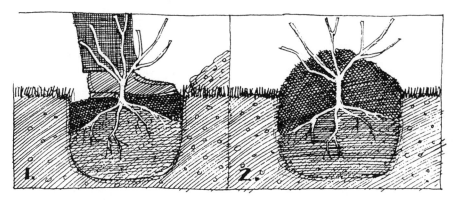

Planting a bare-root rose: (1) Spread the roots over the mound in the planting hole so the bud union is positioned 1 inch below ground level. Firm the soil well around the roots and then water it. (2) Pile soft soil 6 inches over the crown of the new plant to protect the top from drying while the roots become established. Remove the mound after growth begins.

Heartland of America as it was then in Pliny's Herculaneum. Roses respond to thorough preparation of soil. Double dig it to at least 12 inches deep; incorporate lots of peat, leaf mold, or compost—the more the better. At the same time, scatter and incorporate rose fertilizer (sold in granular form at garden stores) at the rate suggested on the box. Do all this well in advance of receiving your roses, so the ground has time to settle.

PLANTING YOUR ROSES

The best time for planting bare-root stock in the Heartland is mid-March to mid-May. If the bed is already prepared, there usually need be no delay in planting. It can well happen, though, that a sleet storm arrives the same day as the roses, with the mercury on a slide into the teens. In such a case, take the roses to a cool basement or garage, unwrap and inspect them, remoisten any packing around them, and put them back in their wraps. Move them to any sort of cold storage you can devise: buried in the compost pile, deep enough not to freeze; or placed in a spare refrigerator (not the freezer) until a better day for planting.

Soak roots overnight in a tub of water just ahead of planting. Keep roots covered while you dig planting holes in the area prepared. For each plant, dig a hole wide and deep enough to accommodate roots without cramping. Prune off any broken roots. Pull together a mound of loose soil at the center of the hole on which to rest the root crown. Lay a yardstick across the hole to show where ground level is, and hold the plant up to it so the bud union (the thick joint where the roots meet the top) is about 1 inch below. This is the recommended level for most of the Heartland, although at northern extremes you could set the union as deep as 2 inches below ground level as a precaution against freeze damage.

Fill in soil around the roots, firming it with your hands and then treading it lightly. Before completely filling the hole, pour in a bucket of water to which you have added 1 tablespoon of soluble fertilizer, 10-10-10 or similar. Let it sink away while you go on to the next plant. Finally, fill the hole up to ground level. If all went well, the bud union should be buried and hidden from view. A finishing touch, one that really pays off in our region where hot spring winds can turn living stems into dead sticks, is to mound 6 inches of soil or compost over the newly planted crown. Later, after new shoots show that the roots are taking hold, simply pull away the mound and smooth it out around the plant. Newly planted roses are likely to begin blooming six to eight weeks after planting in spring. You should not expect to see them at their full potential, however, until the second or third year when they are well established.

CARING FOR YOUR ROSES

FEEDING. A packaged rose fertilizer, applied as directed, should keep your roses growing through summer up to frost. Make the first feeding in spring as plants are setting on their first buds. Feed again about August 1. Some rosarians give plants in-between boosts with foliar (or through-the-leaf) feeding—a small amount of a soluble product like Miracle-Gro added to the regular multi-purpose spray used for insects and diseases. After August 1, let up on all fertilizer so that plants will slow down naturally and begin to harden themselves for winter.

WATERING. The standard rule on watering roses is 1 inch a week, whether it comes from rain or from your hose. When rains fail and droughts develop, you'll need to irrigate roses in some manner. Of the many methods of applying water, the least desirable for roses is the overhead sprinkler, which not only wastes water but encourages disease. In the Heartland, a drip irrigation setup with an emitter beside each plant is the ideal method, as it eliminates waste and puts water directly where plants can use it. Soaker or weeper hoses of various sorts are also practical for roses growing in rows.

SPRAYING. If you want flawless roses, regular preventive spraying is a necessity. Several kinds of insects love roses; if unchecked, they can ruin a planting. Currently, a favored insecticide is Orthene, which works systemically throughout the rose plant. In addition to insects, roses get diseases. Most are prone to a defoliating and ugly leafspot disease called blackspot, and to mildews that gray and distort leaves and stems. As both are fungus diseases, they are ordinarily fought with a fungicide added to the spray being used against insects. Funginex is currently the fungicide of choice for controlling rose diseases. Some fanciers alternate it with other fungicides (such as benomyl [Benlate]) to deter the disease organisms from acquiring any sort of resistance or immunity to one control. For mixing and using these, read and follow package directions. Also add a spreader-sticker, perhaps just a drop of dishwashing detergent, to the solution

DEADHEADING ROSES

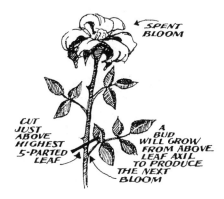

SPENT BLOOM

CUT JUST ABOVE HIGHEST 5-PARTED LEAF

A BUD WILL GROW FROM ABOVE LEAF AXIL TO PRODUCE THE NEXT BLOOM

Do not leave long stubs.

as you mix it in the pump-up sprayer. This will make it spread more easily over leaf surfaces and cling to them longer. Roses are also susceptible to stem cankers and scale insects. You can prevent these troubles simply by spraying with a dormant-season lime-sulfur solution in early spring, the same as the one used for fruit trees. Many growers simply make it a habit to spray the roses with lime-sulfur at the same time they dormant-spray their apples in March.

MULCHING. Mulching is an important part of summer care. Mulch seems to help roses in several ways—it cuts down on diseases, discourages weeds, holds in soil moisture, and stabilizes soil temperature. Which mulch is best? Almost anything derived from some sort of plant tissues. Each grower has his or her own favorite. Sometimes it is a case of what is available. Cocoa-bean hulls from the garden store are a deluxe topping with handsome chocolate-brown color, and they smell good. Some gardeners use shredded tobacco stems, on the theory that they have an insecticidal effect. Don't depend on it, however, to relieve you of the job of spraying. Wood chips are good, although they may get in the way of winter mounding. Just rake them off to the side. Pine needles are perfect if you can get them. Grass clippings from your lawn, if free of herbicide, serve well also.

REMOVING SPENT FLOWERS. Deadheading is another necessity if you want to keep blooms coming. Once a week go over the bed with hand pruners, removing blooms whose petals are ready to fall. Watch for any needed light remedial pruning you can do at the same time. To remove the spent flower head, simply follow the stem down to the nearest five-parted leaf and sever it just above that point. A vigorous bud, probably already evident in the axil of that leaf, will produce a replacement cane and another bloom in four weeks or so. The five-parted leaf rule is not immutable. Often just below the rose flower will be one or more three-parted leaves, with a lusty growth bud already showing where the leaf joins the stem. If so, select one of these in a good position to be the replacement. Generally, the higher on the stem the renewal bud is, the sooner it will produce a bloom, although such blooms may lack the long, sturdy stems and full-size flowers preferred by growers intending to enter them in flower shows. Collect deadheads in a paper bag for removal from the premises. Allowing petals and diseased foliage to fall among the plants sets up a breeding ground for diseases and insects, so it is best to clean away any such debris.

After late September, do no more pruning or deadheading. You have already stopped fertilizing; stop watering as well. It is time for plants to harden, and allowing seed hips to develop is one way of encouraging maturity in the plant.

WHICH ROSES SHOULD YOU PROTECT FOR WINTER, AND HOW SHOULD YOU DO IT?

Kinds particularly needing winter protection in the Heartland are hybrid teas, grandifloras, and floribundas. Shrub roses such as 'Harison's Yellow' and polyanthas such as 'The Fairy'

usually survive winters unaided by us. In the southern parts of our region, the floribundas might also get by without special protection, but if you dislike taking chances, mound them. Likewise, the miniatures—although surprisingly hardy—are on a borderline here, so to take no chances you should mound them and lay an airy mulch over them. Tree roses—those produced by budding a bushy top onto a long, bare trunk connected by another graft to roots at the bottom—seldom survive our winters unless they are buried. Dig a trench that is long, wide, and deep enough to tip the

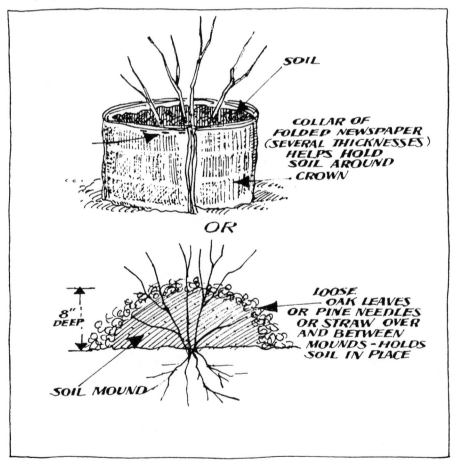

SOIL

COLLAR OF FOLDED NEWSPAPER (SEVERAL THICKNESSES) HELPS HOLD SOIL AROUND CROWN

OR

8" DEEP

SOIL MOUND

LOOSE OAK LEAVES OR PINE NEEDLES OR STRAW OVER AND BETWEEN MOUNDS—HOLDS SOIL IN PLACE entire plant over into it; then put the excavated soil back over the plant. Most shrub roses and polyanthas will survive our winters unaided. Climbers vary in hardiness. 'New Dawn,' a light-pink climber with double flowers of moderate size, is a time-tested variety that seldom shows much winter damage here. In northern Zone 4 areas, however, it is wise to mound the crown. Large-flowered climbers such as the dark-red 'Don Juan' or the yellow 'High Noon' are essentially high-growing hybrid teas and are best winter protected as such. They are likely to kill back to the soil mound most winters.

Mounding with soil or well-decomposed compost is a favorite form of winter rose protection. The farther north or west you are, the deeper the mound should be. At a minimum, aim to make it 8 inches deep. As I noted earlier, it is standard practice in Minnesota to bury the whole plant; in our latitudes we need not go that far. The purpose of the soil mound is to protect that vital crown area where the stems emanate just above the graft (bud union). If that area is killed, you have in effect lost the whole plant, because even if it sends up shoots from below the graft, they will be from the wild

---

Some of the Heartland's Favorite Modern Roses

(based on reports of regional rosarians and observations in area gardens)

HYBRID TEAS
Chrysler Imperial (dark red)
Double Delight (red blend)
Garden Party (white)
Granada (red blend)
Miss All-American Beauty (dark pink)
Mister Lincoln (dark red)
Olympiad (medium red)
Peace (yellow blend)
Pristine (white)
Red Masterpiece (dark red)
Tiffany (pink blend)
Touch of Class (pink blend)
Tropicana (orange-red)

GRANDIFLORAS
Electron (dark pink)
Gold Medal (dark yellow)
Montezuma (orange-red)
Queen Elizabeth (medium pink)
White Lightnin' (white)

FLORIBUNDAS
Betty Prior (medium pink)
Iceberg (white)
Ivory Fashion (white)
Showbiz (medium red)
Sun Flare (medium yellow)
The Fairy (light pink; polyantha)

SHRUBS
Bonica (light pink)
Carefree Beauty (medium pink)
Simplicity (medium pink)

CLIMBERS
America (orange blend)
American Pillar (pink blend; rambler)
Blaze (medium red)
Don Juan (dark red)
Golden Showers (medium yellow)
New Dawn (light pink)

rootstock incapable of blooming as before.

For mounding, bring in soft soil from somewhere else—not from the rose bed itself, or roots will be exposed and damaged. As a preliminary to the mounding process, many gardeners install collars of newspaper (several thicknesses folded together and stapled) around the base of plants to hold the soil around the crown. Strips of building paper are also used this way. After mounding, many growers add loose straw, hay, or oak leaves between mounds for further insulation. If we could depend on deep, lasting snow cover in the Heartland, this would not be necessary. However, since we know our winters are likely to be open and snowless much of the time, we need to cushion rose crowns against the wide temperature fluctuations.

TIMING WINTER PROTECTION. November, around Thanksgiving, is when most Heartland gardeners go about protecting roses. This is easier to do after a few light freezes have killed the leaves. Do no real pruning in autumn; it is all right to remove the tops of long, waving branches, or to gather the tops and tie them with twine so you can work among the plants. Ideally, rose crowns should be snugly mounded before severe wintry blasts arrive; but these are hard to predict in our region, and sometimes we have to hurry out in mid-November to do this work in the face of icy gales sweeping in from the north, dropping the temperature from the balmy seventies to single digits in a few hours. Extreme freezes in fall before there have been any gentle ones

are hard on roses and other plants. Another danger period is late winter—February and March—when longer days bring warmth that thaws and then nights that freeze, along with occasional deep plunges of temperature. Take care not to unhill roses too soon. When, in early April, your sixth sense tells you that the worst is over, begin the process. Do it gradually, not all at once, just in case you are wrong. Watch for developing new shoots inside the mound, so you do not inadvertently break them.

SPRING PRUNING. After unhilling, when you can see all of the plant, assemble your pruning tools and start restoring your roses for another season of growth. The canes will probably have died down nearly to the soil mound or beyond. You can identify dead wood by its dry light-brown look. Cut all of it out down to the green. Take out any canes that look diseased, deformed, or in the wrong place. Also take out any that are obviously very old, as you are trying to renew the plant. Aim for a balanced, vase-shaped framework of three to five husky green canes free of twiggy growth. Prune away all that does not fit this design. Some springs you may not find much still alive above the crown, a signal that you should mound it more deeply the next year. There may be other springs, after a rare gentle winter, when canes are alive several feet upward. In that case, prune to leave canes about as tall as your loppers. In cutting back, strive for slanting cuts just above outward-heading buds to encourage an open, spreading shape.

Remove suckers, the shoots that come from below the bud union. These are from the rootstock, which is a wild rose (a specially selected species) different from the upper plant. They look different—the leaves are smaller and duller. If you let a sucker grow, it soon overwhelms the rest of the plant and you are left with only the wild growth. If it blooms at all, the flowers will be small and completely different from those of the rose variety you planted. Dig down and remove it at the source, where it comes out from below the bud union.

In making pruning cuts as large as a dime in diameter, it pays to daub the ends with tree wound paint to keep stem borers from tunneling down into the pith, killing the upper part of the stem. Sometimes these insects tunnel all the way down into the crown. Instead of tree wound paint, some growers use Elmer's Glue-All or other glue that won't wash off. Also, the most ardent and careful growers cover cuts of any size, not just the large ones.

Climbing roses, ramblers, and large shrub roses are pruned mainly to remove dead wood or the oldest, woodiest canes, perhaps one or two a year. Few gardeners bother to deadhead roses of this type unless they are repeat bloomers. The red seed structures ("hips") that follow the blooms are an attractive and desirable fall feature of many types of shrub roses—for example, *Rosa rugosa*.

In spring pruning of miniature roses, carefully study the plant and cut

Rose Gardens to Visit in the Heartland

IOWA

Iowa State University Horticultural Gardens, Ames

Bettendorf Park Board Municipal Rose Garden, Bettendorf

Noelridge Park Rose Garden, Cedar Rapids

Vander Veer Park Municipal Rose Garden, Davenport

Greenwood Park Rose Garden, Des Moines

Dubuque Arboretum Rose Garden, Dubuque

Weed Park Memorial Rose Garden, Muscatine

Grandview Park Rose Garden, Sioux City

State Center Public Rose Garden, State Center

KANSAS

Memorial Rose Garden, Fort Hays State University, Hays

E. F. A. Reinisch Rose Garden, Topeka

Botanica, The Wichita Gardens, Wichita

MISSOURI

Capaha Rose Display Garden, Cape Girardeau

Laura Conyers Smith Municipal Rose Garden, Loose Park, Kansas City

Missouri Botanical Garden, St. Louis

NEBRASKA

AARS Constitution Rose Garden, Boys Town

Lincoln Municipal Rose Garden, Lincoln

Memorial Park Rose Garden, Omaha

back to live wood. If necessary, shorten branches to balance the shape. As miniatures are on their own roots, they can renew themselves from severe freeze damage to come back and bloom as before.

Things Nobody Ever Tells You

❧ It is generally (but not universally) true that yellow-flowered roses are more susceptible to blackspot leaf disease than roses of other colors.

❧ Sprays are far more effective and waste less material than dusts in combating rose diseases. As the spores of the rose blackspot disease are spread in water (including dew), it is well to apply fungicide a day ahead of the rain to make sure it sticks or is absorbed, ready to protect the leaf at its most vulnerable time. Cover both sides of foliage. Systemics such as Funginex and Benomyl are more effective than surface-type fungicides, because they actually enter plant tissues and do not wash off. Nevertheless, they should be renewed at intervals given on the labels, usually every ten days.

❧ From all viewpoints—environmental, economical, and for the health of roses—the best way to apply protective fungicides and insecticides through summer is with a portable pump-up hand sprayer with a rotating nozzle that can be directed upward against the undersides of leaves. Reserve the sprayer just for this purpose, and never use it for weed killers.

❧ Lime-sulfur spray can stain painted surfaces. In close quarters, prevent this problem by temporarily shielding the nearby wall, fence, or whatever with plastic sheeting or other cover.

Trees, Shrubs, and Vines

In planting a new place, start with the woody plants—trees, shrubs, and woody vines. They are the longest-term plants, needing years to reach the expected size, form, and potential beauty. They have many uses in home gardens—as shade, windbreaks, havens and food for wildlife, screens, backdrops or frames for views, and color all year. Woody plants earn their keep. Life without them is unthinkable.

Most of the Heartland's tree-filled scene is recent—it has developed only over the past century or so. When settlers began arriving in the 1800s, trees were few and far between. The prairies offered no shade until you came to a watercourse. Pioneer women wrote about how, upon coming to a tree after days of not seeing one, they had an urge to hug it.

The reason for the sparseness of trees was the same as for the abundance of prairies—fire. Before settlement, prairie fires were common. Whether started by lightning, deliberately set by Indians, or accidentally ignited by campfires, these wildfires raced on the winds, fueled by the dry grasses. With few wide rivers or anything else to stop them, they ran for many days before dying out in a rain or wind shift. The perennial grasses quickly regrew, but woody plants stood little chance.

Pioneer nurserymen loaded wagons with planting stock of favorite hardy trees and drove from farm to farm, offering ponderosa pines, fruit trees, American elms, black walnuts, lilacs, black locusts for fence posts, and Osage orange trees, which were promoted as useful for posts and stock-tight hedges. The settlers lost no time in planting them.

As these trees matured and scattered seeds, the landscape changed. Volunteer trees appeared, and by then there were few prairie fires to threaten them. Woodlands spread throughout the region and are spreading still. Gardeners continue to play a role in altering the Heartland landscape.

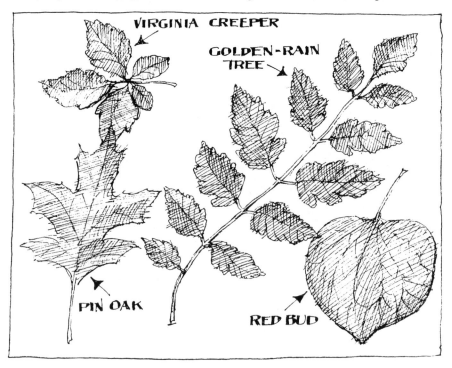

VIRGINIA CREEPER

GOLDEN-RAIN TREE

PIN OAK

RED BUD

How to Choose Suitable Trees and Shrubs

In selecting trees and shrubs, our main concern is to choose kinds suited to the climate, the site, and the purposes intended. Our list of possibilities is so long that choosing is not easy. Several arboretums already exist in the Heartland, and the number of such institutions is growing. Nebraska has a unique statewide arboretum system consisting of forty-two locations throughout the state. Significantly, Nebraska was the birthplace of Arbor Day. The main useful purpose of an arboretum is to help people choose trees intelligently. If the tree grows nearby, in climate and soil similar to your own, it should also grow for you. Moreover, you can get an accurate impression of its size, growth style, foliage, flowers, and fruits and its storm and wind tolerance. Other places to study adapted trees are old cemeteries and public parks. They usually contain time-tested plants of many sorts.

Do not expect woody plants to be without faults. There is no tree beyond reproach. There will always be leaves to rake, litter to scrape out of gutters and downspouts, limbs or other debris to pick up, suckers to prune out, or various maladies to cause concern. In our region, some trees have more faults than virtues. Kinds with overwhelming problems were intentionally omitted from my descriptions of trees, shrubs, and vines for the Heartland later in this chapter. This accounts for the absence of seemingly prominent trees such as the American elm, whose susceptibility to Dutch elm disease is

as yet unremedied, and the Siberian elm, which is so prone to storm damage and infestation by insects.

List the trees and shrubs you find in your area. Study what local nurseries offer, confident that the kinds they sell will grow locally. Look at the Plant Hardiness Map (see endsheets) so you understand what is meant by hardiness zones mentioned in catalogs or books and know which one you are in. Such maps, however, are only general guides. Many other factors play roles in determining what should, or will, grow.

Keep in mind the eventual size a considered tree will reach. If you can foresee that someday it might have to be removed because of outgrowing its site, it is best at the beginning to choose a smaller kind. Consider also whether the tree will get along with its neighbors. Some kinds, such as the surface-feeding maples, elms, and hackberries, do not allow other plants to prosper within their root runs.

Soil is another factor. Clay soil brings difficulties in establishing many trees. In wet weather, clay becomes waterlogged, suffocating roots; in dry weather, it shrinks, opening deep cracks and exposing roots to drying. If this is the kind of soil you have, expect to give extra effort in watering, drainage, and mulching to enable new trees to get established. You might decide to limit your number of plantings to what you can care for in the early stages. If your garden lies in the flood plain of some nearby river, the soil may be so alkaline as to produce chlorosis (leaf yellowing due to lack of available iron) in susceptible kinds like pin oaks. A preliminary soil test could help you avoid that type of mismatch. Or you might be forewarned of chlorosis problems merely by looking carefully at plants in your neighborhood.

While making your choices, consider microclimate situations around your yard. They may suggest possibilities. A familiar example is the northeastern corner of a house, unreached by sun on winter afternoons. Such a site would be favorable for small smooth-skinned trees such as crab apples, cherries, and Japanese maples, which suffer from winter sunscald if planted out in the open. Possibly it offers a place for borderline broadleaf evergreens like mountain-laurels, which might tolerate our cold temperatures but not our zooming fluctuations. There are other ways to minimize sunscald damage to smooth-barked trees, but it is far less work if you capitalize on a naturally favorable site.

Windbreaks are another way to widen planting possibilities. They may consist of a tree-shrub planting, a hedge, a trellis with vines where space permits, or something more structural. A board or picket fence, especially one running north and south, also expands planting possibilities. The east side, with shade in the afternoon and shielded from those withering southwestern winds, might provide a site for some plant such as rhododendron or holly that otherwise would be out of its range. Heartland gardeners are notorious gamblers on "iffy" plants; they can greatly improve their odds with clever use of windbreaks and sunbreaks against the extremes of both winter and summer.

ABOUT BROADLEAF EVERGREENS

Broadleaf evergreens are a group of trees and shrubs that hold their leaves through winter or most of it. Gardeners value them for sustaining touches of green in winter's landscape. Unfortunately, the Heartland list of plants for such service is short. Our open winters—dry, windy, and sunny as well as cold—are beyond the endurance of many broadleaf evergreen plants widely grown to the south and east of us and along the West Coast.

The farther north and west you are in the Heartland, the fewer your options in broadleaf evergreens. At the northwestern extremes, the list may offer only the yuccas for green broadleaf touches in a winter garden. In those areas, gardeners must rely on needle evergreens—pines, spruces, junipers, and the like—for winter landscape color.

Since a few miles can make a great difference between growing many of these broadleafs or not, your local nursery or garden shop probably offers the best advice you can get on them.

A few kinds, such as Mentor barberry and varieties of *Euonymus kiautschovica*, may hold green leaves some winters but not others, depending on weather. The plants themselves usually survive and leaf out again in spring. Even hollies may drop leaves after a rough winter, but eventually they revive. Be patient with winter-damaged broadleaf shrubs or trees. Hold off on pruning or replacing until spring is well advanced. The plant may not be as dead as it looks. Euonymus 'Manhattan' and 'Jewel' varieties, for example, will recover from severe winter leaf burn after sometimes shedding all their battered foliage by early spring.

ABOUT AZALEAS AND RHODODENDRONS

Members of the genus *Rhododendron*— shrubs universally prized for their splendid flowers and handsome foliage—are out of their element in much of the Heartland, although in favored places some are grown. Only one species occurs naturally in our region— specifically, in the Ozarks: *R. nudiflorum roseum*, called "mountain honeysuckle" by local people.

"Azalea" is the name commonly given to small-leafed deciduous kinds (those that shed their leaves in winter) and also to some kinds that are evergreen. "Rhododendron" is the name usually reserved for those with large, thick evergreen leaves. Distinctions are not absolute, but you can call any of them rhododendrons and be botanically correct. All azaleas are rhododendrons but not all rhododendrons are azaleas.

In the Heartland, many climatic and soil factors work against this group of plants. They need acidic soils; many of ours are alkaline (the opposite of acidic) or neutral. They need a calm, steady, tempered climate with reliable moisture year-round. Only rarely does our climate meet these requirements. Nevertheless, rhododendrons and their subgroup, azaleas, are growing in

thousands of Heartland gardens because their owners have made commitments in care, remedying conditions toward what the plants require. The gardeners provide organically enriched acidic soil, correct drainage, wind-protected sites with the right degree of shade in summer and winter, and faithful watering during our inevitable periods when things go dry. Examples can be found westward almost to the one-hundredth meridian.

Missouri and most of Iowa have soils generally somewhat acidic (pH 6.5 or below), more suitable for rhododendrons than the soils of Kansas and Nebraska, which tend toward neutral or alkaline as you go west. Most rhododendrons grow best in soil pH between 5.0 and 5.5. Your nearest state university extension center can tell you how to get soil tested or may even provide that service. To make soil more acidic (that is, to lower the pH), you can add agricultural sulfur or iron sulfate. Here are the amounts of either one to add to lower the pH level one unit on the scale in a silt loam soil: agricultural sulfur—2½ pounds per 100 square feet; iron sulfate—5 pounds per 100 square feet.

If you go in for rhododendrons, it is most practical to prepare the soil of a bed all at once, either several weeks before planting or the previous autumn. Dig or till it 1 foot deep, adding lots of organic material (brown premoistened peat or oak-leaf compost). Aim for equal parts by volume of organic material and topsoil. If the native topsoil is dense and heavy, lighten it by generous addition of sand, about one-quarter of the total volume. Discard any clay you encounter in excavating. Till all this together with the added sulfur or iron sulfate. The finished level will be a few inches higher than before—a help for drainage, although after it stands a few weeks it will settle.

Finally, at planting time in spring, open planting holes slightly shallower than the balled and burlapped or container-grown plant and set the plant so its crown is about 2 inches *above* ground level. This allows for settling and provides surface drainage. Roots must not be buried deeply. A loose mulch, such as pine needles or rotted coarse sawdust, is a good topping to preserve moisture and slow down temperature fluctuations. Never cultivate around these shrubs.

Check the soil pH around rhododendrons every year or two, as it may change. Irrigation water in the Heartland is usually quite alkaline, especially in summer, and is one of the forces at work continually neutralizing the acidic soil you provided. Regular surface applications of sulfur or iron sulfate may be needed, a little at a time, to maintain soil acidity. Commercial fertilizers packaged especially for azaleas and rhododendrons also are useful in helping hold the acidity.

The southeastern part of the Heartland can grow a very wide selection of rhododendrons and azaleas, including evergreen types. Visit local nurseries in that area in spring to see the kinds they recommend. Their advice for their own localities is probably the best available. If you select plants while they bloom, you can be sure about colors.

Hybridization goes forward at some horticultural institutions to develop forms more tolerant to the midcontinent climate. This seemingly assures that despite all the odds more azaleas and rhododendrons will color Heartland gardens in the future.

There is always a vanguard of gardeners set on having these plants where nobody else does, with full knowledge of the chance of failure. They may be so removed from rhododendron country that their local nurseries offer very little in either plants or guidance, so mail-order sources are the next resort. As advice in that case, here are the hardiest and most widely adapted varieties for the outer limits or beyond, all rated winter hardy in Zone 5 unless otherwise described: Exbury hybrids (including Knaphill hybrids)— 'Gibraltar' (orange), 'Cecile' (salmon-pink), and 'Whitethroat' (white); 'P. J. M.' rhododendron (rose-lavender, very early); 'Northern Lights' rhododendron series from the University of Minnesota (several colors, rated hardy through Zone 4); *Rhododendron mucronulatum* (rose-lavender); and *R. schlippenbachii* (pink).

THE PREPARATION FOR AND PLANTING OF MOST TREES, SHRUBS, AND WOODY VINES

For trees, dig ample holes. A general rule is to make the hole 1 foot wider than the diameter of the root ball (whether the tree is balled and burlapped, container grown, or bare rooted) and deep enough to accommodate the full depth of the roots so the plant stands at the same level it did in the nursery, as indicated by bark color at the soil line.

For shrub beds where many plants will be used, improve the entire bed area first by tilling in, as deeply as possible, such improvements as organic material and sand or gypsum if needed to break up clay. Then grade the bed to

Four ways nursery plants are sold.

correct any drainage problems. Finally, after the entire bed is prepared, dig planting holes for each plant.

When to plant depends on the kind being planted, and on how or when the plant arrived from the nursery. The most practical planting times are spring and fall.

Woody plants come from the nursery in several ways:

Balled and burlapped ("B&B" in nursery parlance) plants have an undis-

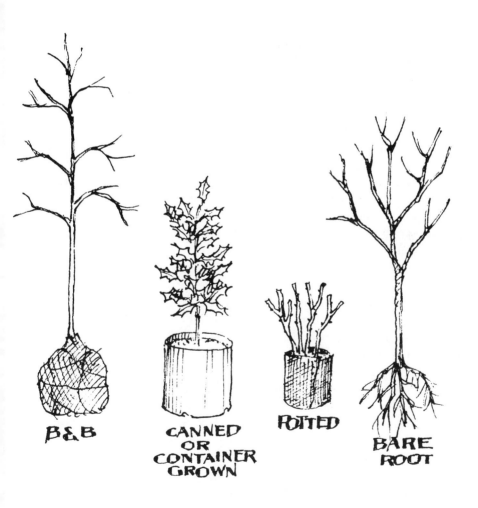

B&B

CANNED
OR
CONTAINER
GROWN

POTTED

BARE
ROOT

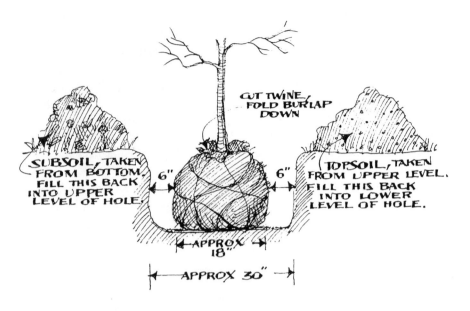

CUT TWINE,
FOLD BURLAP
DOWN

SUBSOIL, TAKEN
FROM BOTTOM,
FILL THIS BACK
INTO UPPER
LEVEL OF HOLE.

6"

6"

TOPSOIL, TAKEN
FROM UPPER LEVEL.
FILL THIS BACK
INTO LOWER
LEVEL OF HOLE.

←APPROX→
18"

←APPROX 30"→

Planting a balled and burlapped tree.

turbed earth ball around their roots that is held by burlap tied and pinned into place. Nurseries use this method for handling larger trees and shrubs. Plants delivered in this form may be planted nearly any time a hole can be dug, but August to November and late February to May are favorite times.

As the earth ball is heavy, usually 80 pounds or more, you will need help to handle it. Take care not to drop or otherwise break the ball on such a plant, as the damage may prove fatal. Never grasp the plant by its trunk, but instead hold onto the ball and its wrappings. Measure the diameter of the ball and dig the planting hole 1 foot wider. Measure the depth of the ball and dig the hole just that deep. As you work, place topsoil in one pile and subsoil in another so as you refill you can put the more workable topsoil into the lower root zone and the subsoil nearer the surface. Before lowering the root ball

into the hole, decide which way you want the plant to face. Because of the sunscald threat in winter, it is a good idea to face the branchier side to the southwest. This also helps balance the tree against our prevailing southwestern winds. When the ball is in place, check to be sure the plant is at the depth it grew before. Make any adjustments while wrappings are still intact. When ready to refill soil, cut the twine holding the burlap around the roots and trunk and over the ball. Roll the burlap down and away, removing as much as you can without disturbing the earth ball. The burlap eventually disintegrates, but if there are any wires that have been used to reinforce the ball, they should be removed to prevent possible future problems. Also remove any plastic twine that may not rot. At the same time, fill in soil, tamping it into the voids with a stick. Finish by watering the hole to settle soil. Finally, form a wide saucer around the outside of the planting hole to conserve water for the plant. On slopes, raise the saucer on the downhill side to catch water so it will soak in around the ball instead of running off.

In southern areas of the Heartland, planting of balled and burlapped plants goes on even in December and January if the soil is unfrozen. An exception is for broadleaf evergreens, which are so susceptible to damage in our open winters that it makes sense to wait until spring to plant them. Remember the need for watering plants set out in fall, winter, or very early spring. This is especially important with needle evergreens—pines, junipers, yews—whose needles continue to expire moisture. As our winters are usually dry, we cannot depend on nature to provide the needed moisture for newly set plants of this type that are never really dormant.

Plants grown in containers (cans) likewise may be planted almost any time you can dig the hole. Canned or container-grown plants are in large, often metal or plastic containers of soil where they have grown since they were small. Hard-to-transplant kinds like pyracantha are often sold this way. Though lighter and easier to handle than a balled and burlapped plant, the canned plant presents the initial problem of getting it out of the can. Nurseries have a device that slits the metal can, thereby easing the plant's removal. Ask the nursery to slit the can before you take it home if the store employee does not volunteer to do it.

If the container is a pressed-fiber type, you can probably cut it off with a sharp knife without undue disturbance to the root ball. Fiber pots are not readily biodegradable, so do not mistakenly suppose you can plant pot and all. The plant must be removed from the container. Follow the same procedure as described for planting balled and burlapped stock. When the container has been removed so you can inspect the roots, check to see if any are circling the mass, indicating a root-bound condition. Such roots would choke off future development if allowed to remain. Remedy this by vertically scoring the root mass in five or six places with a sharp knife. This should cut free the entwiners and stimulate new roots to grow outward.

Potted nursery stock, like container-grown stock, may be planted almost any time other than the dead of winter—except for broadleaf evergreens, which are better put off until spring. Potted nursery plants are similar to container-grown ones, but the pots and plants are usually smaller, because the plants have not been growing there more than a season or so. Shrubs, small evergreens, and many other kinds of plants in small sizes are sold this way. Because of the smaller size, removal from the pot is no problem. The network of roots often holds the ball together. Fiber and plastic pots can usually be slit with a sharp knife if necessary, or removed merely by inverting and tapping out the plant. Set out potted shrubs and trees the same as those from the larger containers. Again, check for any rootbound instances, and if you find some, comb a few of the root strands outward to encourage them to reach into the new soil around them. Scoring with a knife helps loosen a tightly bound root mass.

Bare-root stock is best planted in the dormant season, usually early spring (up to early May in the Heartland). Many kinds—lilacs, for example—can also be planted bare root in fall if you can obtain freshly dug dormant stock in time to plant before freeze-up. Exceptions are magnolias, dogwoods, redbuds, sweet gum trees, and oaks, which might not regenerate damaged roots quickly enough before deep freezes to sustain life until spring. Fruit trees also belong on this spring planting preferred list, including flowering fruit trees such as crab apples and cherries.

"Bare root" means just that. Plants are dug up while dormant, cleaned of soil, and then stored at the nursery in a cold, humid area that will keep them fresh but not allow them to grow. Bare-root stock has the advantage of being light and easy to handle and transport. This is usually the way in which trees and shrubs ordered by mail are delivered. Local nurseries also handle many kinds this way. Another advantage is that you can see exactly what you are getting, as nothing is hidden.

If planted right and without delay, bare-root nursery stock should grow well. The main threat to these plants is drying out somehow before they are finally planted. This can happen during transit, during delays before planting, or even while you are doing the

planting. Unwrap new arrivals immediately and inspect them. If you can plant that day or the next, stand the roots in a tub of water to soak for up to ten hours. When you take the plants outdoors, lay wet toweling or gunny sacks over their roots to keep sun and wind from drying them.

If you have a lanky young tree to plant, study its branch structure to decide the best position. Look for the best branch extending from midway down the trunk or lower, and turn the plant so this branch is on the southwest side. This strategy enables shade cast by the branch to help prevent frost cracking while the tree is young.

If the plant's roots flare out from the crown in a downward cone, draw up a mound of soil at the center of the planting hole over which to spread them. Arrange roots evenly. Holding the main stem so the crown is at ground level, refill soil in the hole halfway. Work it down with fingers or a stick, then tread it lightly to compact it. Pour in a pail of water and let it soak away. After the water is gone, finish refilling all soil, using the cloddy subsoil last. As a finishing touch, draw up a shallow saucer-shaped ridge around the outside of the planting hole to trap water and direct it downward to the root zone. Add another pail of water. Mulch the inner area to conserve moisture and keep weeds down. As the plant begins to grow, see that it does not ever want for moisture throughout its first season.

In the case of trees with taproots, such as walnuts, shape the planting hole to accommodate the entire central root length without cramping or cutting.

Most bare-root dormant trees need pruning at planting time. Sometimes the nursery has pruned the plant for you. If not, you should prune out about one-third of the branch structure to balance roots lost in digging and to help the plant recover from transplanting. Do not cut back the leader (central trunk) or small twigs, but reduce major side branches, cutting to a smaller, outward-pointing branch so there will be no stubs. This initial pruning should suffice for two or three seasons, while the tree is allowed to grow with all the leaves it can make.

STAKING AND OTHER PROTECTION. Install a strong, rot-resistant stake about as long as the tree is tall, at the time the tree is planted. Position the stake on the south side, the direction from which we get the hardest winds. Use baler wire or rot-proof twine to tie the tree trunk to the stake using a figure-eight loop, which gives the tree a bit of play while keeping it from whipping or breaking in violent winds. Where the tie passes around the tree trunk, thread it through a section of hose or tubing to cushion the tender bark against cutting or girdling.

Safeguard the tree base from bark injury. Several kinds of injuries threaten this area: gnawing by mice and rabbits, carelessness in mowing around the base, carelessness with string trimmers, sunscald in winter, or damage from borers. A tree wrap installed right after planting is the first line of defense. The commercial tree wrap made of stretchy waterproof pa-

per is satisfactory. Cover at least the lower 2 feet of trunk or up to the lowest branches. Fasten the wrap with plastic tape at the lower end, then wrap the paper spirally up to the lower limbs and fasten again with tape there. Before winter add a screen wire or hardware cloth collar so it loosely encircles the base of the tree up at least 18 inches and anchor it firmly in the ground; this stops mouse and rabbit depredations in winter and protects against string trimmer or mower damage in the mowing season. Keep grass and weeds cleared away from the tree base to further discourage animals and reduce mower damage.

WATER CONSERVATION FOR TREES AND SHRUBS. In our region, drip irrigation systems are ideal for new tree and shrub plantings, as they enhance survival while conserving water and time. Such a system installed right after planting, and left in place for two years with an emitter over the root area of each tree or shrub, relieves you of manually watering each plant and almost guarantees better coverage and survival. For shrubs installed under eave overhangs, the system should remain permanently to make up for the lack of natural rainfall reaching such spots. Program it to provide the equivalent of 1 inch of rainfall per week. A coarse mulch, such as pine bark or wood chips, is good topping for the base area over the roots, but draw it back a few inches from direct contact with the trunk to discourage mice and insects. Mulch conserves moisture and inhibits weeds. For watering individual, widely scattered new trees or shrubs, an excellent tool is the hose-end spike root feeder or waterer that you spear into the ground. By delivering the water directly to the root zone, this device saves water by avoiding waste and gives immediate relief to drought-stressed plants.

PRUNING POINTERS

Woody plants of any sort eventually call for pruning to correct a variety of conditions aside from the need to reduce the size at planting time. Pruning is too big a subject to deal with extensively here; good books are available on it. (See Chapter Twelve for a few more details.) Here are some good basic guidelines.

Equip yourself with good tools: hand pruners, lopping shears, a pruning saw with a curved blade that cuts on the pull stroke, and hedge shears. These are the essential pruning tools for home gardeners. Jobs that require climbing into trees via ropes or ladders are best left to professionals.

Early spring while plants are still dormant is the best time for pruning most leaf-shedding trees and shrubs. For spring-flowering types, wait until after they bloom so you don't lose the flower effect that season.

Plan each cut with future growth in mind. Cut just beyond a healthy outward-facing bud.

Plan each cut to avoid tearing bark down the trunk and to leave no stubs that cannot heal over. This often means removing heavy limbs in two stages, starting with an underneath cut outward on the limb.

Make final branch cuts nearly flush with the adjoining trunk or just at the edge of the "branch collar" (the little wrinkles ringing the base of each limb). This area produces a fast-growing callus to cover the wound quickly.

Coating cuts with tree wound paint or dressing is no longer considered necessary and is thought by some even to slow the healing process.

Never "dehorn" or "top" a tree or allow this to be done to any of your trees. The dehorned or topped tree is doomed to an ugly, shortened life beset with troubles, including the broomlike growth of weakly attached water sprouts and dead stubs that spread disease down through the trunk. Qualified arborists know how to down-size mature trees by correct pruning without disfiguring them this way.

PRUNING NEEDLE EVERGREENS.

Junipers and arborvitae. These trees are best pruned in March or April, although it does no harm to prune off tips in December for holiday greens. These two types of shrubs or trees have a common characteristic: a dead zone at the center of the plant where new growth will not regenerate. Therefore, they cannot be severely pruned back to control size, or the plants may be killed. Instead, prune them moderately each year to keep them dense and the size you want. To retain the graceful appearance, do the job with hand pruners, not shears, reaching back along each branch to shorten it just beyond a growing shoot. Some green growth must remain on each branch or it will die entirely. On upright types, beware of cutting the leader (central upright growth) back to the dead zone, as no new leader can develop to replace the old one. You can safely reduce the height of these plants by about 20 percent.

Yews. The best pruning time for yews is spring. Summer pruning is also possible, as well as late fall for holiday greens. But avoid doing any heavy pruning from August up to freezing weather, or you may prompt tender new growth that will die back in winter. Yews, unlike junipers, have latent growth buds low on branches capable of sending out new growth; so they may be pruned severely. To preserve appearance, reach back to a growing

Some Favorite Heartland Shrubs for Hedges

SHRUBS FOR UNTRIMMED HEDGES: *Abelia grandiflora* (glossy abelia); *Berberis thunbergii* (redleaf barberry); *Berberis mentorensis* (Mentor barberry); *Euonymus alata compacta* (dwarf winged euonymus) *Lonicera* x *xylosteoides* (Clavey's dwarf honeysuckle); *Potentilla fruticosa; Lonicera fragrantissima* (fragrant honeysuckle); *Buxus microphylla koreana* (Korean boxwood); *Lonicera tatarica* (Tatarian honeysuckle).

SHRUBS FOR TRIMMED HEDGES: *Ligustrum amurense* (Amur privet); *Buxus microphylla koreana* (Korean boxwood); *Taxus* x *media* 'Hicks' (Hicks yew); *Juniperus keteleeri* or other upright-growing type of juniper; *Euonymus alata compacta* (dwarf winged euonymus); *Euonymus kiautschovica* (varieties such as 'Jewel' and 'Pauli'); *Berberis mentorensis* (Mentor barberry).

side branch that will cover the cut. Avoid shearing, unless you are really trying for a formal effect. Once you start shearing, it is almost impossible to return the yew to its natural form.

Pines, spruce, fir, and Douglas-fir. If planted where space is adequate, these trees seldom need pruning. Sometimes tip pruning is done to increase density; if necessary, do this in early summer. Christmas tree plantations are usually tip pruned annually for this reason. It is a simple process of removing about half of the length of the new "candles." If desired you can merely snap them off by hand while the emerging new needles are still short. This shortens the distance between "spokes" along the branch and creates a fuller looking tree. It is a useful way to keep mugho pines low and dense. If the central leader (highest tip on an upright-growing tree) is damaged so that competing shoots develop, select the strongest shoot to be the replacement and pinch out the competitors. If it veers off at an angle, train it upright by tying it temporarily to a splint fastened vertically from below. Old wood on trees of this type does not have many (if any) dormant buds from which new growth can emerge, so refrain from cutting them back heavily. To be safe, cut no further than two-year-old wood.

FERTILIZING TREES AND SHRUBS
Recent plantings benefit from annual fertilization. Mature plantings whose growth has slowed will improve in color and vitality if given fertilizer every two or three years. Use a balanced

fertilizer strong in nitrogen, the first number in the formula given on the box or bag. For example, a fertilizer with a N–P–K (nitrogen-phosphorus-potash) ratio such as 10–6–4 would be suitable. This is the same ratio often used for lawn fertilizer. In fact, trees growing on regularly fertilized lawns are well enough provided that they probably do not need any extra feeding.

Estimate the root area of the tree or shrub to be fertilized; usually it can be assumed that roots spread out as far as the tops, sometimes farther. You will need to distribute the fertilizer evenly throughout this zone. Estimate the amount of fertilizer needed based on the trunk diameter and vigor of the tree. Allow 1 to 2 pounds of complete fertilizer for each inch of trunk diameter. The fertilizer is to be placed in 1-

Things Nobody Ever Tells You

❧ Needle evergreens do shed their leaves, or needles. Some pines may do it twice a year. For example, white pines, as well as others, may turn some needles yellow-brown and shed them in early summer and again at mid-autumn. When they do this, they usually alarm gardeners, who assume it is a disease. These are the older needles whose times have come; they are well back from the growing tips of branches. This is a sign of health and growth and is nothing to worry about. Pine needles, incidentally, make the best long-lasting mulch you can get for roses, blueberries, and other shrubs. Rake them up and use them.

❧ Hedge-type yews and euonymus are easy to propagate from cuttings. You can easily start your own hedge at no cost by rooting some prunings—perhaps a neighbor will give you some. Summer tip prunings are preferred, shortened to about 8 inches. Strip needles or leaves from the lower half, dip the base in a rooting hormone (from a garden shop) and bed the lower half in a moist half-and-half mixture of

clean sand and brown peat. Keep these shaded and enclosed in clear plastic to hold humidity and water them regularly. If necessary, hold them over winter in a cold frame or in a cool area indoors that has fluorescent lighting. After two months, test them for roots. When you find some, pot the plantlets individually for gradual hardening and growth before moving them during the growing season to their outdoor garden destination. Plant them about 1 foot apart to make a tight low hedge. Keep them watered for the first year.

❧ The Keteleer juniper (*Juniperus chinensis* 'Keteleeri') makes one of the very best sheared evergreen hedges in Heartland gardens where apple or hawthorn trees are growing, as it is not a host for cedar-apple rust. Many other junipers considered for hedge uses, especially those derived from native species, are prone to harboring this disease, which trades back and forth between junipers and apple/hawthorn trees. The Keteleer descends from a Chinese ancestor that is genetically resistant.

inch-wide holes drilled or driven 2 feet apart in concentric circles around the trunk, reaching 1 foot deep or more. Soil augers are useful for this, or you can make holes with an iron rod of suitable diameter. Choose a time after rains or extensive watering, while the soil is soft. Often the fertilizer is mixed half and half with sand or peat for more-even distribution. Pour a heaping ½ cup of mixture into each hole. There is no need to refill the soil in holes. If rains do not come soon afterward, water the area.

Tree-care firms can save you all this work by bringing their special equipment for injecting liquid fertilizer over the area. Another alternative is to use a spear-type home root feeder with tree fertilizer cartridges that connects to your garden hose. Even distribution of the total feeding over the entire root area is still the objective.

Train clipped hedges to be wider at the bottom than at the top—this allows light to reach all areas, making a dense hedge.

HARDY FLOWERING SHRUBS, THE GARDENER'S FRIENDS

These woody plants, smaller than trees but nearly as permanent and pleasingly colorful when they bloom, are important fixtures in Heartland gardens. They serve many useful purposes. Some of them, such as bridalwreath spirea (*Spiraea* x *vanhouttei*), have become so established in the Midwest that they seem always to have been here.

From the garden culture standpoint, shrubs are easier to care for than trees, because they are smaller. They may live just as long or longer than trees. Planting, pruning, watering, and other care follow the same guidelines

as for trees. Many shrubs are so self-sufficient that once established they require little special attention. By careful selection you can have sustained color from shrubs over a long interval, with heights and growing habits to fit many situations.

HEDGES, THE FRIENDLY FENCES

Hedges are of two broad types: the informal or untrimmed, which are allowed to attain their natural height and spread; and the clipped, which are held to certain dimensions and shapes. In these busy times we do not see neatly trimmed hedges as often as we once did. The idea still serves many occasions, however, when no other planting seems as appropriate. Hedges of both types are useful for delineating areas, providing gentle barriers, framing or protecting a garden or furnishing a background for it, or screening off an objectionable view. The following lists suggest favorite kinds of untrimmed

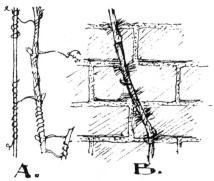

A.   B.   C.   D.

and trimmed hedges used in the Heartland. Descriptions can be found in the shrub lists on pages 165–69.

Hedges intended to be kept trimmed start with small plants set closely together. For example, a privet or juniper hedge would start with the smallest sizes available at nurseries, and the plants would be set 12 to 15 inches apart. Cut them down at planting time to only a few inches high to encourage low branching, which results in a dense hedge. Clipped hedges require faithful attention from the gardener, because if they ever "get away" (are allowed to outgrow the intended height and width) it is difficult to get them under control and back to their former fine appearance. Trimmed hedges are high-maintenance features.

WOODY VINES

Vines provide drapery for a garden. They add color and interest without demanding much horizontal space. Their one basic requirement is the right sort of support. Some can cling to stone or woody surfaces; some (such as

How vines climb determines the type of support they need. A—Tendrils wrap themselves around wires or twigs. Examples: grapes and clematis. B—Aerial rootlets attach themselves to wood, stone, brick, and other surfaces. Example: climbing hydrangea. C—Twining stems encircle any nearby support of appropriate diameter, such as tree/shrub branches, trellises, or arbors. Example: wisteria. D—Holdfasts are special tendrils with disclike tips that cling to surfaces such as stone, concrete, and wood. Example: Virginia creeper.

bittersweet) must twist their way upward along some narrow upright; some (such as wisteria) need the sturdiest of supports. Some (like the hybrid clematises) have dramatically colorful flowers; some (like the native Virginia creeper) put on a foliage colorfest each autumn high in the treetops. The vine list on pages 180–82 gives information on these and other favorite vines in the Heartland. Plant them as you would a shrub or small tree; early fall or spring are suitable times.

Deciduous Shrubs Recommended for the Heartland Area

Abelia x *grandiflora*
(glossy abelia)

Only for milder or protected areas. Grows to 4'. Pink flowers all summer; purplish fall foliage. May die back in cold winters, but regrows and blooms from new wood. Makes pleasing low untrimmed hedge in shade.

Acer palmatum
(Japanese maple)

Only for milder or protected areas. Grows to 12' but usually is lower. Many varieties exist; most have open purple-red lacy leaves; provide spring to fall foliage color. Good choice as a specimen plant.

Berberis x *mentorensis*
(Mentor barberry)

Takes cold down to -25 degrees. Reaches 5' if untrimmed. Dark-green foliage from spring to late fall. Heat tolerant. Good choice for sheared formal hedge; accepts sun or part shade.

Berberis thunbergii atropurpurea
(redleaf Japanese barberry)

Hardy throughout. Available forms range from 15"–4'; 'Crimson Pygmy,' the shortest, is good for edging or as red accent. Spring to fall reddish foliage. A yellow-leaf form, 'Aurea,' is also available.

Caragana arborescens
(pea shrub)

Hardy throughout but performs best in northern areas. Grows to 12' unless trimmed. Yellow flowers in spring; green foliage through summer. Best as hedge, background, or windbreak. In warmest areas, may be ruined by spider mites and leafhoppers.

Chaenomeles speciosa
(flowering quince)

Plant hardy throughout, but flower buds may freeze in northern areas. Available forms range from 3–6'. White, pink, orange, or red flowers in early spring. Can be clipped into hedge. Spreading root suckers and early leaf shedding due to leafspot disease sometimes are problems.

Cornus alba
'Sibirica,' 'Elegantissima'
(Siberian dogwood)

Hardy throughout. Grown for its red stems in winter on 8' shrubs. Small yellow flowers in spring; white berries in fall. 'Elegantissima' is a variegated form with green-white leaves.

Cornus mas
(Cornelian cherry)

Hardy throughout. This tree-shrub grows to 12'. Grown for its small umbels of yellow flowers in earliest spring and red fruits later. Good as screen or shrub border.

Cornus sericea stolonifera
(Redosier dogwood)

Hardy throughout. Spreading shrubs reach 7'. Bright-red twigs are showy in winter. Small white flowers in spring and white fruits in fall; grown mainly for winter twig color. Used for backgrounds. A yellow-twig form is also available.

Cotinus coggygria atropurpurea
(purple smoke bush)

Takes cold down to -20 degrees, but not for High Plains. Reaches 10'. Purple foliage and fluffy bloom panicles through summer give variety in shrub landscapes. Needs full sun.

Cotoneaster apiculatus
(cranberry cotoneaster)

Takes cold down to -20 degrees, but not for High Plains. Reaches 2–3'. Small pink flowers in spring and red berries in fall; small shining foliage on wide, arching branches. Good on slopes or for draping retaining walls.

Cotoneaster divaricatus
(spreading cotoneaster)

Takes cold down to -20 degrees, but not for High Plains. Reaches 4' in upright habit. Small pink flowers in spring and red berries in fall. Turns red in fall; fine texture. Tolerates part shade.

Deciduous Shrubs Recommended for the Heartland Area continued

Cotoneaster horizontalis (rock-spray cotoneaster)	Takes cold to down to -20 degrees, but not for High Plains. Semievergreen and spreading; stays under 2'. Useful on banks or in rock gardens. Red berries in fall.
Deutzia x *lemoinei* (Lemoine deutzia)	Hardy throughout and believed hardier than similar Deutzia gracilis. White flowers in early summer on 6' shrub. A compact form is also available.
Elaeagnus umbellata (autumn olive 'Cardinal')	Hardy throughout. Dense spreading shrub that grows to 12'. Silvery foliage all summer; red fruit in fall; inconspicuous yellow spring flowers. Drought tolerant. Used for screens and as wildlife shelters.
Euonymus alata compacta (dwarf winged euonymus, burning bush)	Hardy throughout. Grows to 8'. Neat accent plant or hedge; may be clipped if desired. Flowers are inconspicuous; shrub is grown for its brilliant red fall foliage.
Forsythia x *intermedia* (forsythia, golden-bell)	Though hardy, flower buds are killed below -15 degrees. A favorite for early spring because of its yellow flowers on shrubs that grow to 5'. Recent varieties 'Meadowlark' and 'Northern Gold' have extra bloom hardiness for northern areas.
Hibiscus syriacus (Althaea, rose-of-Sharon)	Not satisfactory north of Zone 5. Upright shrub that grows to 10'. Grown for showy blooms in white, pink, rose, or blue in late summer. Tolerates heat but not drought. Sterile varieties that avoid self-seeding nuisance are available.
Hydrangea arborescens (hills-of-snow)	Hardy throughout, but not drought tolerant. Grows fast to 4' high in formal-looking mound. Carries white-to-tan flower clusters June to fall. Takes part shade.
Hydrangea paniculata grandiflora (hydrangea peegee)	Hardy throughout. Spreading low-branched form that may grow to 7' or more, but is usually lower. Oldtime favorite for long-lasting showy white flowers in late summer. Tolerates shade but not drought.
Ilex verticillata (winterberry)	Hardy throughout, but not drought tolerant. A leaf-shedding holly, rounded in form to 10'. Grown for red berries on bare branches over fall and winter. Best in shrub borders or as background. Both male and female needed for fruit effect.
Kerria japonica	Hardy down to -20 degrees, but not for High Plains. Green stems effective all year; showy yellow flowers in April and May on 4' shrub that spreads by root suckers. Blends well into background of perennial gardens or foreground of shrub border.
Kolkwitzia amabilis (beauty-bush)	Hardy through Zone 5, but not for northernmost areas. Grows to 8' in vase shape. Profuse pink flowers in May and June. Makes splendid display as specimen shrub if allowed space for full expansion in width and height.
Lagerstroemia indica (crape-myrtle)	This tree-shrub of the South has been developed into dwarf shrub forms valued in southern parts of Heartland for white, pink, red, or purple flowers in midsummer and later. Can be grown even in north-

Deciduous Shrubs Recommended for the Heartland Area continued

	ern areas if hilled for winter like roses and cut back to crowns in spring. Reblooms from new wood. Inquire at local nurseries about adapted varieties.
Ligustrum amurense (Amur privet)	Hardy throughout. Grows to 10' if unclipped. Fast-growing fine-textured green foliage through season; much used for clipped hedges. Small white flowers in spring.
Ligustrum x *vicaryi* (golden privet)	Hardy throughout. May grow in vase shape to 8' but easily kept short by pruning. Shows yellow foliage through growing season. Widely used in our region; no major problems evident.
Lonicera fragrantissima (winter honeysuckle)	Hardy in Zone 5, but not for northernmost areas. Grows to 6'. Semi-evergreen in mild winters and southern part of Heartland. Fragrant, creamy-white flowers in late winter; not showy, but appreciated for earliness.
Lonicera maackii (Amur honeysuckle)	Hardy throughout. Grows to 10'. Whitish flowers in spring; red berries from autumn to winter until birds take them. Grown for windbreaks or screens.
Lonicera tatarica (Tatarian honeysuckle)	Hardy throughout. Grows to 12' but can be kept clipped. Pink-to-red flowers in May; red berries in summer attractive to birds. Used also for informal hedges or backgrounds. Susceptible to a gall-producing aphid; consequently is less recommended now than formerly.
Lonicera x *xylosteum* (Clavey's dwarf honeysuckle)	Hardy throughout. Gray-green foliage through summer on mounded spreading plant that seldom exceeds 5'. Little pruning needed; few problems. Whitish flowers. Used for low informal hedge. 'Emerald Mound' is a smaller, darker green form used for accents or foundation plantings.
Myrica pensylvanica (bayberry)	Believed hardy throughout, but not for alkaline soils. Grows to about 5'. Not evergreen for Heartland, but grown for its interesting branching and gray berries that hold through winter; aromatic gray-green foliage in summer. Used in shrub borders and bank covers. Need several plants together to get fruit set. Spreads by root suckers.
Paeonia suffruticosa (tree peony)	Hardy except in extreme north of region. In western areas, water through dry summers. Grows to 4'. Large early blooms in all peony colors, including yellow, on permanent woody plant covered with handsome blue-green foliage until frost. Use as accent in featured place or in garden settings.
Philadelphus coronarius or *P. virginalis* (mock-orange)	Hardy throughout region. Upright shrubs up to 7' high grown for showy white flowers in late spring. Since these are often leggy at base, they need something lower planted in front. Some varieties, especially *P. coronarius*, are fragrant. Use in shrub borders.
Physocarpus opulifolius (ninebark)	Hardy throughout region. White-to-pink flowers in clusters in spring on spirealike shrubs that grow to 7' high. Gold-leafed form ('Luteus') and dwarf ('Nanus') are available. Use in shrub borders.

Deciduous Shrubs Recommended for the Heartland Area continued

Potentilla fruticosa (cinquefoil)	Hardy throughout region. Summer-long yellow-gold flowers on low shrubs 2–3' high. Many named varieties. Give full sun for best bloom. Use these in low hedges, foundation plantings, or among perennials. Adapted well in western areas, and fairly drought tolerant.
Prunus x *cistena* (purpleleaf sand cherry)	Hardy throughout region. Red foliage all season on 6' plant; pink-white flowers in May followed by edible black-purple fruits. Use for color effect in screens or windbreaks.
Pyracantha coccinea (firethorn)	Only for southern part of region; even there, use hardiest varieties such as 'Lalandi' and 'Kasan.' Though considered to be broadleaf evergreens, they often are brown by spring in this region. Showy orange berries persist through winter unless eaten by birds; white flowers in spring. Can be trained on trellis, fence, or wall or allowed to grow naturally.
Rhododendron species and hybrids (azaleas, hardy kinds)	See discussion in this chapter on pages 153–54. With proper preparation of soil and careful selection of site, a few may be grown over much of this region.
Rhus typhina (staghorn sumac)	Hardy throughout region. Grows to 10' high. Foliage turns bright red in fall; seed heads are showy through winter. Spreads by underground suckers. Use in naturalized areas or on banks, where it can move around without invading valued plants. Varieties available with deeply cut leaflets. Fairly drought tolerant.
Rhus aromatica (fragrant sumac)	Hardy throughout region. Low, spreading shrub that grows to 5' high and expands to form colonies. Scarlet fruits in summer, red foliage in autumn. Drought tolerant. Use for area cover or on banks.
Salix caprea (pussy willow)	Hardy throughout region, this willow is grown primarily for its silvery furry catkins in early spring. Grows fast to 20' high. To keep it in bounds and to encourage more "pussies," cut it to the ground every few years. Belongs in background or shrub border where other plants will blend with it.
Spiraea species (white-flowering) (bridal-wreath spirea)	Hardy throughout region. Several in this group, all spring blooming: Japanese White (*S. albiflora*), only 18" high, blooming in June; 'Garland' (*S. arguta*), 5' high, blooming in May; 'Bridal-wreath' (*S. prunifolia*), blooming in April–May; 'Thunberg' (*S. thunbergii*), 3' high, blooming in April; 'Vanhoutte' (*S. vanhouttei*), 5' high, blooming in May; 'Snowmound' (*S. nipponica*), 5' high, blooming in late May.
Spiraea species (pink-flowering) (Bumalda or Froebel spireas)	Hardy throughout region; all are summer blooming, some to August or even later if earlier blooms are removed. Because of their small size, they are often grown in groups. Tolerate part shade. 'Anthony Waterer' (*S.* x *bumalda*), 3' high; 'Froebeli' (*S.* x *bumalda*), 3½' high.

Deciduous Shrubs Recommended for the Heartland Area continued

Spiraea japonica 'Alpina' (Alpine spirea)	Hardy throughout region. Only 1' high, this dainty plant excels in rock gardens or foreground plantings, making a low mound with pink flowers in May, sometimes repeating. Gold-leafed form available.
Symphoricarpos orbiculatus (coralberry)	Hardy throughout region, this native is useful as bank cover, spreading by suckers and runners and averaging 3' high. Tolerates shade. Gray-green foliage; small pinkish flowers in June not showy, but purple fruits clustered at leaf axils hang on through winter giving interest and wildlife forage.
Syringa meyeri (dwarf Korean or Meyer's lilac)	Hardy throughout region; grows to 5' high. Small panicles of lilac flowers in April–May. Use as foundation plant or in shrub borders where compact habit useful.
Syringa x *persica* (Persian lilac)	Hardy throughout region; grows to 6' or more. Pale-lavender flower clusters in May; plants smaller in all respects than common lilac. Use in shrub borders, hedges, or backgrounds.
Syringa vulgaris (common lilac)	Hardy throughout region. Showy flower panicles in April–May on plants that grow to 12' high. Many named varieties in white to deep purple, even cream-yellow; some fragrant. Use in shrub borders and backgrounds of spring gardens.
Tamarix ramosissima (pentandra) (Tamarisk or Tamarix)	Hardy throughout region. Drought tolerant. Fine-textured feathery foliage in summer, dense pink flower panicles at ends of branches in July. Needs sharp pruning each spring. Use as thin screens or backdrops in summer; not effective in winter.
Viburnum carlesii (Korean spicebush or pink snowball)	Hardy down to -20 degrees, but not for High Plains. Light-pink flower clusters in early spring on rounded 4' high shrub; fragrant. Blooms with tulips; good in spring garden.
Viburnum x *carlcephalum* (fragrant snowball)	Hardy except on northern edge of region. Plant and flower clusters larger than *V. carlesii*—grows to 6' or more; also has better foliage and is healthier; flowers not quite so fragrant, however.
Viburnum dentatum (arrowwood)	Hardy throughout region. Vigorous plants grow to 10' high. Creamy flower clusters in midspring; red foliage and blue berries in fall. Use as screens or backgrounds.
Viburnum lantana (wayfaring tree)	Hardy throughout region. Grows to 12' or more. Creamy flowers in May; red foliage with yellow, red, or black berries in fall. Use in shrub backgrounds or for winter bird forage.
Viburnum plicatum mariesii (doublefile viburnum)	Hardy down to -20 degrees, but not for High Plains. Grows to 8' or more. White flowers in layered clusters—effective in May; in fall red fruit that eventually turns black. Refined appearance suits this for garden background or as specimen.

Deciduous Shrubs Recommended for the Heartland Area continued

Viburnum opulus (European highbush cranberry)	Hardy throughout region. Grows to 10' high and wide. White flowers in May; red berries and red foliage in fall. Use in shrub borders or backgrounds.
Viburnum opulus 'Compactum' (dwarf European cranberry)	Hardy throughout region. White flowers in May and red berries in fall on dense 4'-high plant. Fits small landscapes better than the regular form.
Weigela florida (weigela)	Hardy down to about -15 degrees; not for northern extremes of region. Pink-red flowers in early summer on 6' shrub. Not drought tolerant; needs part shade. Some varieties ('Bristol Ruby') will rebloom into autumn. 'Red Prince' is especially hardy.

Recommended Shade Trees for the Heartland

Acer ginnala (Amur maple)	Small rounded tree that grows to 20' high. Any soil or exposure. Red fall foliage.
Acer platanoides (Norway maple)	Oval tree that grows to 60' when mature; moderate to fast growing and shallow rooted. Needs sunny place; soil and wind tolerant. Turns gold in fall. Protect against sunscald when young.
Acer rubrum (red maple)	Rounded tree that grows to 70' when mature; moderate to fast growing and shallow rooted. Needs sunny place and slightly acidic soil. Use a hardy northern strain. Brilliant red fall color.
Acer saccharinum (silver maple)	Wide-spreading tree that grows to 75'; fast growing and shallow rooted. Needs sun; tolerates any soil. Not drought tolerant and breaks in storms.
Acer saccharum (sugar maple)	Upright or rounded tree that grows to 65' when mature; moderate growing and shallow rooted. Does best on north-facing slope in clay loam soil. Bright yellow-red fall color. Not drought tolerant. In northern areas, choose black maple (*A. nigrum*).
Aesculus hippocastanum (horse-chestnut)	Oval tree that grows to 65' when mature; moderate growing. Tolerates any soil, but gets leaf burns in hot exposures. Showy flowers and brown nuts.
Betula nigra (river birch)	Often in clump form, the tree grows to 70' when mature; moderate growing. Has peeling two-tone-tan bark. Tolerant of wind, soil, and moisture and resists birch borers; has no serious faults.
Carpinus betulus (European hornbeam)	Fine-textured, narrowly upright tree that grows to 30' when mature. Tolerates any soil or exposure; no serious faults.
Celtis occidentalis (hackberry)	Oval-topped, moderate-growing tree that reaches 90' when mature. Tolerates any soil or exposure; drought tolerant and shallow rooted. Berries are liked by birds. Sometimes affected by witches'-brooming of top twigs.

Recommended Shade Trees for the Heartland continued

Cladrastis lutea (yellowwood)	Vase-shaped tree that grows slowly to 35'. Needs wind-sheltered site and protection from sunscald. White pealike flowers in clusters in early summer. A good small accent tree.
Elaeagnus angustifolia (Russian olive)	Small, open, irregularly shaped tree that grows to 20' when mature. Silvery-gray foliage and fragrant flowers. Heat and drought tolerant but not long lived.
Fraxinus pensylvanica (green ash)	Rounded, oval, or columnar, this tree is moderate growing and reaches 60' when mature. Tolerates any soil or exposure; drought tolerant. Seeds create litter unless it is a seedless form such as 'Marshall.'
Fraxinus americana (white ash)	Oval-topped, moderate-growing tree that reaches 60' when mature. Tolerates any soil or exposure. Seeds create litter except in seedless forms (for example, 'Rosehill'). Noted for its purple fall color.
Ginkgo biloba (ginkgo)	Forms upright pyramid that reaches 80' when mature. Slow growing, tolerant of wind and any soil or exposure; no pests or diseases. Plant only male trees to avoid messy fruit. Gold color briefly in fall.
Gymnocladus dioicus (Kentucky coffee tree)	Grows moderately in angular style to 70' when mature. Tolerates wind and any soil or exposure. Female trees have large seed pods, so plant only males if seeds not wanted.
Gleditsia triacanthos inermis (honey locust)	Forms loose, open head and grows to 60' when mature. Fast growing and tolerates wind and any soil or exposure. Lacy foliage is susceptible to mimosa webworm. Select improved varieties (such as 'Skyline') that are thornless and seedless.
Juglans nigra (black walnut)	Open-formed tree that reaches 65' when mature. Moderately fast growing and accepts any soil or exposure. Roots are toxic to some neighboring plants. Edible nuts.
Koelreuteria paniculata (golden-rain tree)	Has rounded top and grows to 55' when mature. Accepts any soil or exposure and is pest free and drought tolerant. Showy yellow flowers in summer.
Liquidambar styraciflua (sweet gum)	Rounded top when mature and reaches 75'. Moderately fast growing and shallow rooted; avoid dry, alkaline soil. Wind tolerant. Seed balls create litter. In northern areas of the Heartland, give it a protected site.
Liriodendron tulipifera (tulip tree)	Cylindrical tree that grows fast to 85' when mature. Needs sun, but tolerates any soil. Wood is brittle and breaks often in winds.
Phellodendron amurense (Amur cork tree)	Has wide-spreading crown and reaches 25' when mature. Moderate growing; tolerates any soil or exposure and temperature extremes. Has small white flowers in early summer and interesting branching.

Recommended Shade Trees for the Heartland continued

Populus deltoides (eastern cottonwood)	Has spreading, open crown and reaches 90' when mature; fast growing. Makes quick shade but roots may heave sidewalks or invade sewers; plant only in open areas. Weak wood may break in storms. Use male form to avoid flying cottony seeds.
Platanus occidentalis (sycamore)	Has rounded or open head and grows fast to reach 85' when mature. Needs moisture at roots. White blotchy bark is showy in winter. Large leaves create litter; anthracnose disease often hits spring foliage.
Quercus alba (white oak)	Has upright oval form and reaches 75' when mature. Accepts any soil or exposure and tolerates wind. Splendid purple-red autumn foliage; may create acorn litter. Transplant only when young.
Quercus bicolor (swamp white oak)	Has rounded canopy and reaches 75' when mature. Moderate growing, accepts any soil or exposure and is wind tolerant. Litter from large acorns in autumn. Not noted for fall color.
Quercus rubra (northern red oak)	Has rounded top and reaches 60' when mature. Grows fast, accepts any soil or exposure, and is wind tolerant. Susceptible to oak wilt disease. Rust-red foliage in autumn; acorns create litter.
Quercus coccinea (scarlet oak)	Has rounded crown; though slow to establish, it eventually grows to 80' when mature. Tolerant of soil, site, and winds. Bright-red foliage in autumn; coloring best in acidic soil.
Quercus macrocarpa (bur oak)	Has spreading crown and grows moderately to 90' when mature. Widely tolerant of soil, site, and wind. Fall foliage not showy; acorns create litter.
Quercus palustris (pin oak)	Pyramidal when young and rounded in age; grows to 85' when mature. Low-hanging limbs require pruning; reddish fall foliage. Avoid planting in alkaline soil.
Quercus robur (English oak)	Various forms available from narrow to spreading. Grows moderately to 75' when mature. Accepts any soil or site and tolerates wind. Not noted for fall foliage.
Taxodium distichum (bald cypress)	Upright pyramidal leaf-shedding conifer that grows moderately to 60' when mature. No serious problems; accepts any soil, but prefers moist. In northern areas, give it winter-protected site. Serves best as specimen.
Tilia cordata (littleleaf linden)	Dense upright oval or pyramidal tree that grows moderately to reach 60' when mature. Tolerates most soils and is fairly drought tolerant; needs sun. Turns yellow in fall.

Flowering Trees Recommended for the Heartland

Albizia julibrissin
(mimosa or hardy silktree)

Not really hardy in this region, but grown across southern Missouri and Kansas. Though winters may kill it to the ground, it regrows from root or trunk base and blooms in July on new growth. Fluffy round brushlike clusters of pink stamens always admired. Not recommended for landscapes because of annual brush with death and necessity of starting over each year. Are undeniably part of scenery across the southern part of region.

Amelanchier laevis
(serviceberry)

Hardy throughout region, but protect it from hot winds in western areas. Grows to under 10' in Heartland. Does best in part shade and deep soil. Grown for its white flowers in earliest spring, edible purple fruit, and orange fall foliage. Has root suckering habit, so is best placed in background where can spread.

Cercis canadensis
(eastern redbud)

Hardy down to -20 degrees. Low, spreading flat-top tree that grows to 10–20' when mature. Pink-purple or white flowers open before leaves come out in April. Does best in part shade. Iowa and Nebraska gardeners should inquire at nurseries about hardier forms being developed. Elsewhere investigate newer foliage forms. Plant in spring only.

Cornus florida
(flowering dogwood)

Rated hardy in Zone 5 (-20 degrees); state tree of Missouri and does best in southern half of that state. Not for northern areas of Heartland or High Plains. Reaches about 15' high and wide in our region. Needs neutral or slightly acidic soil; shade tolerant but not drought tolerant. Valued for showy white or pink flower bracts in midspring; red foliage in fall followed by red berries. Plant in spring only.

Cornus kousa
(Japanese dogwood)

As hardy as *C. florida* but more pest resistant and slightly less spreading; grows in same area. Reaches 18' when mature. Not for windy dry plains. White starlike flower bracts open in June; showy pink-red fruit and red foliage colorful in fall. Low branching gives shrubby appearance. Plant in spring only.

Crataegus species
(hawthorn)

Hardy down to -30 degrees; come in confusing number of species and varieties generally growing into small thorny trees about 20' high and 25' wide when mature. Produce showy white flowers in dense clusters in spring; in fall produce set of lasting red or orange berries gradually devoured by robins, waxwings, and other birds. Most kinds of hawthorns beset by various leaf diseases and pests, although they survive; *C. crusgalli* (cockspur hawthorn) is one of the most resistant. Best planted in spring. Use as landscape specimens or screens.

Magnolia x *loebnerii*
('Merrill')

Hardy down to -25 degrees (Zone 4). Although wood is hardy, open flowers are killed by late frosts about every other year throughout Heartland. This hybrid between *M. stellata* and *M. kobus* is more upright than most magnolias, grows to 20', and bears white many-petaled flowers in early spring; flowers are larger than those of *M. stellata*. Plant in spring only. In northern areas, place in sheltered location.

Flowering Trees Recommended for the Heartland continued

Magnolia x *soulangeana* (saucer magnolia)	Hardy down to -20 degrees (Zone 5). See preceding note about dangers of late frosts to flowers. Flowers are large, saucer-shaped, and white to purple-pink in color on wide-spreading trees that grow to 25' when mature. Difficult to grow lawns under these trees, so plan on another type of ground cover. Plant in spring only.
Magnolia stellata (star magnolia)	Hardy down to -25 degrees (Zone 4). Often the earliest magnolia to open. See *Magnolia* x *loebnerii* for dangers of late frosts to flowers. Usually grows slowly to about 15' high and wide when mature. Starry white flowers, 4" across, with many narrow petals in early spring. Plant in spring only. Use as specimen in protected site.
Malus species and varieties (flowering crab apple)	Hardy throughout region; best flowering trees for Heartland. White, pink, and red-to-purple flowers open at tulip time in spring, followed by red and yellow fruits in fall-winter. Many sizes and shapes are available for various landscape needs; also disease-resistant cultivars. Study examples in arboretum near you to aid in selecting. Use as specimen trees, in tree-shrub borders and backgrounds, and as backdrops for gardens.
Prunus species (flowering cherry)	Recommended only for milder areas of region or with protection. The prized Oriental cherry cultivars such as grow around the Tidal Basin in Washington, D.C., have not usually been long lived in our region and the blooms are often spoiled by late frosts. In successful sites they make 15–25' trees, some in weeping forms and with double flowers in delicate pink-white tones.
Prunus species (flowering plums)	Purpleleaf sand cherry-plum, *P.* x *cistena*, is a small (8') purple-leafed tree that keeps its foliage color through summer. This cherry-plum produces pink blooms in May and is hardy throughout our region. The 'Blireiana' plum, another hybrid, is less hardy and so is risky in northern reaches of the Heartland. It grows to 15' and bears double pink flowers amid purple foliage. The 'Thundercloud' plum grows to 15' when mature and is hardy throughout our region. It bears single pink flowers amid purple foliage. Protect its trunk from sunscald, and prune it annually. Use any of these as accent trees.
Prunus persica (flowering peach)	With a profusion of double red-pink flowers in early spring, these trees are as showy as any that flower, but they are no hardier than peaches grown for fruit and just as subject to insects (especially borers) and diseases. Even in southern (Zone 6) parts of the Heartland, they may last only a few years. They grow fast. Many gardeners are willing to replant them just for the brief lift they give in a spring garden.
Pyrus calleryana (Callery pear or Bradford pear)	Considered hardy down to -20 degrees, this ornamental pear from China has changed cityscapes in southern half of Heartland because of its wide use as street tree. Its narrow upright tailored form reaches 30' and is suitable for medians and parking strips; a neat habit and three-season color effects add to its usefulness. White flowers cover it in early spring, clean shining green foliage in summer, and varnished red leaves in late fall; fruits tiny. 'Bradford,' the original cultivar, was

Flowering Trees Recommended for the Heartland continued

	prone to splitting in winds and is now yielding to improved forms with stronger branching (for example, 'Whitehouse').
Sorbus aucuparia (European mountain-ash)	Hardy throughout region, but does best in colder areas of Heartland. White flower clusters in spring followed by orange berries and leaves in fall on trees reaching about 25' high. South of central Iowa, it is increasingly affected by borers and fire blight. Alkaline soils in western areas retard its growth. An alternative for warmer Heartland areas and those with alkaline soils is *S. alnifolia* (Korean mountain-ash), which offers borer resistance. Both kinds good as specimen trees.
Syringa reticulata (tree lilac)	Hardy throughout region. Rounded tree grows to 25', with shiny cherrylike bark attractive in winter. Large panicles of creamy white flowers cover tree in early summer. Use as specimen tree or in tree borders or screens. Protect from lilac borers.

Needle Evergreens Recommended for the Heartland

TREES (UPRIGHT FORMS)

Abies concolor (white fir)	Hardy throughout region. Not for High Plains. May reach 30' high and 12' wide. Beautiful specimen tree resembling blue spruce but more adaptable. Symmetrical and upright when mature.
Juniperus chinensis ('Keteleer' juniper or 'Ames' juniper)	Hardy throughout region. This species apparently does not harbor cedar-apple rust. May reach 15' high and 6' wide if permitted. Bright-green color holds through winter. May be sheared; makes good hedges. Guard against bagworms.
Juniperus scopulorum (Rocky Mountain juniper; 'Blue Haven,' 'Welch,' 'Wichita Blue,' and others)	Hardy throughout region. May reach 15' high and 5' wide. Most in this group have blue-green foliage that is attractive in tree borders. Drought tolerant and adaptable. Guard against bagworms.
Juniperus virginiana (Eastern red cedar; 'Canaertii,' 'Burkii,' and many others)	Hardy throughout region. May reach 20' high and 8' wide. 'Canaertii' is dark green and dense and has profusion of grapelike cones. 'Burkii' has blue-green foliage that turns purplish in winter. All play host to cedar-apple rust. Well adapted in our region.
Picea abies (Norway spruce)	Hardy throughout region, but suffers in hot, dry summers; best in cooler parts of region. May reach 50' high and 20' wide. Has dark-green pendulous branches and large cones.
Picea glauca 'Conica' (dwarf Alberta spruce)	Hardy throughout region, but in western areas it needs protection from dry winds and winter sun. A dense conical tree that grows slowly to perhaps reach 5' in 15 years. Used in dooryards, Oriental gardens, and small area landscapes for fine-textured green effect.
Picea glauca densata (Black Hills spruce)	Hardy throughout region. May reach 30' high and 20' wide. Dense, often blue-green foliage good for screens and tree borders. Grows slowly.

Needle Evergreens Recommended for the Heartland continued

Picea pungens (Colorado blue spruce)	Hardy throughout region; widely adapted. Green or blue needles in stiff, upright habit. Silvery blue forms are used as landscape accents. May reach 30' high and 20' wide.
Pinus nigra (Austrian pine)	Hardy throughout region, widely adapted. Coarse stiff needles on upright tree that may reach 40' high and 25' wide. Used in shelterbelts and tree borders. Deer do not browse this pine as much as they do those with softer needles.
Pinus ponderosa (Ponderosa pine)	Hardy throughout region; well adapted in western areas. Grows fast when young; mature trees become irregular, often rounded in crowns, with bare brown trunks. May reach 45' high and 25' wide. Use in tree borders or as windbreaks.
Pinus resinosa (red pine)	Hardy throughout region, but protect young trees from winter sun. Has long, slender needles and red-brown bark; may reach 45' high and 25' wide.
Pinus strobus (white pine)	Hardy throughout region; protect from hot winds. Needles are soft, long, thin, and dark green; trees grow fast when young and may reach 70' high and 25' wide. Valued in backgrounds, tree borders, screens, and windbreaks.
Pinus sylvestris (Scotch pine)	Hardy throughout region. Has short stiff needles and orange-brown bark; top becomes open, irregular, and picturesque with age. May reach 50' high and 25' wide. Use in tree borders or garden backgrounds. A blue-needled form also available.
Pseudotsuga menziesii (Douglas-fir)	Hardy throughout region, but needs consistent moisture; not for High Plains. May reach 50' high and 20' wide. Short stiff shining needles are fine textured and medium green. Use as specimens or in backgrounds.
Taxus cuspidata 'Capitata' (Japanese yew)	Hardy throughout region, but protect from hot winds and winter sun; not drought tolerant. Best to give it north or east exposures and part shade. Offers fine-textured dark-green needles. Pyramidal form may reach more than 8' high and 3' across, but may be controlled by pruning. Often used in foundation or dooryard plantings.
Taxus x *media* 'Hicks' (Anglojap yew)	Hardy throughout region, but protect as described for *Taxus cuspidata*. Hicks yew has columnar habit and fine-textured dark-green needles. Reaches 10' high and 4' wide if permitted; may be pruned to contain size. Use as foundation plant or in backgrounds or screens.
Thuja occidentalis (arborvitae)	Hardy throughout region, but needs moist soil and humidity; not for High Plains. Many cultivated varieties, from tiny to huge, are available. Use as foundation plants, hedges, or accents. Study varieties at nurseries before purchasing.
Tsuga canadensis (Canada hemlock)	Cold hardy throughout region, but not for dry, hot, windy areas or alkaline soils; shade tolerant. With graceful, often drooping branches and dark-green needles, these trees may grow to 50' high

Needle Evergreens Recommended for the Heartland continued

and almost as wide; readily controlled by pruning. Northeastern part of Heartland offers best prospects for hemlocks. Use as hedges, screens, foundation plants, or accents.

Shrubs (Low, rounded, spreading forms)

Juniperus chinensis ('Hetz,' 'Mint Julep,' 'Pfitzer,' 'San Jose,' 'Armstrong,' and 'Maney')	Hardy throughout region; widely adapted. Sizes vary; study varieties at nurseries before purchasing. Most give spreading, layered effect. Some show blue, gold, or purple tones. 'San Jose' is 10" high and 6' wide. Plant in sunny locations. Use as ground covers, foundation plants, or garden backgrounds.
Juniperus horizontalis ('Andorra,' 'Blue Chip,' 'Blue Rug,' 'Bar Harbor,' 'Hughes,' 'Prince of Wales,' 'Webberi,' and others)	Hardy throughout region; widely adapted. All grow wider than high; seldom more than 1' high. 'Andorra' turns purplish in winter; most others show bluish tint. Plant in sunny location. Use them for ground covers or shrub foregrounds.
Juniperus procumbens (Japanese garden juniper)	Hardy throughout region; but in open winters it may suffer winterburn. Blue-gray-green foliage under 1' high but wide spreading, to 5' or more. Makes a dense mat.
Juniperus sabina ('Arcadia,' 'Blue Danube,' 'Scandia,' 'Broadmoor,' and others)	Hardy throughout region; widely adapted. All are low spreaders, 2' high or less, spreading to 5'. Fine textured and dense, they vary in color from dark green to gray-green.
Pinus mugo (mugho or Swiss Mountain pine)	Hardy throughout region. Forms a cushion-shaped slow-growing mound about 5' high and 5' wide. To control size, pinch back "candles" (young growth) in spring. Often used as accent or doorway planting.
Taxus x *media* ('Brown's,' 'Ward's,' and 'Densiformis' yews)	Hardy throughout region, but protect from hot winds and winter sun. Fine-textured dark-green shrubs will grow in part shade; best in north or east exposures. 'Brown's' is largest, up to 6' high; 'Densiformis' is smallest, only 3' high. All spread to about 6'. May be held to size by pruning.

Broadleaf Evergreen Trees and Shrubs Recommended for the Heartland

Abelia x *grandiflora* (glossy abelia)	See under "Recommended Deciduous Shrubs" on page 165. Hardy down to -10 degrees (Zone 6). Evergreen only in mild winters.
Azaleas	Except in the extreme southeastern arc of our region, few azaleas are reliably evergreen in the Heartland. Breeders continue to work toward hardier ones. Among those currently most likely to overwinter with foliage intact (Zone 6 or protected places in Zone 5) are the Robin Hill hybrids and some of the Gable, Girard, and Shammarello hybrids. Ask your most respected local nursery for advice on these.
Berberis julianae (wintergreen barberry)	Hardy down to -10 degrees (Zone 6); usually keeps dark-green foliage through winter. Has rounded form up to 4' high, spine-edged leaves, and spiny twigs. Useful for barriers or hedges.

Broadleaf Evergreen Trees and Shrubs Recommended for the Heartland continued

Berberis x *mentorensis* (Mentor barberry)	See under "Recommended Deciduous Shrubs" on page 165. Evergreen only in mildest areas and winters.
Buxus microphylla var. *koreana* (littleleaf boxwood or Korean boxwood)	Hardy down to -20 degrees (Zone 5); protect from harsh winter winds and sun. Grows slowly in dense mounded form up to 3' high; has tiny leaves that may turn bronzy by late winter. Accepts part shade.
Buxus sempervirens (common boxwood)	Hardy down to -10 degrees (Zone 6); protect from harsh winter winds and sun. Shining green foliage forms dense mounded shrub that grows up to 4' high; in good conditions it grows larger. Seek hardiest cultivars, such as 'Vardar Valley.'
Cotoneaster dammeri (bearberry cotoneaster)	Hardy down to -10 degrees (Zone 6) and shade tolerant; not drought tolerant or for far western areas of region. Trailing, low ground cover has small smooth bright-green leaves that give fine texture; may lose leaves some winters.
Daphne cneorum (rose daphne)	Hardy down to -20 degrees (Zone 5); not drought tolerant or for High Plains. Shade from winter sun and protect from wind; keep soil moist. Forms a spreading mat that grows to 1' high. Fragrant, pink flowers in spring.
Euonymus fortunei vars. (wintercreeper; 'Gaiety,' 'Sunspot,' 'Emerald 'n' Gold,' and 'Jewell')	Hardy down to -20 degrees (Zone 5); fairly drought tolerant. Upright if supported, otherwise low and spreading. Many forms available, some vining. Some have variegated leaves. Scale insects often a problem. Fairly drought tolerant.
Ilex x *cornuta* (Chinese holly hybrids; 'China Boy' and 'China Girl')	Hardy down to -20 degrees (Zone 5). Remarkably widely adapted and soil tolerant; benefits from part shade. Compact, upright plant that grows quickly to 6' high and wide. Stiff, shiny green foliage; small vivid-red berries on females (both sexes needed for pollination). Worth trying in areas previously thought beyond holly country.
Ilex cornuta (Chinese holly)	Hardy down to -10 degrees (Zone 6); needs sun or part shade. Shiny green leaves with spiny tips; bushy to 6' or more and vigorous growing where winter hardy. Makes dense year-round screen or hedge. Red berries on females.
Ilex crenata 'Convexa' (Japanese holly)	Hardy down to -10 degrees (Zone 6); not drought tolerant. Small, rounded boxwoodlike small leaves and black berries; may be clipped. Best in north and east exposures with part shade. Much used in southeastern part of region as foundation plant or low hedge. Recent hard winters have pushed back limits for using this.
Ilex glabra 'Compacta' (inkberry)	Hardy down to -20 degrees (Zone 5). Tough and widely adapted, but not drought tolerant. Oval, lightly spined dark-green leaves on loose, upright shrub that grows to 6' or so; can be pruned to encourage density. Small black berries on female plants. Use for year-round screen or as dooryard or foundation planting where space permits.

Broadleaf Evergreen Trees and Shrubs Recommended for the Heartland continued

Ilex x *meserveae* hybs. (blue hollies; 'Blue Boy,' 'Blue Girl,' 'Blue Princess,' and 'Blue Stallion')	Hardy down to -20 degrees (Zone 5). Widely adapted in both climate and soil; tolerates part shade. Small, glossy blue-green leaves, lightly prickled; vigorous growers that spread; may reach 10' high; but not likely in western areas of region. Readily controlled by pruning. Female varieties bear abundant small red berries; 'Blue Stallion' is a pollinator. Use for year-round screens, shrub borders, or dooryard or foundation plantings.
Ilex opaca (American holly)	Hardy down to -15 degrees (Zone 5); in western areas, amend soil to acidify. Upright conical tree that grows to 18' or smaller as it nears hardiness limit; can be clipped. Typical holly-shaped foliage; red berries on females. Needs protected site. Use as specimens, foundation plants, screens, or hedges.
Ilex x *fosteri* (Foster's holly)	Hardy down to -15 degrees (Zone 5); acidify soil in western areas. Narrow glossy leaves, not prickly, on upright tree that grows to 8' or more; may be pruned to tighten shape. Small red berries. Needs protected site; winter sun may burn foliage.
Kalmia latifolia (mountain-laurel)	Hardy down to -20 degrees (Zone 5); not drought tolerant. Shiny leathery leaves on rounded shrub that grows to 5' across. Pink flower clusters in spring. Acidify soil; supply ample organic matter; protect from winter sun and harsh winds; keep mulched and watered. Use in dooryard gardens or as special accents. Northeast exposure best.
Leucothoe fontanesiana (drooping leucothoe or Catesby's leucothoe)	Though hardy down to -10 to -15 degrees, this shrub requires moist acidic soil and year-round partial shade. Low, spreading plant with arching branches that grows to 3' high. Racemes of white flowers in spring. Useful for fronting evergreen shrub borders or as backgrounds for perennials.
Magnolia grandiflora (southern magnolia)	Hardy down to -10 degrees (Zone 6). Upright tree that grows to 15' or more, depending on climate. Large leathery green leaves. To prevent disfiguring winter leaf damage, plant in protected place out of winter sun and winds. White flowers in summer.
Mahonia aquifolium (Oregon grape-holly)	Hardy down to -20 degrees (Zone 5); not drought tolerant. Upright shrub that grows to 6' high and 4' wide; stiff hollylike leaves turning bronzy in winter. Yellow flowers in spring and blue berries in late summer-fall. Give part shade in our region. A good year-round ornamental; use as foundation plants, dooryard accents, or shrub borders to lend variety.
Nandina domestica (nandina or heavenly bamboo)	Hardy down to -10 degrees (Zone 6). This small upright shrub is not evergreen in most of our region and often succumbs to winters; it is grown anyhow for its unmatched Oriental effect. Grows to about 3' high and accepts part shade and most soils; not drought tolerant. Needs protected site. Green bamboolike leaves turn red in autumn and remain until spring; red berries through winter.

Broadleaf Evergreen Trees and Shrubs Recommended for the Heartland continued

Pieris japonica (lily-of-the-valley bush)	Hardy down to -10 degrees (Zone 6). Upright plant that reaches 5' high; needs slightly acidic organic soil, consistent moisture, and protection from winter sun. Shining green ovate leaves in rosette effect, and white bellflowers in drooping clusters in spring; new foliage in spring is bronze-red. Use as garden backgrounds, accent plants for doorway gardens, or in front of shrub borders.
Pyracantha coccinea (Firethorn varieties 'Gnome,' 'Kasan,' and 'Lalandei')	Hardy down to -15 degrees (southern edge of Zone 5); tolerates most soils. Southern areas of region have more choice of varieties. Thorny mounded growth that reaches up to 7'; may be pruned as desired. Showy orange berries in autumn–winter; white flower clusters in late spring. Useful as hedges, barrier plants, espaliers (trained on walls or fences), specimens, foundation plantings in sun or part shade (dwarf forms), or shrub borders. Difficult to transplant and should not be disturbed once established.
Rhododendron (Catawbiense hybrids; 'P.J.M.')	Hardy down to -20 degrees (Zone 5). Grown primarily for their spring flowers, these plants also offer evergreen foliage. Give north or east exposures, organic soil, mulch, and reasonable moisture through droughts; acidify soils in western areas and protect from drying winds and winter sun. Catawbiense hybrids grow to 8' with large foliage; 'P.J.M.' to 5' with small foliage that turns bronzy in winter; mounded habit. Southeastern parts of region have much wider choices in kinds to grow.
Viburnum rhytidophyllum (leatherleaf viburnum)	Hardy down to -10 degrees (Zone 6). Protect from harsh winds so leaves will not be tattered by spring; otherwise widely adapted. Upright rounded shrubs grow to 6' high and wide, plants are fairly coarse and leaves are large and crinkled. Use in shrub borders or as screens.
Yucca filimentosa (Adam's needle)	Hardy down to -20 degrees (Zone 5) or below. Native yuccas exist throughout most of the Heartland. Form mounded rosettes up to 2' high and wide of stiff pointed green leaves; variegated yellow-green form is available at nurseries. Provide green foliage through winter and spires of white flowers in early summer. Use as garden accents or barriers or grouped in sunny shrub borders.

Woody Vines Recommended for the Heartland

Actinidia arguta (Bower actinidia or hardy kiwi)	Hardy down to -20 degrees (Zone 5). A vigorous twiner with shining green leaves and red stems. Fruits are 1 inch long, edible, and borne only on female vines. Use for screens on sturdy trellises or arbors.
Akebia quinata (five-leaf akebia)	Hardy down to -20 degrees (Zone 5). Grows fast and climbs by twining; readily controlled by pruning. Delicate fine-textured foliage in 5-parted semi-evergreen leaves; small purple flowers. Use on trellises, arbors, or walls.

Woody Vines Recommended for the Heartland continued

Ampelopsis brevipedunculata (porcelain vine)	Hardy down to -20 degrees (Zone 5); tolerates heat and wind. This Asiatic plant has naturalized in our region. Vigorous fast-growing grapelike vine has shining turquoise or lavender berries in fall; needs pruning each spring. Use for high screens or fences (climbs by tendrils).
Aristolochia durior (Dutchman's-pipe)	Hardy throughout region. Dense vine with large glossy leaves and odd brownish flowers in summer; needs strong support. Slow in starting, but vigorous once established. Use as screen for porches or on high fences.
Campsis radicans (trumpet vine)	Hardy throughout region; tolerates heat and wind. Showy red-orange flowers all summer and fall and lacy foliage. Can climb trees; clings by holdfasts to masonry and wood. Vigorous grower that spreads underground and may need control. Flowers attract hummingbirds. A yellow form and other improved varieties are available.
Celastrus scandens (American bittersweet)	Hardy throughout region. Vigorous twining vines may climb to 25'; will ascend trees, but may damage them. Colorful orange berries last most of winter. Use as screens or winter accents; will attract birds.
Clematis x '*jackmanii*' and other named hybrids	Hardy throughout region. Large showy flowers of purple (or blue, pink, rose-red, or white) in May–June and later; climbs by leaf petiole tendrils. Vines grow to 10' long, but are not massive; suitable for fences, post supports, screens, vine houses, trellises, or ironwork. Have top in sun and base in shade; mulch over roots.
Clematis paniculata (*maximowicziana*) (sweet autumn clematis)	Hardy throughout region; heat and drought tolerant. Clouds of small fragrant white flowers in September, then fluffy seed heads through early winter. Climbs by leaf petiole tendrils; may die back in harsh winters but quickly regrows. May reach 20' long. Remains green well into winter. Use as screens on fences, trellises, brush piles, or old buildings. Trouble free.
Euonymus fortunei radicans (wintercreeper)	Hardy down to -20 degrees (Zone 5); heat and drought tolerant but needs shade. Evergreen, but the *coloratus* form turns purplish in winter. Comes in many varieties. Will climb (by holdfasts) trees and stone or brick walls; may be trained on fences or trellises. Also used as ground cover. Shearing helps appearance. Guard against scale insects.
Hedera helix (English ivy)	Hardy throughout most of region, but in northern and western areas, it needs a protected site; seek best-adapted varieties. Evergreen foliage is thick, shining, and refined; will climb trees and wood or masonry walls. Choose north or east exposure to minimize winterkill. May be slow to establish; watering advised. Also used as ground cover in shaded locations.
Hydrangea anomala petiolaris (climbing hydrangea)	Hardy down to -20 degrees (Zone 5). Shining, deep-green foliage; large flat white flower clusters in early summer. Clings by holdfasts

Woody Vines Recommended for the Heartland continued

	along stem; will climb trellises, wood fences, arbors, and masonry walls and can ascend trees. Although it may be slow to establish, it grows large; branches may reach outward 1 foot or more, so allow clearance. Give part shade and water through droughts; mulch over roots.
Lonicera heckrottii (goldflame honeysuckle)	Hardy throughout region; dies back in Zone 4 winters but regrows and blooms. Large yellow-purple trumpet-shaped flowers all summer and blue-green foliage. Semi-shrubby plant is easily controlled. Use on trellises or keep pruned as shrubs.
Lonicera japonica halliana (Hall's honeysuckle)	Hardy throughout region; heat and drought tolerant. Semi-evergreen with fragrant white-yellow flowers in summer. Climbs by twining so use on trellises, fences, porch rails, or terraces; also used as ground cover. May spread or become invasive.
Lonicera sempervirens (trumpet honeysuckle)	Hardy down to -20 degrees (Zone 5). Orange-scarlet trumpet-shaped flowers in summer; twining semi-evergreen foliage. Its hybrid, 'Dropmore Scarlet' (*L.* x *brownii*), is thoroughly hardy throughout region; has bright-scarlet trumpet-shaped flowers. Needs sturdy support.
Parthenocissus quinquefolia (Virginia creeper or woodbine)	Hardy throughout region; native to Heartland. Leaves are 5-parted and turn crimson in autumn before they fall; blue berries of autumn attract birds. Climbs high into trees or on walls.
Parthenocissus tricuspidata (Boston ivy)	Hardy throughout region; tolerates urban conditions. Shining 3-lobed dark-green leaves turn gold and red in autumn; blue-black berries remain into winter. Climbs by holdfasts; clings to stone, concrete, wood, trees, or bricks.
Polygonum aubertii (silver-lace vine)	Hardy throughout region. Widely adapted, fast-growing vine may die back in winters in northern areas, but soon regrows; does best in sun. Dense foliage and frothy white summer flowers extend into fall. Use for screens, to cover arbors or shade houses.
Vitis (grape; native spp. such as *V. riparia* [riverbank grape] or cultivated varieties such as 'Canadice')	Hardy throughout region. Riverbank and other wild grapes, as well as cultivated varieties, can be used ornamentally. Fruits in late summer or fall are an added feature. High-climbing vines ascend by tendrils on trellises, fences, or pergolas. Dense green foliage easily controlled by pruning.
Wisteria floribunda (Japanese wisteria)	Hardy throughout region. Heavy, high-climbing wooded twiner, with panicles of lavender flowers in spring, needs strong support; may be slow to begin blooming. Use on arbors, architectural features designed for vines, or arcades.

CHAPTER ELEVEN

Dealing with Adversities

*History attests to the trials and
tribulations farmers and gardeners of the
Heartland have endured. Early settlers soon
realized they were not in the Garden of
Eden. But even Adam and Eve, gardening
in Paradise, probably found a few things
to complain about.*

Most of our woes relate to weather—relentless seasonal winds, especially withering hot spring winds; bright, dry, cold, and windy winters with scanty snow cover; weather extremes, often long lasting, of heat, cold, wetness or drought; and occasional wild and sudden temperature fluctuations. Erratic weather is characteristic of a continental climate. Such a climate is expected in places like the Heartland that are far inland on a huge land mass, with no great bodies of water to cushion the temperatures and no mountains or other influences to tame the winds or offer early relief when weather patterns become entrenched.

Many people find beauty and majesty in the great air systems that roll across our region and sometimes collide in furious storms. Although gardeners may not manage such a detached view, most will affirm the overall goodness of our land. It is well within the requirements for fine gardens. Its main challenge to gardeners is to prepare against the problems that will come. The first way is by wise choices of plants. The rest is by being alert and resolved to leave no more to chance than necessary.

DROUGHT

Like pain, drought is forgotten as soon as it is over. But in the Heartland, periodic droughts are realities to remember. We should often remind ourselves of the preciousness of water. Gardeners especially should heed every water conservation rule, lest someday the privilege of watering a garden be taken away.

Study how water behaves in your garden soil. How long does your soil hold moisture after a rain? How deep does 1 inch of moisture penetrate? Clay holds more moisture than sandy loam, takes longer to dry out, and requires more to penetrate the depths. Dig a few experimental excavations to understand what really happens. This knowledge will guide your subsequent watering practice and help avoid waste.

IRRIGATION SYSTEMS. Sometimes we apply more water than is really needed. Annual flowers and early vegetables— marigolds, squash, and cucumbers, for example—do not need deep watering. They are shallow rooted, going about 2 feet deep. Most moisture is absorbed in the upper half of their root systems, so it is the upper 12 inches or so where moisture is important for them. Below that, the moisture (in this case) is wasted as far as the plants are concerned. For deep-rooted perennial plants—trees, shrubs, and fruits—the case is different. For them it is efficient to use a lance-type watering tool that injects water into the depths.

For surface watering, the trickle irrigation systems are the most efficient yet known. The least efficient are the various types of overhead sprinklers, which waste water to evaporation. Trickle or drip irrigation systems are a permanent investment of time and money. They are highly practical in vegetable gardens, orchards, vineyards, shrub beds, even perennial flower beds and rose gardens. The components are easy to assemble and they last for years. These systems are available by mail or through local dealers.

Double potting is a way to protect outdoor container plants from drying out or overheating in summer.

DOUBLE POTTING. Double potting is a method of protecting outdoor container plants—such as potted roses or impatiens—from the stresses of drying out or overheating in summer. Merely place the growing pot inside another pot one or two sizes larger and pour sand, vermiculite, or a fibrous mulch into the space between them. Of course, both the outer pot and the inner one must have drain holes.

CISTERNS. Where space and circumstances permit, cisterns are an old idea with new appeal. They have long been used in many desert areas of the world, collecting rain from roofs, driveways, or other hard surfaces to save for dry times. They were common on early farms and rural homesteads throughout the Heartland and could be used again today as a water supply for gardens if not for human needs. It is amazing how much water runs from downspouts in even a light shower. Collecting and sav-

ing this water for plants makes sense. Connect your cistern to a drip irrigation system and you have the ultimate in garden watering efficiency.

MINI-TERRACES AND CHECK DAMS. Gardens or plants sited on slopes are at a disadvantage in dry weather because what little moisture does fall runs off quickly. With a shovel, it is easy to create a temporary low bank or semicircle on the downhill side of the chosen tree or shrub to detain runoff water long enough to sink in where roots are. On sloping cultivated areas, it is good practice to create such low berms or terraces all the way across on contours at least every 12 inches of drop. If space permits, make these berms permanent by seeding grass on them to stop erosion. They will serve as rain savers and access paths into the future.

FLOODS AND GULLY WASHERS

Our counterpoints to drought are the occasional wet periods that go on and on, drowning gardens and plants. Daily rains may continue for weeks, even months, creating havoc far beyond your garden. Vast floods have long been a part of Heartland realities.

You cannot stop the rains, but you can reduce damage from the excess. Inspect plantings after rains to see where water stands. Possibly you can lead it off by cutting shallow drainage channels to a lower level. Or perhaps you can divert it somehow from above. Places that regularly wash out in fast runoff can be stabilized by placing some immovable but porous obstruction in the channel: stones of sufficient size or well-anchored brush and straw.

Sediment collecting behind such barriers will eventually raise the level. Then grass seed sown over them should result in a sod, making the retainer even more stable. Where rushing water continually reopens gullies or washes out retainers, you might resort to the ancient idea of gabions. These rock-filled cages of woven-wire fencing hold the stones in place while letting the water flow slowly through.

In poorly drained, tight soils that seem to create water-holding "tubs" around the planting holes of trees or shrubs, a special technique is sometimes used by professionals. The basic idea is to lay a 6-inch layer of coarse (2- to 3-inches thick) stones at the bottom of the planting hole. Then in a side trench lay a connecting lead-off drain line gently sloped down to an outlet at a lower level.

EXCESSIVE HEAT, EXCESSIVE COLD

At the time either of these adversities strikes, you can do little about it. But you can prepare for either eventuality. In the first place, when you selected plants for your garden, let's hope you considered their tolerances to heat and cold. And next, in placing them in your design, let's hope you positioned them in favorable spots.

For heat stress, an immediate remedy is to apply an organic mulch (compost, shredded leaves, bark chips, or dried grass clippings) over the root zones of susceptible plants. Also, pay careful attention to watering. Temporary shading is another possibility. You may have seen dahlia fanciers, on hot

August days, affixing umbrellas over promising plants being coddled for September shows. Most gardeners, bent merely on seeing their gardens survive until cooler days, will do best by mulching and watering.

In winter and early spring when the temperature takes murderous plunges, the fate of your cold-susceptible plants, such as roses and crape myrtles, may rest on your foresight in hilling and mulching them the previous fall. Even quite hardy perennials like ajuga and coralbells might be loosened from rootholds and killed by repeated swings of freeze and thaw. Again, mulch helps. If you hesitate to submerge a leafy crown in organic mulch, you can instead pour a pint of dry sand over the crown and brush it in. Sand not only buffers against cold but leads away moisture that might freeze against stems. Many good gardeners routinely pour a cup or two of sand over every clump in the perennial garden each autumn.

In spring vegetable gardens, unseasonable cold may delay germination or rot seeds, resulting in poor stands. You can warm cold soil with clear or black plastic mulch—not white. Before planting, lay it between rows or over the entire area to warm it. Sun warmth trapped under the plastic raises the temperature many degrees during the day. Some of the warmth is retained at night. Remove any plastic over seed rows as soon as you see sprouting. If you lay black plastic beside the row rather than over it, it can remain through the season as a mulch. It will conserve moisture and keep down weeds.

Another of technology's gifts to gardens is the spunbonded lightweight "fabric" (pressed together, not woven) available in various lengths and widths to lay directly over emerging seedlings, or even over well-developed perennial plant clumps, for protection from threatening weather. In cultivated soil, the material is anchored at the edges by ridging soil over them. This porous white synthetic material permits air, light, and moisture to pass but buffers temperature changes, making several degrees of difference on frosty nights or days. It is so nearly weightless that plants can grow beneath it. The same material is also useful for protecting strawberries, grapes, even fruit trees of a coverable size. After cold weather ends, you can still use this fabric as an insect shield—it will ward off many insect pests such as squash bugs that otherwise might have to be controlled with chemical sprays. Ask at garden stores for the spunbonded "floating" covers or watch for them in garden supply catalogs.

SPRING WINDS. Spring winds are hard on newly set transplants of all sorts—tender tomato or pepper plants in vegetable gardens and many kinds of transplants in flower gardens. Canny gardeners have long used the "shingle method" to protect such plants temporarily while they get established. They simply sink a cedar shingle into the soft soil on the windward side or sometimes on all sides. The shingle not only quiets the wind around the plant but also provides an interval of shade as the sun moves across, improving conditions as the plant adjusts to its new location. After two or three weeks the

Shingles give temporary wind and sun protection while tender transplants become established.

shingles are removed and stored again for another such occasion.

FROST CRACKS. Frost cracks are serious problems with young trees in the Heartland. They are largely preventable by wrapping the trees' lower trunks with tree wrap as soon as you plant them, or by whitewashing them as our ancestors did. When trees reach the age to produce ridges or shadow-casting texture in their bark, they can get along without this help. Frost cracking of tree trunks occurs on very cold days or nights in winter, usually (but not necessarily) when snow is on the ground, and in clear weather when the sun has shone brightly. As the sun sets, the sudden drop in temperature on the previously sun-warmed bark results in tearing stresses on the living tissues, usually on the side most exposed to winter sun. The vertical split reaches inward to the wood. It may escape your attention at first, but you will notice it as spring advances. Al-

ROTTED WOOD

ORIGINAL TRUNK LAID BARE BY FROST CRACK

A cross section of a maple tree trunk about ten years after it suffered a frost crack on its southwest side. New bark partially enfolds the dead wood but has not closed the wound. Rot has advanced inward. This often fatal problem is prevented by wrapping the trunks of young smooth-barked trees in winter.

though the resulting gash may heal over in time, it leaves a lasting scar that mars the tree's beauty and impedes its full development. Arborists call this "southwest disease" because it nearly always is on that side of the trunk. Of course, it is not really a disease, but the home owner may think so. Here are a few of the more-susceptible trees: fruits (apples, pears, cherries, including ornamental forms); tulip-trees (*Liriodendron*); young walnuts (black and Persian); and young maples of several sorts. In addition to wrapping trunks of susceptible young trees, you can reduce this frost-crack damage by leaving lower branches unpruned on the sunny side so their shadows cross the trunk by day, reducing those drastic temperature differentials.

WINTER BURN. Winter burn usually refers to the browned edges (sometimes whole leaves) of broadleaf evergreens or tips of needle evergreens. The causes are much like those of frost cracks—extreme temperature changes. In the case of winter burn, temperature fluctuations cause parts of winter foliage to die and turn brown. March is when most winter burn shows up on yews, pachysandra, *Euonymus kiautschovica*, leatherleaf viburnum, evergreen types of rhododendron, and many others—even junipers. Drying winter winds contribute to the problem, but you will notice that most damage comes on plants exposed to winter sun. Placing susceptible plants where they will be shaded in winter is the easiest solution. If it is too late for that, another way to reduce damage is to provide any sort of screening for shade or simply to wrap the plants in burlap. The spray-on antidesiccant products applied to foliage and buds in late autumn may also help some in this. Follow label directions and repeat treatment as recommended.

BUD BLAST. Yet another manifestation of hard Heartland winters, "bud blast" refers to the aborted flower buds of fruit trees or flowering trees and shrubs. A familiar example is azaleas. They may have gone into winter with a promising set of bloom buds at the tips and carried them through until spring. But as days grow warmer and growth begins, the bloom buds brown and fall off even as little new leaves emerge up and down the stems. The plant is telling you that if you want to see it bloom regularly, you will probably have to visit it in some other garden in a zone where winters do not get so cold.

ICE/SNOWSTORMS

The Heartland is notoriously susceptible to ice storms. They are most dreaded because they cause power outages, but gardeners also fear broken trees and shrubs from the weight of ice. If winds come, breakage is even worse. As it is clearly impossible to prepare against such disasters, our best response is to choose strong-structured trees. Glance around the neighborhood after such a storm and you will see what not to plant. Siberian elm (*Ulmus pumila*) suffers terrible breakage, one of the reasons landscapers here no longer recommend it. Any trees with weak V-shaped crotches and lots of twiggy surfaces are prone to splitting from ice accumulation. Should any of your really prized and valuable trees be damaged this way, the best course is to call a qualified arborist to assess the situation and carry out remedial pruning. It is good policy to keep large trees regularly pruned by professionals who know their business. They can install cables or braces in weak places and in other ways head off potential storm damage.

Breakage from snow is less common in our area. When it does occur, it usually happens close to the ground on spreading evergreens overburdened by drifts or the sheer amount of snow or sometimes by careless snow removal tactics. Foundation plants may be split by avalanches from the roof. If this happens frequently, you should provide some type of guard over the plants. Hardy souls concerned about their evergreens can go out during snowstorms and brush off overloads they see accumulating. Be gentle, because frozen branches are brittle and easily damaged. Spreading evergreens near driveways can be flagged for snow plow or blower operators to avoid dumping snow on them. After such damage occurs, the only remedy is to prune out torn branches in spring.

SUMMER STORMS

In the Heartland, summer storms roll in from the West, often approaching with an ominous navy-blue roiling sky presaging wind in the low-hanging clouds and sometimes hail with driving rain. Fearing tornadoes, we seek safety for ourselves and leave the garden to its fate. Summer wind storms can happen anywhere in the region, and can inflict as much damage as ice storms, but usually not over such wide areas. Sometimes these wind storms completely uproot trees from ground softened by rain. They may even bring hail.

Heavy hail, propelled by wind, scours the landscape—shredding plants, blasting bark from trees, piling up against stems of tender plants, pounding the ground into bricklike hardness. After such devastation you may as well wait a few days to assess the garden damage. You will probably have other things to do, such as repairing roofs and windows. Trees and shrubs stripped of their leaves in the growing season will usually start again and send out a new set. Nature seems to prepare for this sort of disaster, giving trees and shrubs secondary leaf buds that come into action if somehow the first leaves are destroyed. Of course, loss of spring foliage is a setback for the plant. It needs moisture and a boost with mild fertilizer as it starts over, so do not neglect those requirements. If days are long and hot and dry periods loom ahead, watchful care is needed even more. Prune out wind-broken branches and study each tree individually to decide what to do. Perhaps some cannot be salvaged.

Following hailstorms in vegetable and flower gardens, practicality guides your decisions. Beans slashed off near ground level or frozen back may as well be dug up and reseeded if enough growing days remain for the crop to mature. Sweet corn, cucumbers, summer squash, and lettuces also might be replanted with hope of a harvest. It may be too late to restart tomatoes or peppers. The best option for them is to trim off breakage, straighten up the plants as well as you can, boost them with mild fertilizer, and encourage them to regrow. Root crops—carrots, beets, potatoes, onions, and the like— may take a setback but should soon regrow from the crowns and make some sort of yield.

In the flower garden, trim off battered foliage and blooms. This immediately improves appearance, and with first aid in the form of fertilizer and watering, most plants will revive and eventually once again make a good show.

Could you prevent hail damage? Possibly, if you knew for sure it was coming. But most of us, understandably, trust to luck that such storms will pass by—and most of the time we are right. The one most feasible and practical protective measure is a soft surface mulch such as shredded leaves or grass clippings to cushion the ground. If we kept this always in place throughout the growing season, our gardens would stand a better chance whether it hails or not. Also, timely and consistent staking of young trees would greatly reduce the chances of their breaking in summer wind storms.

INSECT PESTS

Heartland gardens confront a flourishing set of insects, but at least we need not worry much about Japanese beetles. These imported pests stay mainly east of the Mississippi River. The lists on pages 192–93 give the worst of our garden insects, grouped according to the parts of the garden they prey upon.

In the section following the lists, I suggest ways to control each kind of insect. There are three general approaches to reducing insect damage in gardens. The first is cultural—giving good care to your plants to encourage healthy growth. Some insects, such as tree borers, actually seem to pick on plants already in trouble. Cultural methods include rotating crops as best you can, handpicking insects from plants, and removing weeds and trash that harbor insects (sanitation).

The second approach is to use biological methods—a term heard more and more, broadly meaning enlistment of other living organisms to work with us in controlling the "bad" insects. An example is *Bacillus thuringiensis* (B.t.), a microbial pesticide introduced about midcentury to kill cabbage worms and similar caterpillars by making them sick. Derived from bacterial cells, it can be applied as a dust or mixed with water and applied as spray. *B.t.* is considered harmless to birds, bees and other beneficial insects, and mammals. Dipel and Thuricide are two prevailing trademarked product names for it at this time. Several strains of it now exist.

Biological controls of a different sort are the parasitic or beneficial insects sold for release at strategic times to attack certain pests. For example, Trichogramma wasps—so small you can barely see them—will seek out the eggs of caterpillar-type pests such as codling moths (apple worms) and armyworms. The wasp lays her own egg inside the moth egg, and her larva, soon hatching, feeds on the host egg, destroying it.

Some garden supply firms sell beneficial insects by mail and send them at your most favorable dates for release in spring. In some cases you can order a timed series of releases. All you do is open each container when it arrives and hang it where the beneficial insects can escape and go about their business.

Here are some other beneficial insects that are currently available.

GREEN LACEWING. Its larvae prey on soft-bodied insects (aphids, thrips, and leafhoppers) and spider mites.

LADYBEETLE. This insect preys on aphids, scale insects, spider mites, and the larvae or eggs of many other insect pests.

PRAYING MANTIS. This insect preys on caterpillars, aphids, spider mites, maggots, borers, and a range of others.

BENEFICIAL NEMATODES. These tiny "eel-worms" prey on soil stages of grubs, caterpillars, weevils, and the like.

Though biological insect controls at first may seem expensive compared with the chemical mode of curtailing insect pests, they look better when all costs of the chemical approach are added up—your time, necessary equipment, and environmental hazards. Without doubt, the biologicals have a promising future. Be realistic in your expectations of them, realizing that beyond introducing these beneficial insects to your premises, you have no say in what happens next. The ladybugs you unleash in your backyard may look for greener pastures before the day is over. Benefits from using beneficial insects may not be dramatically visible.

Another pesticide sold among the biologicals—diatomaceous earth—kills its insect victims by a mechanical process. This dust consists of the fossil remains of single-celled algae that lived in ancient oceans. The tiny particles have uniquely sharp edges that slice into the outer skins of insects and literally dry out their innards. Many kinds of insects, ticks and mites are susceptible to the action of diatomaceous dust. It can be applied in dust form with a regular garden duster (be very careful not to breathe any or get it in your eyes) or in liquid form through a hose-end sprayer. Most garden stores carry it.

The third mode of insect control—chemical sprays or dusts—is the traditional method. These are products you buy in a bag, can, or bottle at a garden store and apply according to instructions on the label. Some of them, such as rotenone, pyrethrum, and sabadilla, are very old and come from natural sources, but most are synthesized. Unless properly handled, some—for example, dimethoate (Cygon) or carbaryl (Sevin)—could do harm to the user, to the garden, or to the environment; thus it is important to read and follow label directions carefully. It is because of possible hazards and the need for great care that chemical insect controls are less favored than they once were.

Insect Pests of Vegetable Gardens

NAME	TARGET PLANTS
Aphids	Many, especially beans, broccoli, peas, brussels sprouts
Asparagus beetle	Asparagus
Blister beetles (black and gray)	Many, especially tomatoes, melons
Cabbage worms (loopers)	Cabbage and its relatives
Colorado potato beetles	Potatoes
Corn earworm, tomato fruit worm (same)	Corn, tomatoes
Cucumber beetles (spotted and striped)	Cucumbers, beans, corn, squash, melons, pumpkins
Cutworms, armyworms	Many, especially tender transplants, succulent seedlings
Flea beetles	Eggplant, potatoes, spinach, radishes
Grasshoppers	Many leafy plants of late summer
Harlequin bugs	Cabbage and related plants, including mustards
Leafhoppers	Many, especially tomatoes, beets, potatoes
Mexican bean beetles	Green beans, lima beans
Spider mites	Beans, tomatoes, many others
Squash bugs	Squash, pumpkins
Squash vine borers	Pumpkin, squash, cucumber, melons
Tomato hornworm	Tomatoes
Whiteflies	Many, especially tomatoes

Insect Pests of Fruits

NAME	TARGET PLANTS
Aphids	Many, especially apples, cherries
Borers	Many, especially apples, cherries, peaches, plums
Canker worms	Many, especially apples, cherries
Codling moths	Apples, pears
Mealybugs	Apples, grapes
Scale insects	Most fruit trees, berries, grapes

Insect Pests of Flower Gardens

NAME	TARGET PLANTS
Aphids	Many, especially nasturtium, roses, chrysanthemums
Borers	Irises, roses, others
Cucumber beetles (spotted and striped)	Many, especially roses, chrysanthemums, zinnias, dahlias
Flea beetles	Many
Grasshoppers	Many
Leafhoppers	Many
Mealybugs	Many
Spider mites	Many, especially roses, marigolds, verbena, phlox, violets

Insect Pests of Ornamental Trees and Shrubs

NAME	TARGET PLANTS
Aphids	Many
Bagworms	Junipers and others
Borers	Lilacs, dogwoods, flowering peaches, apples
Canker worms	Elms, oaks, others
Cicadas	Many
Elm leaf beetles	Siberian and American elms
Fall webworms	Many, especially walnuts, oaks, ash, linden
Mimosa webworms	Honey-locust
Scale insects	Most shade and flowering trees, shrubs, evergreens, roses
Spider mites	Evergreens
Tent caterpillars	Many trees

Practical Insect Controls for Home Gardens

Aphids	Small, soft-bodied, green, pink, or brown sucking insects. Basic chemical controls: malathion dust or spray; insecticidal soap. Also, dormant spray. Follow labels.
Asparagus beetles	Small, dark with yellow spots. Clean off infested foliage in fall and burn. Also keep bed cleaned of weeds.
Bagworms	Dangling twiglike bundles with caterpillars inside. Handpick and destroy as soon as you see them. Spray with *Bacillus thuringiensis* every five days. Follow label. Junipers of many sorts are severely attacked by bagworms and may be killed unless the insects are controlled.
Blister beetles	Slender, active, 1 inch long, gray or black. Handpick (wear gloves). Clean up plant debris where they hide.
Borers	A general term for larvae of moths or beetles that tunnel into plants beneath bark. Keep trunks of young trees wrapped. Mothballs or crystals at the tree base (but not touching it) have a repelling effect. Watch for entry holes in susceptible trees and probe with wire for the grub. Chemical control for woody plants: Dursban (chlorpyrifos) sprayed or painted on trunks; follow label. For iris borers: lift and divide clumps every two or three years to avoid crowding; spray in midspring with dimethoate (Cygon)—a systemic to be used with caution; follow label. Clean the bed of old foliage in autumn to get rid of eggs. Iris borers foster the spread of the destructive soft-rot bacterial disease.
Cabbage worms	Slender, greenish, loop shaped, on leaf undersides. *Bacillus thuringiensis* spray or dust. Follow label.
Canker worms	Small green-to-gray measuring worms; they hang from silky threads in spring. Band trees in February with Tanglefoot.

Cicadas (locusts)	Heartland species most destructive to trees and shrubs is the periodic seventeen-year cicada. Each spends seventeen years in the soil, feeding on tree roots, before emerging as an adult. However, there are different broods in different areas emerging every few years on a predictable basis. Thousands may emerge from the ground beneath a single tree, all within a day or two, from the third week of May through early June. Tree trunks will be littered with their cast skins. Females soon climb into low trees and shrubs to lay eggs, slashing twigs in rows where eggs are deposited. Branches are severely damaged or killed. If local authorities warn of a severe cicada year, protect prized young trees with mosquito netting, cheesecloth, or spunbonded floating covers. After egg laying ends, prune off and burn damaged twigs, eggs and all, to help trees heal quickly and reduce future numbers of periodic cicadas in your garden. In addition to the seventeen-year locust, many parts of the Heartland also have a thirteen-year type.
Codling moths	Best recognized as the worm in apples. A regular fruit tree spray applied according to package directions will control this. Or for a biological control, use *Bacillus thuringiensis* (follow label), or releases of trichogramma beneficial wasps.
Colorado potato beetles	Striped, pinkish, rounded, ¼ inch long. Handpick and destroy. Basic chemical control: rotenone dust or spray; follow label.
Corn earworms	Yellow, green, or brown caterpillars ¼ to 1 inch long; they devour young kernels. Squirt several drops of mineral oil into silks as ears begin to fill. Early maturing ears are more likely than late crops to escape damage. The same insect (a moth) also produces the tomato fruitworm. Keep corn and tomatoes apart in the garden.

Practical Insect Controls for Home Gardens continued

Cucumber beetles, spotted	Small, yellow-green, with twelve black spots. Larvae feed on roots in spring; beetles spread wilt and virus diseases. Basic chemical controls: rotenone dust or malathion spray; follow labels. Protect young plants in spring with Hotkaps or row covers.
Cucumber beetles, striped	Small and yellow, with three black stripes; similar to spotted cucumber beetle (above) in control.
Cutworms, armyworms	Soft, smooth, gray, brown, or black ground-dwelling caterpillars. Use *Bacillus thuringiensis*; follow label. To protect tender transplants, place a cardboard collar around each as you set it out. Worms will not crawl over.
Elm leaf beetles	Olive green, slender, striped, ¼ inch long; they infest elm trees and overwinter in houses. Ask professional arborist about systemic injection for these. Treatment of mature trees is impractical for home gardener to attempt.
Fall webworms	Green-yellow or gray-red-black striped, hairy caterpillars inside webs at branch tips; they devour foliage. Cut off and burn webs. *Bacillus thuringiensis* is biological control; follow label.
Flea beetles	Tiny, black, active; they eat holes in leaves. Use rotenone dust; follow label.
Grasshoppers	Usually worse in dry years; populations grow as summer progresses. They prefer grassy areas so keep grass mowed around gardens. A biological control called "grasshopper spore" consisting of a disease culture (*Nosema locusteae*) affects grasshoppers ingesting it and is passed on to succeeding hatches. It does not entirely rid a garden of hoppers, but an early application reduces the population. This product is available by mail from certain garden supply firms or perhaps from your local dealer if you ask for it.

Harlequin bugs	Flat, black with red areas, ⅜ inch long. Readily controlled with sabadilla dust, an organic insecticide, or rotenone; follow labels.
Leafhoppers	Small, sucking, flying, wedge shaped, in various colors; they spread diseases among plants. Basic chemical control: diazinon spray or dust; follow label. "Sticky stakes"—yellow boards coated with sticky Tanglefoot—will attract and trap many. Place close to target plants.
Mealybugs	Soft scale insects with white waxy covering. Control with insecticidal soap spray or diatomaceous earth; follow labels.
Mexican bean beetles	Small, round, red with black spots, resemble ladybugs. Use rotenone dust; follow label.
Mimosa webworms	Brown ½-inch long worms in webs spun over leaves. Use *Bacillus thuringiensis*; follow label.
Scale insects	Brown, gray, or white bumps plastered on stems or leaves. Use dormant or growing season oil spray or lime-sulfur; follow labels.
Spider mites	Not really insects. Dust-size mites best seen by tapping plant foliage over sheet of paper; watch for movement. A strong stream from the hose will wash them off, but this must be repeated every day or two. Use insecticidal soap spray, lime-sulfur spray, or diatomaceous earth; follow labels. Dormant oil spray kills overwintering eggs; follow label.
Squash bugs	Angular, gray-brown, ⅝ inch long or smaller; they spread wilt disease. Mash brown egg clusters whenever you see them on undersides of squash/pumpkin leaves.

Practical Insect Controls for Home Gardens continued

Squash vine borers	White caterpillars inside stems. Locate the entry hole near the base of the vine and dig the worm out carefully with a pen knife; heap earth over the stem and water it to promote rooting there.
Tent caterpillars	Hairy caterpillars that cluster in webs at tree crotches. Prune out the branches to which the tent is attached and burn everything, tent and all, if possible. *Bacillus thuringiensis* is a biological spray or dust for these; follow label.
Tomato hornworms	Large, fleshy, green, striped, with "horn" at end. Handpick. If you find small white cocoons (like rice grains) attached to their flesh, leave them. From them will emerge new parasitic wasps that prey on hornworms and help control them. Bacillus thuringiensis spray or dust is a biological control; follow label.
Whiteflies	Tiny white insects that swarm about when plants are rustled. "Sticky stakes"—yellow boards coated with sticky Tanglefoot—will attract and trap large numbers of these. Place them close to target plant. Or spray plants with insecticidal soap.

ANIMAL PESTS

Your garden undoubtedly supports more inhabitants than you realize—a large cast of visiting or resident animals. Many are harmless or even beneficial, but others rank as pests. Br'er Rabbit and the wily crow are legendary figures for engaging gardeners in battles of wits and always winning. Rural gardens get more variety in animal visitors than city gardens, but both have their share.

BIRDS. Crows seem to be hatched with a sixth sense about where corn and peas are newly planted. The news spreads fast. They might steal the seeds soon after you plant them or more likely, wait until green shoots emerge and then pull them out, kernel and all. Old World gardeners invented and named the scarecrow precisely for this problem. A good scarecrow does as well as anything to discourage crows and provides entertainment besides. The spunbonded floating row covers will defend any sort of seedlings against bird damage.

Sapsuckers damage pine trees. They

drill rings of small holes evenly around the trunks to obtain the sap. These small, shy members of the woodpecker group, though rarely seen, are common throughout the Heartland. They seldom kill a tree but might weaken it. Unfortunately, you can do little about it.

Woodpeckers of several other species drill holes in main branches of fruit trees, especially apples, apparently for the sap. Drought times are when this trouble seems most common. Again, little can be done to prevent it, although you might provide another source of water in hope the peckers will prefer it. Another idea is to hang scare devices—foil pans or imitation snakes or owls in trees they have been attacking.

The inflatable snakes and owls are sold in garden stores primarily to scare fruit-eating birds away from cherry trees, blueberry and raspberry beds, and strawberry patches while they are in fruit. Thse devices work to varying degrees, depending on the hunger of the birds and the length of time they are left in place. To save fruit and berry crops from birds, netting is also available to drape over bushes and small trees to prevent bird access.

CATS. Cats get into garden trouble by their digging habits. Otherwise, except for preying on birds, they do little harm and may actually do good by reducing populations of mice and other rodents. For gardeners who cannot abide cats, a practical way to repel them is to scatter mothballs or crystals (naphthalene or paradichlorobenzene) in their paths. Commercial repellents, many containing naphthalene or paradichlorobenzene, are available.

DOGS. If free to run, dogs can cause havoc in a garden. They wear paths along fences, uproot plants by digging, and leave a wake of broken foliage after plunging through beds. Urination by male dogs produces burned foliage on shrubbery, particularly evergreens; female dogs cause brown spots in lawns. There are ways to cope—put special guards around prized plants; use repellents to keep dogs away from shrubbery (try mothballs); or tie the dogs up.

DEER. As threats to gardens, deer are relatively recent in our region. Urban gardeners need not be much concerned, but those in suburbs and especially rural areas near grasslands or timbered watercourses see increasing numbers of deer. The first thrill of finding their tracks on your property fades when you see similar tracks in your vegetable garden where the rhubarb was chewed off, or find a young pine with bark shredded after a buck polished his antlers on it. Vertical fences are no barrier, as deer bound over them with ease. Some gardeners report success from woven wire fences stretched horizontally just above the ground, as deer fear entangling their feet in the mesh. This idea is impractical where space is limited. Thus far, most of the efforts toward keeping deer away have been in scaring them off or applying repellents. Garden or farm supply stores sell deer/rabbit repellents for spraying on trees, shrubs, vegetable crops, grape vines, and the like to prevent browsing. Retreatment is needed after heavy rains. Labels on these products also suggest that you apply them *before* the animals start eating the plants. Most deer damage from browsing happens in early spring when the animals are hungry; their favorite targets include apple trees, grapes, hazelnuts, and white pines. Stiff-needled pines are not so tempting. In vegetable gardens deer go for rhubarb when it first comes up and early seeded crops such as beets, lettuce, chard, and peas.

A home-style repellent used even in botanical gardens to protect trees is soap. Motel-size bars in their wrappers are drilled through the middle, threaded on string and hung in trees. They will last nearly a year, and the odor, apparently, keeps deer away. For a scare device many hang aluminum foil pans in shrubs or fruit trees. The flashing reflections and banging sound produced by these keep deer away at least for awhile.

GOPHERS. Pocket gophers are not seen much in cities, but gardeners in new developments should be on watch for them. They feed on bulbs, the roots of many plants, and even trees; they can kill trees of fairly good size by their underground chewing. Aboveground evidences of their presence are the conical mounds of fine soil pushed up at intervals along the connecting tunnels. Sometimes they tunnel along vegetable rows, eating the roots or even pulling the tops down into the burrow. Some gardeners drop "bombs" into the tunnels where they generate sulfur smoke that permeates the tunnel system. A high-tech gopher repellent is a sound-emitting device speared into the ground. It drives away burrowing rodents with irritating sound emissions delivered at intervals. Battery powered, it remains on guard through the season. The barely audible sound is

---

Things Nobody Ever Tells You

❧ Tobacco is hazardous to the health of garden tomatoes. Those who smoke or handle tobacco products should stay away from tomato plants. Smoking tobacco carries the tobacco mosaic virus, an incurable plant disease readily spread to tomatoes.

❧ The letters V, F, and N, appearing in catalog or seed packet descriptions of tomato varieties, mean that the variety is genetically resistant to the diseases verticillium and fusarium and to root-knot nematodes (microscopic soil eel worms). These abbreviations are universally used in the seed trade to designate such varieties. Although there are still other diseases that may affect your tomatoes, heeding these signals in selecting varieties is one way to avoid those three problems.

❧ Wilting of plants on hot summer afternoons is normal to some extent and does not necessarily mean drought stress. If plants have not recovered by the next morning, however, they are in trouble and need watering. Brown edges on leaves, called scorch, are another indicator of drought at the roots and the need for watering.

not injurious to pets or annoying to people. It covers a wide area and reportedly works well.

MICE. Mice do more damage and are more numerous than usually supposed. There are several species. They damage or kill young trees and shrubs by chewing on bark at ground level, even working under snow. Keep grass and weeds pulled away from the bases of woody plants and anchor a cylinder of window screen or ¼-inch hardware cloth around the trunks, tight against the ground. Make the cylinder high enough to reach above the expected snow line. Mice also move into mole runs, where they feed on roots and probably bulbs. Valuable bulbs such as lilies are worth protecting at planting time by a wire mesh cage sunk all around them in the planting hole.

MOLES. Moles burrow underground like gophers but feed primarily on insects instead of plants. Nevertheless, they raise long mounds in lawns or flower beds, uprooting plants or undermining them and providing runs later taken over by mice. Trapping with regular mole traps is the most recommended way to eliminate them, but it takes much observation to be successful. You can drive moles away with the smoke bombs and sonic devices recommended for gophers.

RABBITS. The surest way to bar these abundant pests from vegetable gardens is by using close-mesh wire poultry netting with the base buried a few inches in the ground. A repellent widely reported to work all season is human hair (from barber and beauty shops) tied into net bundles and dis-

A chicken-wire fence 24 inches high holds off nibbling rabbits. For temporary protection of prized specimens, you can put it up quickly and just as easily take it down when the emergency is over.

tributed along rows. Blood meal sprinkled along lettuce and beet rows spooks rabbits and feeds nitrogen to the plants. Floating row covers protect young vegetables. Rabbits damage or kill trees by chewing bark in winter; protect the bases with mesh collars as suggested for mice.

RACCOONS. These well-known thieves of sweet corn at its tenderest stage are difficult to thwart. Here are some ways to try: place an electrified fence around the patch—the lowest wire should be 6 inches aboveground, the upper wire about 16 inches above; surround the corn plants with pumpkin or winter squash vines to form a leafy jungle through which the coons will be reluctant to wade; sprinkle hot pepper on silks of ripening ears.

SLUGS. Commercial bait granules or

pellets—also liquids—are available to place under inverted pots or in other dark moist places accessible only to slugs. Scatter bands of dry sand or ashes around slug-tempting plants such as hostas. Trap slugs in saucers filled with stale beer—attracted by the malt, they crawl in and drown. Or dust the area around plants with diatomaceous earth.

SQUIRRELS. In cities where squirrels face no predators (except cars), they are too numerous and become garden pests, digging up bulbs or plants, making craters in lawns, sometimes eating bloom buds and flowers, cutting tree or shrub twigs for dens, and littering lawns. Trapping is about the only way to control them. Humane traps for squirrels are sold by garden suppliers. Peanuts are good bait. Visit the trap daily, and take your catch to the woods for release. Some say the squirrel may beat you home.

TURTLES. Mysterious holes chewed in cantaloupes the day they ripen may turn out to be the work of our friendly ornate box turtle or the Carolina box turtle found in this region. Remember that these shy creatures live mainly on insects, especially grasshoppers, and can be forgiven for sampling your cantaloupes. If the turtle tries a new one every day instead of finishing the first, you might save remaining melons by either placing a mothball beside each one while it matures to pickable stage or by encircling them with wire.

WOODCHUCKS. Woodchucks, or groundhogs, although seldom seen, help themselves to many vegetables in rural gardens, working at dawn or

dusk. They especially favor sweet corn and green beans. These sizable animals are well equipped to climb and can hardly be fenced out. They refuse to cross black plastic, however, so you can possibly exclude them by laying a black plastic zone all around the garden. See also the suggestions given for gophers, as the same controls can be applied.

DISEASES

Although plant diseases are hard to define and diagnose, they are nonetheless real. The twentieth century has seen Dutch elm disease change the landscape dramatically. In the previous century, a disease affecting potatoes changed the history of Ireland as it brought about famine and mass migration. Blights mentioned in the Bible may afflict your Heartland garden today.

Plant diseases are caused by fungi, bacteria, viruses, nematodes, and sometimes other factors in the environment classed as physiological. The substances used in treatment or prevention run the gamut of those used in human medicines—fungicides, bactericides, antibiotics, fumigants, and disinfectants.

The general classes of ailments include leaf spots, wilts, blights, mildews, cankers, declines, damping-off, leaf curl, galls, rots, rusts, scab, smuts, mosaics or "yellows," and others. Complete cures are unlikely, although symptoms may be controlled; so the gardener's best course is either to try for prevention or, if that fails, to arrest the spread of the ailment. Preventive steps begin with choosing disease-resistant varieties. Be watchful so you can spot early symptoms and banish the infected plant before it involves its neighbors. Control of insects is very important, as many plant diseases are spread by them. Sanitation is a "health habit" in the garden as well as in your house. Awareness and prevention of some of the interactions between plants that "set up" diseases—such as the relationship between native junipers and apple trees—will help. As you tend your garden, keep the cultural needs of each plant in mind.

Diseases to Watch for in Your Garden

DISEASES IN FLOWER GARDENS

Aster (annual or China —*Callistephus*) Aster yellows virus; spread by leafhoppers. Also affects marigolds, zinnias, many other flowers, and occasionally vegetables. Symptoms: Yellowing of young foliage, growth stiff and stunted, flowers turn greenish and are dwarfed, or blooming ceases. Control: As it is incurable, try to control leafhoppers; watch for any plants that look infected and get rid of them (burn or bury them) before the disease spreads to others.

Chrysanthemum Septoria leaf spot. Symptoms: Leaves turn progressively brown up the stems; spots start small and yellow, then enlarge and darken; browned leaves often hang down on stems. Control: Remove affected plants as soon as you see them; avoid working around them when foliage is wet; keep cultivation to a minimum.

Clematis Leaf and stem spot. Symptoms: Stems die back from ground up. Control: Remove infected stems/leaves; spray with a fungicide such as benomyl—follow label.

Gladiolus Botrytis blight. Symptoms: Starts as small spots on leaf, then spreads to stems; petals get watery spots; corms may soften or mold. Control: Rogue out affected plants; spray with a fungicide such as benomyl—follow label; clean off and burn all plant tops in fall.

Diseases to Watch for in Your Garden continued

Hollyhocks   Rust. Symptoms: Leaves turn yellow on top, with orange spores (sometimes gray) beneath; leaves die; disfiguring to the plant. Control: Clean plants thoroughly in fall (remove dead leaves); dust with sulfur in fall and early spring.

Iris   Bacterial soft rot. Symptoms: Follows borer invasion of stem and root; plants collapse, with rhizomes wet and smelly. Control: See under "Insects" (page 194) on how to control borers; dig out affected plant clumps, seek any sound part to save, and discard rest; disinfect saved portion in Lysol solution and allow to dry in sun several days before replanting.

Lily   Botrytis blight; Madonna lilies especially susceptible. Symptoms: Starts as leaf spots, then spreads to entire leaf, working up stem; buds and flowers distorted; grayish spore bodies. Control: Promptly clean off diseased parts; apply fungicide spray such as Bordeaux mixture. Many people with roses routinely spray lilies at the same time and with the same multipurpose spray used on roses.

Marigold   Aster yellows virus. Symptoms: Greenish, distorted blooms and upper foliage. Control: See suggestions under "Aster."

Peony   Botrytis blight. Symptoms: Buds darken while small and fail to develop; dark-brown splotches on leaves, sometimes affecting most of plant. Control: Use strict sanitation; cut plants off at base in late autumn and remove all debris; as shoots emerge in spring, spray ground area with Bordeaux mixture. This disease is worse in wet weather.

Phlox   Powdery mildew. Symptoms: Usually starts on leaves of summer phlox in June and continues with summer; causes leaves to yellow and die from base upward. Control: Give phlox space from other plants to aid air cir-

culation; spray with a fungicide such as benomyl sold
for powdery mildew—follow label.

Roses   Black spot. Symptoms: Dark spots on green leaves,
followed by leaf turning yellow and eventually falling. Control: Avoid planting highly susceptible varieties together (see Chapter Nine for other means of
control).

Tulip   Botrytis blight. Symptoms: Similar to the botrytis
blight that affects lilies, so can control it in same way;
avoid planting tulips where other tulips or lilies grew
as recently as two or three years earlier.

Zinnia   Aster yellows virus and powdery mildew. Symptoms:
See under "Aster" and "Phlox," respectively. Control:
See under "Aster" and "Phlox," respectively. Select
zinnia varieties described as disease resistant.

DISEASES IN VEGETABLE GARDENS

Sweet Corn   Smut. Symptoms: A disgusting gray fungus eruption
on forming corn ears; fungus (called "boil smut") is
transported by wind; hot humid weather seems to
encourage disease. Control: Some hybrids are resistant, but the best course is strict sanitation—
promptly remove and burn or bag for removal with
trash any infected ears as soon as you find them to
prevent overwintering spores from starting an outbreak the next summer; clean up and remove from
garden all corn plant debris (husks, stalks, and so on).

Cucumbers   Cucumber bacterial wilt; also affects squash and
pumpkins; transmitted by spotted and striped cucumber beetles. Symptoms: Leaves wilt suddenly
and shrivel; stems dry. Control: Try to control the
beetles early on; keep young vines under row covers
as long as possible.

Diseases to Watch for in Your Garden continued

Peppers Fruit, leaf, and stem spot (anthracnose). Symptoms: Dark, sunken spots on green or ripening fruit. Control: Pick off infected fruits as soon as you see them to reduce spread.

Potatoes Scab. Symptoms: Corky areas on surface of tubers; sometimes cracking of surface. Control: Disease is present in most soils but especially in limy ones so grow potatoes in slightly acidic soil; avoid any amendments such as liming that would raise pH of soil; plant more-resistant varieties (study catalog descriptions).

Tomatoes Early blight, which also affects potatoes; tomato fusarium and verticillium wilts; tomato blossom end rot, which also affects peppers and is believed to be caused by soil moisture extremes, from wet to dry or dry to wet; and septoria leafspot, which is common in many areas. Symptoms: Early blight causes brown, roundish spots with concentric rings that start on lower leaves and gradually enlarge to cover leaves, which turn brown and shrivel. Tomato fusarium and verticillium wilts turn older leaves yellow and then gradually wilt the entire plant, moving upward. A dark, sunken, leathery area of tomato blossom end rot at bottom of fruit gradually enlarges. Small gray spots of septoria leafspot on lower leaves darken and then foliage dies upward on the plant. Control: To avoid early blight, rotate plantings so as not to repeat tomatoes (or potatoes) on same ground more often than every three years; clean up and burn or bury diseased foliage. Use varieties, usually so labeled, that are resistant to tomato fusarium and verticillium wilts. To avoid tomato blossom end rot, mulch in early summer to stabilize moisture; it is also helpful to work agricultural lime into soil around plants, ½ cup per plant, early in growing season. Septoria leafspot can be prevented by weekly spraying with chlorothalonil fungicide (follow label), beginning as first fruit clusters appear.

DISEASES IN FRUIT GARDENS

Apples/pears   Fire blight, a bacterial disease spread partially by aphids, leafhoppers, and other insects. Symptoms: Leaves, twigs, or entire branches suddenly turn brown as if seared; leaves shrivel and die while clinging to tree. Control: Plant blight-resistant varieties (particularly pears); immediately prune out affected branches well below the discolored bark area and disinfect pruning tool with household bleach between cuts to avoid spreading; control aphids with dormant oil spray in March and leafhoppers with multipurpose fruit tree spray during growing season—follow labels; avoid feeding with nitrogen fertilizer in spring so as not to promote flush of soft susceptible growth—instead, fertilize in fall.

Apples   Powdery mildew, cedar-apple rust, and scab. Symptoms: Powdery mildew makes whitish spots on leaves and distorts them. Cedar-apple rust, also a fungus, cycles back and forth between red cedar (*Juniperus virginiana* or *J. scopulorum*) and apple. On apples it makes spots on leaves that start out yellow, turn reddish, and then dark; finally, spore organs underneath leaves release spores in fall to overwinter on junipers; leaves also drop early, weakening tree. (The other host, junipers, harbor galls that form on branches, maturing the next spring and releasing spores back to apples. Galls may be handpicked from junipers and destroyed). Scab first shows as blurry dark spots on leaves and fruits, followed by early dropping of leaves and fruits. Control: For all of these diseases, use disease-resistant varieties; use regular multipurpose orchard spray, following label for schedule and mixing directions. Rust disease is reduced if it is possible to get rid of *Juniperus virginiana* (red cedar) in the vicinity, but in urban-suburban circumstances this is impossible. County or area extension offices provide advice about materials approved for spraying and when these sprays should be applied.

Diseases to Watch for in Your Garden continued

Grapes
Black rot. Symptoms: As fruits grow, pale spots appear, then turn brown over the entire berry, which shrivels and hangs on; leaves of the plant may have brown spots. Control: Use a fungicide spray such as Bordeaux—follow label; make first spray just before blooms open, second just after, and another two weeks later; cut off and destroy any old mummy fruits.

Peaches
Leaf curl and cytospora canker. Symptoms: Leaf curl causes young leaves to pucker and curl, turn red on margins, and become bumpy and distorted; no fruits form; tree dies after several successive years of infection. Cytospora canker causes gummy, rough dead ridges in bark and eventually dieback of limbs. Control: For leaf curl, use a lime-sulfur spray in dormant season, just before buds swell—you can spray only during dormancy as no available material is effective later; alternative sprays are ferbam, Bordeaux mixture, or chlorothalonil. For cytospora canker, chlorothalonil as dormant spray is recommended—follow label.

DISEASES IN ORNAMENTAL TREES AND SHRUBS

Crab Apples
See under "Apples" (page 207) in diseases of fruits. Crab apples get all the diseases that fruit apples do. Scab is especially severe. Choose disease-resistant varieties.

Elms (American)
Dutch elm disease. So few American elms are left that this disease is less noticed than it once was, but to elms that remain it is as deadly as ever. The disease invades the conductive system of inner bark, having been transmitted either by a spore-carrying elm bark beetle from an infected tree or by root graft from an infected neighbor. Symptoms: In early summer, "flagging" or yellowing of leaves of one branch after the other occurs until the entire tree is involved.

Control: Injection treatments are available to save valuable trees but must be repeated each year—ask an accredited arborist to do this; another treatment approach is strict sanitation, or the quick removal of branches showing infection—again, call a qualified tree service. Work has been done to develop disease-resistant American elms, but it is too soon to say if that goal has been reached.

Euonymus (especially *E. kiautschovica*)
Crown gall; other plants (such as roses and raspberries) may be affected. Symptoms: Rough, tumorlike rounded globs of corky tissue near soil line (sometimes higher); plants weaken but usually do not die; can spoil appearance of a hedge. Control: Inspect stock before planting and reject any with suspicious-looking knots on stems, crowns, or roots; to prevent spreading disease with tools, disinfect them with household bleach mixed with water.

Hawthorns
Rust, a fungus disease very similar to cedar-apple rust; alternate host is red-cedar juniper (*Juniperus virginiana*). Symptoms and Control: See under "Apples" (page 207).

Junipers (*J. virginiana* or *J. scopulorum*)
Rust galls; this is the other phase of the rust cycle that affects apples, crab apples, and hawthorns. Symptoms: Roundish, wrinkled brown galls appear on twigs of juniper trees in spring; in June they enlarge and transform into a spore-spreading stage with soft gelatinous "horns." Control: If you have only a few trees, pick off galls in late winter.

Bush honeysuckles (*Lonicera tatarica*)
Brooming; believed to be spread by aphids. Symptoms: A recent development, this disease results in "witches'-brooms" or gall-like crowding and distortion at ends of branches. Control: Spray aphids with systemic-action chemical solution such as Orthene; best long-term control is to replace susceptible varieties with resistant forms still to be determined.

Diseases to Watch for in Your Garden continued

Lilacs   Powdery mildew. Symptoms: White splotches coat foliage late in summer. Control: Apparently this fungus does little harm to plants and occurs after flowering, so no control efforts are recommended.

Maples   Maple wilt (verticillium); especially hits silver maples in midsummer, but other trees may also host it. Symptoms: Leaves die, taking one large branch at a time. Control: Prune out affected limbs; it may not be possible to save the tree, as other branches may be affected the same season or in succeeding year—if tree must be removed, avoid replanting another maple (or elm) in that immediate area.

Oaks   Oak wilt; especially hits red oaks, but oaks of all kinds are susceptible. Trees usually die soon after symptoms show, and some may die slowly over a few years. Though more a forestry problem than one of gardens, this does show up in new housing developments that have replaced woodlands. Symptoms: Pale leaves that turn brown from the edges in. Control: Remove infected trees; keep close watch on neighboring oaks that may be connected by root grafts.

CHAPTER TWELVE

Garden Keeping through the Seasons

Whether viewed as useful toil or as recreation, working in the outdoor garden brings personal rewards: the pleasure of watching nature unfold its changes, the satisfaction of viewing a job well done, the sense of participating in elemental processes of the real world. These are a few of the impulses that motivate gardeners wherever they are.

On the more practical side, there are the physical benefits of fresh air and exercise and release from tensions and worries. Gardening has been a link in human history since the beginning. Here in the Heartland, our fast and definite march of seasons gives a watchful gardener much to ponder and to do.

EARLY SPRING

Garden work in spring always exceeds the time available for doing it. Start as early as you can. February usually brings some days suitable for outdoor work.

PRUNING. Even though snow may linger, mild days in February and March are prime times for pruning trees, many shrubs, and woody vines, especially grapes and wisteria. The spring flowering shrubs are usually not pruned until *after* they bloom, so as not to sacrifice the flower display. Aside from the flower consideration, any shrub or tree can be pruned in early

spring. Fruit trees and berry bushes should lead the way.

Experience is the best teacher of pruning, but to avoid serious mistakes, particularly with fruit trees upon which rest great expectations, it is well for beginners to consult any of the basic pruning guides. The main objective is usually to direct new growth into a strong, open structure. Another goal is to foster renewal of the plant. It is al-

Spring shrub pruning. (A) Thinning is a renewal method for shrubs such as lilacs that shoot up many branches from a crown. Take out a few of the oldest branches near the ground each year, leaving the others. A curved pruning saw is the best tool for this. (B) Shrubs that grow too big for their space are reduced by "heading back." This process means cutting back branches to healthy buds at the height desired. Vary the length of branches for a natural look. Flowering shrubs can be pruned just after they bloom, allowing you full enjoyment of the flower effect.

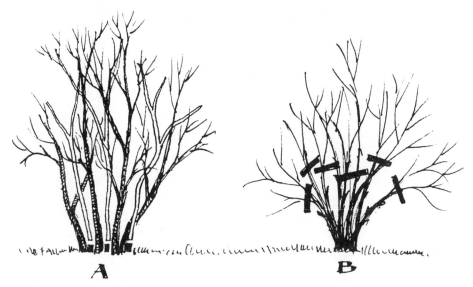

A   B

ways safe to prune out any dead limbs, broken branches, and branches that cross each other, forming tangles. Remove a targeted branch cleanly to the next larger branch, leaving no stub. It is not necessary to paint the cut. Essential tools include hand pruners (the scissors type is best for precision cuts); long-handled loppers; and a curved-blade fine-toothed pruning saw. To reach high limbs you may need a pole pruner.

Renew shrubs such as lilacs, forsythia, and philadelphus (mock orange) by going to ground level and, with pruning saw or loppers, cutting out a few of the largest, woodiest branches entirely. Removing one or two of the oldest limbs each year will keep such shrubs looking full and shapely and blooming well. On lilacs, while you are at it, also remove at ground level some of the suckers that commonly arise like a thicket around the base. A sharp shovel is a good tool for this.

Start pruning grapes in January if weather gives a break (vines should not be frozen). Even grapes grown ornamentally on fences or arbors need annual pruning to keep them vigorous and attractive. A vine decorating an arbor should have the live canes reduced by at least one-third. Remove all the dead ones.

Overgrown wisterias also are just as well pruned back in late winter while you can see the structure, even though you may reduce blooms. Take off about half of the plant each year, pruning back to the main trunks. As plants commence growth, watch for root suckers arising in the vicinity of the trunk, and cut them out with a spade. Unless kept pruned, wisterias may overwhelm and break down the supports on which they grow. It is all right to prune further after plants have bloomed if the growth warrants it.

SPREADING COMPOST. A warm interval in February is a perfect time to begin working down your compost pile with the objective of spreading most of it back on your garden from whence it came. The topmost, undecayed materials placed there only the previous autumn may need to be pitched aside, but underneath you should find the broken-down materials ready to use. Attack the pile with a sharp shovel, making vertical downward slices to reduce the size of pieces further. Put the "made" compost in your wheelbarrow to trundle off to flower beds, vegetable gardens, shrubberies, or whatever needs it. Put shovelfuls over the roots of clematis vines, around emerging rhubarb, over asparagus. Work a coating over ground-cover beds (English ivy, epimedium, pachysandra, hostas, ajuga, lily-of-the-valley, and ferns). Berry patches, fruit trees, grape vines, emerging bulb plants—all can use this compost. Emptying or reducing the pile at this time opens the way for the great additions soon to come with warm weather and the resulting weeds.

DORMANT SPRAYING. This most important spraying of the year comes right after pruning. Do it while buds are still tightly closed. In this stage they can withstand stronger spray concentrations than would be possible later on. There are two general types of dormant spray. Lime-sulfur, a fungicide and insecticide, is used especially to control leaf curl disease on peaches and to control diseases and insects on apples, roses, and raspberries. The second type, dormant or miscible oil (mixed with water according to label directions), is used to get rid of scales, spider mites, and insect eggs on apples, pears, peaches, plums, apricots, cherries, gooseberries, and currants. Don't use lime-sulfur within a month of using a dormant oil spray (injury may occur) and don't use it on apricots. For peach leaf curl, an alternative dormant spray is ferbam, which has proved superior in controlling this disease. A newer recommendation is chlorothalonil as a dormant spray for both peach leaf curl and the cytospora canker, a widespread bark disease of peaches and cherries in our region. Whatever you choose to use, follow package directions.

A 1½ gallon pump-up sprayer is a good tool for spraying if you have only a few dwarf fruit trees and shrubs; a trombone-type sprayer with the intake hose clamped to a bucket containing the desired spray solution is the most economical yet effective spraying tool for a small orchard of standard fruit trees. It will shoot spray to the tops of them.

LAWN WEED PREVENTION. Crabgrass or foxtail invasion of Heartland lawns is very common in summer, but you can prevent this by applying a preemergence crabgrass control product to the lawn just ahead of warm weather. The same week forsythias show color, about the end of March or beginning of April, is a strategic time.

To avoid any skips or misses, set the spreader at half the recommended setting (read directions on the bag for this) and then make two passes over the area—the second at right angle to the first. If you get good coverage and a crabgrass-free lawn, you need not make this treatment again for several years or until you notice crabgrass or foxtail reappearing. Preemergents work by preventing seed germination.

WHEN PLANTS COME UP TOO EARLY. Peonies, daffodils, and tulips, among others, seemingly have their own antifreeze in early spring, and their young leaves survive repeated frosts without much damage. If you feel you want to protect them, as when record lows are forecast, a light covering of leaves should bring them through; or spread a commercial spunbonded covering over them to hold in ground warmth.

CARING FOR PEONIES. When those red new shoots first begin to nose through the ground, apply a Bordeaux mixture spray to them and the surrounding soil to prevent any outbreak of botrytis blight. This fungus disease is a common cause of leaf browning and blasted bloom buds. Other fungicide sprays such as benomyl will also suppress the disease. If any of last year's dead stems remain, cut them off at the ground and remove them from the premises.

REMOVING WINTER MULCH OR PLANT DEBRIS. Clean off perennials and bulb beds gradually. It does not need to be done all at once. Be guided by weather. The same is true for roses that were mounded for winter. Frosts or freezes can revisit even two or three weeks after your average last frost date, so be prepared for emergency protection. In such a situation, spunbonded floating plant covers are ideal to lay over precocious shoots.

FERTILIZING SPRING-BLOOMING BULBS. The time to fertilize spring-blooming bulbs is in early spring while foliage is growing. Use a bulb fertilizer (one high in phosphorus—the middle number of the formula on the bag) and dig it in gently with a trowel worked among the plants. Then water the area to propel the fertilizer downward. Fertilized bulbs bloom better and last longer than bulbs left unaided.

DIVIDING PERENNIALS FOR REPLANTING. For many perennial flowers—chrysanthemums, hardy asters, summer phlox, ornamental grasses, coralbells, daylilies, yarrows, globe thistles, sedums, lythrums, and many more—early spring is the best time to divide and replant. The general rule is to divide mid-summer and late-blooming kinds in spring, and then wait until late summer to divide and reset kinds that bloom in earliest spring.

MIDSPRING

Each passing day now brings new wonders in the garden—and new tasks.

PRUNING SPRING-BLOOMING SHRUBS. As soon as bloom time ends, you can thin and shape azaleas, viburnums, beauty-bushes, spireas, flowering almonds, lilacs, deutzias, and the like without diminishing the bloom display for next year. Midspring is also a good time to trim back or shape hollies, shrub types of euonymus, yews, junipers—almost any of the landscape trees

and shrubs. To preserve the natural and avoid the sheared effect, use loppers or hand pruners rather than hedge shears.

CONTROLLING PERENNIAL WEEDS. Perennial weeds that are are difficult to control, such as bindweed, climbing milkweed, poison ivy, and wild onion, are most susceptible at this time of year to treatment with appropriate herbicides. The safest type to use near valued garden plants is glyphosate—sold under such trade names as Roundup or Kleenup. As it is not selective, it should be carefully applied only to the target plants—by painting it on with a brush or long-handled sponge or by shielding nearby desirable plants while applying it as a coarse spray. Follow the label carefully.

CONTROLLING PERENNIAL GRASS WEEDS. Bluegrass, brome, fescue, and the like coming up in flower clumps (such as creeping phlox) or in ground-covers (such as English ivy or vinca) are particularly hard to remove. The only permanent solution is to lift the flower clump or ground cover entirely, turn it over, pull the grassy invader out by the roots from underneath, and then replant the cleansed clump, perhaps taking the opportunity to divide it at the same time.

INSPECTING FOR WEED TREES. Watch for weed trees in ground-cover beds and shrub borders especially, and pull them out while they are young and the ground is soft. Seedling oaks and walnuts, probably planted by squirrels, are only a slight bother to remove the first spring; but if left to the second year, they will test your determination and strength. To get a firm grip on them, use household pliers. Many other tree seedlings can become weeds—maples, elms, mulberries, hackberries—in fence- or hedgerows or even under the junipers or yews of your foundation or landscape plantings. The earlier they are removed, the easier.

EDGING YOUR LAWN. Done with a simple step-on edger tool with a half-moon-shaped blade, edging is a well-proven way to put a neat finish on established beds of flowers and ground covers while keeping spreading lawn grasses from infiltrating them. Throw the chunk of soil removed from the edge onto the flower bed. Doing this repeatedly gradually raises the center of the bed and deepens the edge, improving surface drainage. Edging a bed is not so laborious as is assumed by those who have never tried it, and the process affords an opportunity to observe and critique your plantings as you go. There are also, of course, many kinds of structural edging materials available from garden stores; or you can design your own using bender boards or regular-dimension rot-resistant lumber, landscape timbers, or even a masonry edge of bricks, stones, or various concrete products.

CHECKING PLANT LABELS. As various plants break through in the perennial garden, check for labels and replace any that are missing. There is no such thing (yet) as an indestructible plant label. Keeping labels legible and in place—positioned uniformly with respect to the plants to aid in finding them—keeps you from accidentally digging into clumps, or walking over them, or planting spreading neighbors too close.

STAKING OR SUPPORTING PLANTS. Even though plants still seem small, midspring is a good time to place supports for any kinds that will need them—some of the true lilies whose stalks grow tall, delphiniums, baptisias, globe thistles—while you can still see what you are doing and have room to move around in the flower bed. See that trellised kinds, such as clematis, still have serviceable trellises. For peony varieties whose stems go down when rain fills their heavy blooms, bud time is the moment to set in place the metal peony rings or supports. The goal in staking is to support the plant beyond its strength without spoiling its natural grace and form. No small task! One of the secrets is to start while plants are small and supple.

SUMMER

MULCHING. With the onset of heat, and premonitions of drought, let mulching take priority among your tasks. Nothing else done in a summer garden can bring more benefits. Mulch preserves moisture, cools the soil, handicaps weeds, and even suppresses insects to some extent. And, finally, as an organic mulch breaks down, it bolsters the humus in the soil. Grass clippings, shredded leaves, compost, wood chips, spoiled hay, pine needles, sawdust, or commercially marketed mulches such as bark slivers are all possibilities. The stony mulches are best reserved for nonplant areas where you want the color effect. They are generally underlain with weed barriers of some kind, such as the landscape fabrics, to prevent grassy weeds or tree seedlings from becoming severe problems. Do not use black plastic. Of the organic mulches (grass clippings and the like), prepare to replenish as needed. Hot weather and rainy spells will speed their disappearance. Observation tells you when they need to be topped up.

WATERING. Heartland summers often turn dry after mid-June, and gardens containing the typical array of flowers and vegetables need occasional watering to prolong growth and preserve flowers and vegetables. Fruit trees and grapes also benefit from midsummer watering through droughty heat waves. Drip irrigation systems, although time consuming to install, are easily the most efficient and water-conserving method for our region. During dog days of summer, watering may become a lifesaving matter. When water is in short supply you may have to choose which plants will receive and which will be passed over. Give preference to the long-term varieties, particularly any newly set ones, and to late-developing and -blooming kinds like chrysanthemums, dahlias, and Japanese anemones that are expected to produce a fall display. Mulches such as dry grass clippings applied around such plants will cut down on water demand.

WEEDING. Summer's long days bring out the great weed scourges of the year. Prepare for the battle. You may need chemical warfare as well as mechanical weapons (hoe, shovel, scuffle tools, tillers, and cultivators) and, ultimately, the human hand. Whatever works! Watch for the first seedling of purslane to appear, and at-tack it. The same goes for crabgrass, foxtail, lamb's-quarter, pigweed, flower-of-an-hour, carpetweed, or galinsoga. If prevented from seeding, these annual weeds will vanish from the garden in a few years. Perennial types such as bindweed, climbing milkweed, horsenettle, and dandelions are a different matter. Rooting them out is the most direct method, but you must continue doing this until the roots are really gone. A tool to probe under the surface, such as a dandelion digger, is good for getting weeds that have underground root networks or taproots. Do not put the seedy weeds (especially purslane and crabgrass) on your compost pile or you will be fighting them for the rest of your life. Better to dispose of them in the trash pickup, to bury them deeply, or to burn them. The systemic herbicide glyphosate (Roundup) is another effective means of combat if you can apply it to the weeds without hitting desirable plants nearby.

LAWN WORK. In high summer you can rest a bit as mowing slacks off. Lawns in the southern half of the Heartland that had much crabgrass the previous year should get a repeat treatment with a preventive about June 15. Where growing seasons are really long, preventives do not remain effective the whole season. This is when string trimmers are often hauled out to smooth away unruly weeds or high grass around tree trunks, shrubs, foundations, and curbs. Protect any tree trunks where you use string trimmers, as real damage is inflicted before you know it. Depending on your lawn standards, you may be battling sod web-worms, lawn grubs, or weed pests. For these the local garden store offers a selection of remedies and free advice, with products changing year by year. Any patches of lawn that look "gone" might be scheduled for fall renovation at the end of August. However, the summer dormancy displayed by un-watered bluegrass lawns may not be the disaster you imagine. Bluegrass revives quickly when fall rains begin.

DEADHEADING. A callous term, "deadheading" is descriptive of the process needed in summer flower gardens to remove spent flowers and prevent seed formation. It not only keeps the garden looking presentable, but in some cases, as with roses, achilleas, and coreopsis, it sets the stage for a repeat of bloom later. There are a few special techniques for certain plants. On true lilies, use hand pruners to snip off the developing seed pods just below the juncture with the main stem. (With experience, you can learn the master gardener's technique of snapping them off with your thumb.) Leave the green main stem with its array of leaves to continue manufacturing nutrients that feed the maturing bulb underground.

On daylilies, deadheading consists of pulling out the brown spent scapes from the plant's crown. To come out cleanly the stems must be mature and dry. Any with seed pods will be the last to ripen. Unless you want the seeds, it is best to cut these out with pruners. After such a cleaning, the daylily clumps look neat and pleasing for the rest of the season.

On tall bearded irises, the bloomed-out scapes should be removed right to the base at the rhizome. Many veteran gardeners accomplish removal by grasping the stem firmly and giving it a brisk jerk outward, breaking it cleanly at the ground. They maintain that this is a more sanitary practice for the plant than cutting off the spent scapes, with the chance that diseases will be introduced by means of the tool or through leaving a soft, watery stem stub.

Remove fading peony flowers before they start to shatter. Use hand pruners for this, and take no more foliage than necessary. Perennials such as monarda (beebalm), columbines, coneflowers, Siberian irises, veronicas, dictamnus (gasplants), coralbells, and hardy geraniums benefit in appearance by having the remains of their early season blooms pruned off. Use hedge

As lilies mature, snap off developing seed pods without removing any of the foliage or main stem. This allows the plant's strength to go entirely to the bulbs for the next year's flowers.

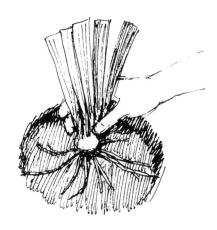

Tall bearded irises need dividing every two or three years. Do this in mid- to late summer. Pull clumps apart into single plants. Lay each rhizome on a low mound in the prepared place; roots should be spread evenly. Cover with no more than 1 inch of soil. Allow 15 to 18 inches between rhizomes, as they increase fast.

shears to save time. Some will respond with a modest set of second blooms.

Roses that "repeat-bloom" need deadheading at the end of each bloom surge—both to encourage new growth for another bloom session and to discourage insects and diseases that may harbor in the old rose heads if you leave them on. Potpourri makers might be eager to harvest your spent rose blooms if you make known their availability.

REMOVING RIPENED BULB FOLIAGE. The shriveled spring leaves of daffodils, tulips, and lycoris are ready for removal as summer sets in. Annual flowers such as nicotiana and periwinkle are good to transplant into the spaces left by tulips and daffodils. But

in the case of lycoris, which vegetates in spring but does not send up blooms until late July, mark the place to protect against accidental digging or trampling while those bloom stems are developing underground.

AUTUMN

Of all our seasons, fall is the most pleasant and beautiful. Often rains come in September, about the time of the fall equinox, prompting the regreening of lawns and a last display of flowers before the shortening days gradually draw plants to a close of activity. Cooler days, deep blue skies, and the glorious colors of tree foliage make this a favorite time to be outdoors.

LAWNS. Fall is the best season to start or repair lawns if they consist of cool-season grasses such as bluegrass or fescue. Experts prefer autumn over spring as the favorable time for fertilizing such lawns and recommend at least two fall feedings, four to six weeks apart, with the first done about Labor Day. A typical lawn fertilizer such as 10-6-4 is as good as any. Fall fertilizing gives the grass a strong push as it heads into winter, thickening the roots and crowns and giving them a "charge" of nutrients that will promote early growth in spring. Aeration is another treatment often given lawns in autumn, and if this is on your agenda, do it ahead of the fertilizing.

Next on the lawn schedule is the annual leaf cleanup. Depending on circumstances this may go on until December or even later. Some oaks release dead leaves all winter. Not only for the sake of appearance but also for the well-being of the grass, it is advisable to remove the leaf blanket from lawns. A thick covering can smother grass. The leaves you "harvest" make valuable additions to compost heaps or may simply be spread over the vegetable garden and tilled into the soil. By spring the leaves will have almost disappeared, but their beneficial effect lasts in your future gardens.

CLEANING UP PERENNIALS. After a few hard fall frosts, most growth and bloom in the perennial garden comes to an end, and you can do any prewinter cleaning you deem necessary. The browning plant tops can be cut off and removed if desired. A case can be made for leaving them on to serve as a snow catch and to shade the ground, preventing some of the thaws that pry out shallow-rooted plants. If much bare ground shows between clumps of perennials, cover it with a protective mulch. Pine needles are excellent; or you could use dry grass clippings, clean straw, or hay. After Christmas, cut up the Christmas tree and mulch with its branches. Pine bark is a favorite product because of its unusual longevity. Not only does it last through winter but most of the next summer as well; its seemingly antifungal properties keep plants healthy.

CLEANING UP PEONIES. Late fall removal of dead peony tops is a sanitation method for preventing botrytis blight among the plants the next summer. So even if you leave all the other plant tops, do cut off peonies close to the ground and remove the tops completely from the garden. Burn them or bury them somewhere away from the

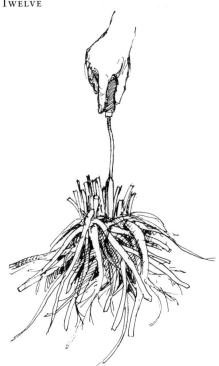

Divide peonies in fall after foliage begins to yellow. Clean away soil and then pry out or cut the crown into sections, each with five or six strong buds and several firm long roots. In replanting, see that the crown is covered with no more than 1½ inches of soil.

garden. October is a good month for planting or replanting peonies in the Heartland. Peony growers or garden shops usually have roots for sale then. Plant the root crowns so the pink "eyes" (growth buds for next year's stems) are just 1½ inches below ground level. Give peonies a sunny location. Although they will survive in shade, they need sun at least half the day to produce good blooms.

DIGGING UP TENDER BULBS. Just after the first hard frost it is time to begin lifting for winter storage the tender corms/rhizomes/tubers/bulbs of gladiolus, cannas, dahlias, tuberoses, *Hymenocallis* (Peruvian daffodils), elephant-ear, caladiums that have been planted in the ground, calla-lilies, and any other "bulbs" of mild climate origins that could not survive our winters outdoors. Clean and cure them by allowing their surfaces to dry, then pack them in vermiculite and store them where freezes cannot reach them. Tuberoses, Peruvian daffodils, and caladiums are best stored in a relatively warm place, 60 degrees or thereabouts. Cannas, dahlias, and gladiolus need conditions that are cooler but not freezing.

PLANTING AND RESETTING BULBS. Autumn is the time to plant hardy bulbs or corms—crocuses, narcissus (daffodils), hyacinths, tulips, muscari, scillas, snowdrops and snowflakes, glory-of-the-snow, wood hyacinths— to name some of the most dependable and long lasting of our bulb plants. The earlier they are planted in autumn, the better, but dealers often do not get their stocks of bulbs until October. Should autumn be dry, water new plantings before freeze-up to get root growth started. Otherwise, if a dry winter ensues after the dry fall, the bulbs may not perform well the next spring. The rule of thumb for bulb planting depth is to make the covering over bulbs three times as deep as the up-down dimension of the bulbs. Which end is up? Usually the most tapered or pointed or sometimes the one showing shreds of last season's foliage. The bases are usually flat or rounded, and sometimes have visible root nubs. Some little tubers—for example, those

of windflowers (*Anemone blanda*)—are so shapeless there is no telling up from down, but it does not matter because they will grow regardless of how they are placed.

WINTER PROTECTION. Roses and crape myrtles are two kinds of woody plants grown in the Heartland that either benefit from being soil mounded in autumn or really require it to survive winter. The usual rule is to put on the soil mound after the ground has frozen; but in the fickle fall weather of recent years, it has been prudent to get the protection in place by December 1 whether the ground is frozen or not. That first hard freeze might prove to be the worst of the winter, and it might arrive with stunning speed. The damage will have been done before the protection was given. Nevertheless, it is usually better late than never, as much winter damage to these plants also occurs in the freezes and thaws of February and March. The purpose of mounding these plants is primarily to keep the cold in the ground rather than preserving warmth. Bring in the soil from some other site; do not scratch it up from between the plants, for shallow roots might be damaged. Some type of collar or retainer around the plant crown is practical to hold the soil in place over the winter. Above the soil mound, a further insulating layer of loose dry leaves (oak leaves are good) or airy hay may be added to further shade plant tops and shield them from drying winds. Do not prune roses in fall. It is all right to draw tops together with twine to prevent whipping in wind.

Different sorts of help are needed to get various plants through our winters. Broadleaf evergreens need screening from winter sun to prevent sunscald on foliage. Burlap wrappings are sometimes used. Ground covering plants like strawberries and epimediums will profit from a loose mulch of clean straw or pine needles.

FALL TILLING AND SPADING. Clean off debris from vegetable gardens, and till or spade the soil in preparation for spring. Work in mulch if you can. If you are hand digging, leave the surface rough and cloddy to catch all possible moisture, whether rain or snow—and to prevent washing. Ground prepared in autumn can be made ready quickly in spring for sowing those earliest crops—potatoes, onions, lettuces, spinach, and peas.

Likewise, empty spaces in flower beds can be dug up in autumn; with compost and fertilizer incorporated, they will be ready to go as soon as spring returns.

WINTER

PLANTING. Heartland winters often offer mild above-freezing periods when dormant woody plants may be planted even in December and January. Nursery stock planted during these winter "windows" shows good survival and has a head start on stock planted later in spring. If winter is dry and open, water evergreens and any fall-planted dormant trees, as they are probably needing moisture since nature is not providing enough.

Inspect plantings occasionally through winter, watching for any whose roots have been exposed by freeze-thaw action (called "heaving"). Gently press them back down to the soil and draw some mulch around them.

Things Nobody Ever Tells You

- Living Christmas trees—balled and burlapped and ready to plant—are a real gamble since there is no guarantee they will survive the holiday inside your house and then the transfer to your lawn outside. Here are some steps to take to give them the best chance. First, dig the planting hole before Thanksgiving and fill and cover the hole and the pile of removed soil with straw or leaves to keep everything unfrozen and workable until planting time. Second, keep the tree's stay indoors very brief, four days at most, and set the thermostat as low as you can live with. Third, be absolutely sure that during its out-of-the-ground time with you, the tree is not allowed to dry out in any part of its root system. Also make sure it does not go dry outdoors in the ground afterward, a real possibility because January and February are often dry months.
- Don't cut off the foliage of bulb flowers—tulips, daffodils, grape hyacinths, and so on—until it turns brown (ripens) naturally.
- Petunias grow easily from cuttings, something useful to know if gaps develop in summer displays or planters. Take a healthy 6-inch stem, strip the leaves from the lower half, and bed it in soft soil where you want it to grow. Keep it watered and shaded a few days.

SALT DAMAGE. Lawns along sidewalks or streets that get heavy doses of salt to melt ice or snow usually incur damage. Shrubs or even trees may also suffer if salty meltwater sinks in around their roots. Leaf edges (on deciduous types) may show browned margins the next spring as if they had been scorched by drought. Needles may turn brown on pines, starting at the tips. Preventing such a calamity is much better than trying to treat it. Avoid using rock salt de-icer if you can. Calcium chloride is less harmful to plants than sodium chloride (salt), but even that may lead to damage. To provide traction on icy walks or drives some gardeners substitute lawn or garden fertilizer (granular type), sprinkled sparingly, or inert materials such as cat litter or sawdust.

Avoid piling salted snow around plants or where runoff will drain onto them. In a case where the ground has already been poisoned by salt, as along streets, you can neutralize the toxic effect somewhat and relieve the tendency to compaction by treating the soil with gypsum, obtainable at garden stores. Spread gypsum at the rate of 200 pounds per 1,000 square feet; repeated treatments may be necessary in subsequent years. Evergreens whose tops have been hit with salt spray are helped a little by hosing them off the first above-freezing day.

WHAT TO DO WITH THE CHRISTMAS TREE. After Christmas, cut up the deposed Christmas tree and use the branches to mulch flower beds. Use your neighbors' trees, too, if they have no plans for them. This is a far better destiny for trees than being sent to the landfill or feeding a bonfire.

WINTER CHECKLIST. During winter inspect young fruit or flowering trees to be sure wire-mesh rabbit guards are in place around trunks and are high enough to prevent rabbits from overreaching them. This is especially important in rural areas where bunnies abound and have the outdoors much to themselves. A young tree can be girdled and destroyed in a single day or night. Cylinders of hardware "cloth" (¼-inch-thick wire mesh) pinned to the ground are effective protectors.

Be sure that smooth-barked young trees have their trunks wrapped up to the lower branches as they go into winter to protect them against frost cracks. An alternative to a tree wrap is a coat of white latex paint. Although some people object to the appearance of paint, it is a method from the past that still works and even has some carryover benefits in summer by repelling insects. Don't use oil-based paint.

You are not the only one who may rediscover in January the bag of bulbs you purchased in fall but never got planted. If you watch for a thaw period when you can dig, go ahead and plant them. They are better off in the ground than in the bag, although because of the late start, they may be slow in blooming the first spring.

Public Gardens to Visit in the Heartland

IOWA

Bickelhaupt Arboretum, 340 South Fourteenth Street, Clinton

Butterfly Garden, Belleview State Park, 1 mile south of city on U.S. Highway 52, Belleview

Des Moines Botanical Center, 909 East River Drive, Des Moines

Dubuque Arboretum and Botanic Gardens, Marshall Park, 3125 West Thirty-Second Street and Arboretum Drive, Dubuque

Earl May Garden, Shenandoah

Iowa State University Farmhouse and Horticulture Garden, Iowa State University, Ames

Pella Tulip Festival, second weekend in May, Pella

Project Green crab apple plantings in Iowa City: U.S. Highway 6 approach to city; Iowa Avenue from Old Capitol to Dodge Street; Gilbert Street from Burlington to Kirkwood streets; Washington Street between Van Buren and Dodge streets; Muscatine Avenue from First to West High streets; Old U.S. Highway 218 from Wardway Street south to Iowa City Airport.

Waterworks Park crab apple trees, Fleur Drive and Locust Street, Des Moines

KANSAS

Bartlett Arboretum, Belle Plaine

Botanica, The Wichita Gardens, 701 Amidon Street, Wichita

Dyck Arboretum of the Plains, Hesston

Eisenhower Museum grounds, Abilene

Gage Park Conservatory, E. F. A. Reinisch Rose Garden, Doran Rock Garden, Gage Park, Tenth Street and Gage Boulevard, Topeka

Kansas Landscape Arboretum, south of Wakefield

Kansas State University Botanic Garden, Kansas State University, Manhattan

Meade Park Gardens and Arboretum, 124 North Fillmore Street, Topeka

MISSOURI

Laura Conyers Smith Rose Garden, Loose Park, 5200 Pennsylvania Street, Kansas City

Missouri Botanical Garden, 4344 Shaw Boulevard, St. Louis

Powell Gardens, east of Lone Jack, just off U.S. Highway 50

Shield of Shelter Insurance Gardens, 1817 West Broadway Street, Columbia

William Rockhill Nelson Gallery of Art grounds, Forty-Sixth and Oak streets, Kansas City

NEBRASKA

Arbor Lodge, just off U.S. Highway 75, Nebraska City

Fontanelle Forest and Nature Center, 1111 Belleview Boulevard North, Bellevue

Nebraska Statewide Arboretum system, forty-two sites throughout the state

University of Nebraska Botanical Garden and Arboretum, City Campus at Thirteenth and R streets, East Campus at Thirty-Eighth and Holdrege streets, Lincoln

Plants That Attract Birds

Most gardeners want the pleasure of songbirds nearby, except when the birds steal their raspberries or cherries. A way to counter any conflicts of interest with birds is to offer other plants as food. For example, a fruiting mulberry somewhere in the yard will lure birds away from raspberries, as they prefer mulberries to any other fruit at that season.

From early summer through the growing season, numerous ornamental trees and shrubs offer food (in the form of colorful berries), nest sites, and shelter for birds. With these, gardeners never begrudge what the birds take, as they receive a rich return of color, activity, interest, and to some extent insect control. Following are lists of the best such plants for the Heartland.

WOODY PLANTS (TREES, SHRUBS, AND VINES) THAT OFFER FOOD FOR BIRDS

Amelanchier arborea (juneberry or serviceberry)

Berberis thunbergii (Japanese barberry)

Celastrus scandens (bittersweet)

Celtis occidentalis (hackberry)

Cornus florida (flowering dogwood)

Cornus alba (redtwig dogwood)

Cornus mas (cornelian cherry)

Crataegus phaenopyrum (Washington hawthorn)

Ilex opaca (American holly and other hollies)

Ilex verticillata (winterberry)

Juniperus virginiana (red cedar or juniper)

Juniperus scopulorum (Colorado juniper)

Ligustrum obtusifolium (Regel's privet)

Lonicera tatarica (tatarian honeysuckle) (and other honeysuckles)

Malus species (crab apples, especially small-fruited kinds)

Morus rubra and *M. alba* (red and white mulberries)

Parthenocissus quinquefolia (Virginia creeper)

Parthenocissus tricuspidata (Boston ivy)

Pyracantha coccinea (firethorn)

Sambucus canadensis (elderberry)

Sorbus aucuparia (mountain-ash)

Symphoricarpos orbiculatus (coralberry)

Taxus cuspidata (Japanese yews; female or fruiting forms)

Viburnum dentatum (arrowwood)

Viburnum plicatum tomentosum (double-file viburnum)

Viburnum prunifolium (blackhaw viburnum)

Viburnum trilobum (American cranberry bush)

PLANTS THAT OFFER SHELTER AND/OR NEST SITES FOR BIRDS

Most of the preceding shrubs and trees, as well as:

PINES
Austrian
Ponderosa
Scotch
White

SPRUCES
Colorado
Norway
Serbian

FIR
Concolor

GARDEN FLOWERS WHOSE SEEDS ATTRACT BIRDS OVER WINTER

Leave the season's growth in place until the following spring.
Asters (all hardy types)
Celosia
Centaureas
Cosmos
Gaillardias
Liatris (gayfeathers or blazing-stars)
Marigolds
Ornamental grasses such as *Pennisetum* (fountain grass)
Portulaca
Sunflowers (both annual and perennial types)
Zinnias

GARDEN FLOWERS THAT ATTRACT HUMMINGBIRDS

These summer residents feed on nectar and are seemingly attracted by tube-shaped blossoms of red, pink, orange, purple, and sometimes blue. The following flowers are noted for attracting hummingbirds:
Canna
Cardinal-flower (*Lobelia cardinalis*)
Columbine (red or pink forms)
Honeysuckle (*Lonicera;* forms such as 'Dropmore Scarlet' [*L.* x *brownii*] and trumpet [*L. sempervirens*])
Monarda (red or pink forms)
Penstemon (especially red, pink, and purple kinds)
Petunia (red-pink kinds)
Salvia (red forms)
Standing cypress (*Ipomopsis rubra*)
Trumpet vine (*Campsis radicans* and hybrid forms)

APPENDIX C

Glossary

ACID. Describes garden soil with pH below 7. See also ALKALINE.

ALKALINE. Describes garden soil with pH above 7. See also ACID.

ANNUAL. Plant that grows from seed, blooms, and dies in one season.

AXIL. Angle where leaf or branch meets stem.

B&B. Balled and burlapped. Refers to trees or shrubs dug with earth ball held together around roots with burlap wrap.

BEARD. Fringelike growth on a petal, as in some irises and orchids.

BICOLOR. Two-colored.

BIENNIAL. Plant that requires two years from seed to bloom, then dies the second year after seeding.

BLAST. Refers to flower buds that dry and fall without opening.

BOLE. Central trunk of a tree.

BRACT. Modified leaf, sometimes resembling flower petals as in dogwood.

CALLUS. Hard surface that grows over an injury or cut.

CALYX. Outer assemblage of flower parts consisting of sepals.

CAMBIUM. Cell layer in trees between bark and wood.

CATKIN. Flower cluster consisting of a scaly spike, as in willows.

CHLOROPHYLL. Green coloring in plant cells.

CHLOROSIS. Condition causing green parts of plants to turn yellow or white.

CLONE. Group of plants derived vegetatively from the same parent.

COMPOST. Vegetation that has decomposed.

COMPOUND LEAF. Leaf consisting of numerous separate leaflets.

CONIFER. Tree that bears seed-cones—for example, pines.

COROLLA. Collective term for the petals of a flower.

COTYLEDON. First leaf of a germinating seed.

CROWN. Place on plant where top stems join roots; or in trees, the upper canopy.

DECIDUOUS. Describes plants that shed their leaves in winter.

DIOECIOUS. Describes plant having male (pollen-producing) flowers on one plant and female (seed-producing) flowers on another.

DISK. In composite flowers like daisies, the collection of small close-set flowers at the center, as distinct from ray flowers.

ESPALIER. System of pruning and training plants to grow in one plane, as against a wall.

EYE. A growth bud, especially on roots—for example, peonies.

FALLS. In iris, the three lower "petals" or sepals of the flower.

FLAT. In horticulture, a shallow box for growing seedlings or cuttings.

FLORET. Individual small flower of a many-parted cluster.

FROND. Leaf blade of a fern.

GENUS. Grouping of plant species that are alike in certain distinguishing characteristics.

GERMINATE. To sprout, as a seed.

GLABROUS. Smooth.

GLAUCOUS. Covered with powderlike "bloom," as on grapes.

GRAFT. Process of joining a bud or stem of one plant to a root of another so they grow together as one plant.

HARDEN OFF. Expose a plant gradually to more adverse conditions such as cold or dry air.

HARDY. Able to withstand adverse conditions, especially cold, without special protection.

HEAVE. Soil action resulting from freezing and thawing that pushes plants out of the ground.

HERBACEOUS. With fleshy, not woody, stems.

HILL UP. To mound soil around plants for winter protection or for support.

HIP. Seed fruit of a rose.

HUMUS. Decomposed vegetable matter in soil.

INFLORESCENCE. Flowering head of the plant, especially a cluster.

LATERALS. Side branches.

LAYER. Rooting of branches of a plant while they are still attached to the parent.

LEACH. To wash out chemical substances in soil by profuse watering.

LEADER. Central upright branch of a tree or shrub.

LEGGY. Stems abnormally long, with few leaves, usually caused by overcrowding or too little light.

MISCIBLE OIL. Oil that will mix with water in a spray.

MONOECIOUS. Plants with pistillate (seed-setting) flowers and staminate (pollen-producing) flowers separate but on the same plant.

MULCH. A covering for soil, to give winter protection, conserve moisture, prevent overheating, or keep down weeds.

NATIVE. Growing naturally in the area, with no human intervention.

NATURALIZE. To adapt to conditions in the area and be self-perpetuating, although not native.

NODE. Swelling or place on stem where growth may develop.

NUTRIENTS. With plants, the minerals that nourish growth.

ORGANIC MATTER. Plant or animal refuse, usually in stages of decomposition, for adding to soil.

PEAT MOSS. Partly decomposed sphagnum moss added to soil for its acidifying, conditioning, and moisture-retaining qualities.

PEDICEL. Individual flower stem.

PERENNIAL. Plant that lives more than two years.

PETAL. One section of the corolla, usually the showy part.

PETIOLE. A leafstalk.

pH. Symbol indicating acidity or alkalinity on a scale in which 7 is neutral, above 7 is alkaline, and below 7 is acidic.

PINCH. Remove growth tips.

PISTIL. Pollen-receiving organ of the flower.

POLLEN. Male reproductive cells that when applied to the pistil begin the process of seed formation.

PROLIFERATION. Offshoot of a plant useful for propagation.

RACEME. Flower cluster in which pedicels are of nearly equal length, as in lily-of-the-valley.

RAY FLOWER. In composites like daisies, the long, narrow petal-flowers around the outside, as distinct from disk flowers at center.

RHIZOME. Thickened rootstem, as in iris.

ROGUE. To weed out unwanted plants.

ROSETTE. Circular cluster of usually basal leaves.

RUNNER. Thin, trailing shoot that takes root, as in strawberry.

SCAPE. Term for a leafless flower stem arising from the plant crown.

SCION. In grafting or budding, the piece that will form the new top.

SEPAL. A separate section of a calyx, at the flower's outer base.

SESSILE. Without a stem or stalk.

SPIKE. Long flower cluster with florets radiating evenly along it, as in hosta or delphinium.

SPORE. Reproductive body of a non-flowering plant such as ferns and fungi.

SPORT. Mutation.

STAMEN. Pollen-producing organ of the flower.

STERILE. In flowers, refers to inability to set seed; in soil, refers to condition free of harmful fungi or bacteria.

STOLON. A runner that will take root and produce a new plant.

STRAIN. A race of similar plants produced from seeds.

SUCKER. Fast-growing shoot from the root or from the trunk or main branch.

TAP ROOT. Central fleshy root that grows downward, as in carrot.

TENDRIL. Twining branch that enables the plant to climb, as in grapes.

THIN. To cut or pull out some plants to make more room for others.

TRUMPET. In daffodils, the long central tube of the flower.

TUBER. A thick underground food storage stem usually containing growth buds.

UMBEL. Umbrella-shaped flower cluster.

VEIN. The line in a leaf, smaller than a rib.

WHORL. Circular cluster of leaves around a stem.

XERISCAPE. Landscape consisting of drought-tolerant plants able to persist without watering.

Bibliography

(See also "Books on Home Landscaping" at the end of Chapter Three.)

Bailey, L. H. *The Standard Cyclopedia of Horticulture*. New York: Macmillan, 1942.

Buchanan, Rex. *Kansas Geology*. Lawrence: University Press of Kansas, 1984.

Clausen, Ruth Rogers, and Nicolas H. Ekstrom. *Perennials for American Gardens*. New York: Random House, 1989.

Dirr, Michael A. *Manual of Woody Landscape Plants*. Champaign, Ill.: Stipes, 1977.

Edinger, James G. *Watching for the Wind: The Seen and Unseen Influences on Local Weather*. Garden City, N.Y.: Doubleday, 1967.

Everett, Thomas H. *The New York Botanical Garden Illustrated Encyclopedia of Horticulture*. New York: Garland, 1981.

Harshbarger, Gretchen F. *McCall's Garden Book*. New York: Simon & Schuster, 1968.

L. H. Bailey Hortorium Staff, *Hortus Third*. New York: Macmillan, 1976.

McLane, Stanley. *Garden Guide by Months for the Midwest*. Kansas City: Frank Glenn, 1950.

Missouri State and Area Extension Horticultural Staff. *Grounds for Gardening—A Horticultural Guide*. Columbia: University of Missouri, 1974 and updates.

National Wildflower Research Center Staff. *Wildflower Handbook*. Austin: Texas Monthly Press for National Wildflower Research Center, 1989.

Olson, Jean E. *Landscape Plants for Iowa*. Ames: Cooperative Extension Service of Iowa State University, 1984.

Phillips, Harry R. *Growing and Propagating Wild Flowers*. Chapel Hill: University of North Carolina Press, 1985.

Rehder, Alfred. *Manual of Cultivated Trees and Shrubs*. New York: Macmillan, 1937.

Settergren, Carl, and R. E. McDermott. *Trees of Missouri*. Columbia: University of Missouri Agricultural Experiment Station, 1962.

Snyder, Leon C. *Gardening in the Upper Midwest*. Minneapolis: University of Minnesota Press, 1985.

Still, Steven M. *Herbaceous Ornamental Plants*. Champaign, Ill: Stipes, 1982.

Taylor, Norman. *Taylor's Encyclopedia of Gardening*. Boston: Houghton Mifflin, 1948.

U.S. Department of Agriculture Soil Conservation Service. *Soil Survey of Johnson County, Kansas*. N.p.: National Cooperative Soil Survey, 1970.

Westcott, Cynthia. *Plant Disease Handbook*. Princeton, N.J.: D. Van Nostrand, 1960.

3M. *The Gardener's Bug Book*. Garden City, N.Y.: Doubleday, 1964.

Wherry, Edgar T. *The Southern Fern Guide*. Garden City, N.Y.: Doubleday, 1964.

Wyman, Donald. *Wyman's Gardening Encyclopedia*. New York: Macmillan, 1971.

OTHER PUBLICATIONS

Publications of the Illinois Cooperative Extension Service, University of Illinois, Urbana.

Publications of the Iowa Cooperative Extension Service, Iowa State University, Ames.

Publications of the Kansas Agricultural Experiment Station and Kansas Cooperative Extension Service, Manhattan.

Publications of the University of Missouri Extension Division, Columbia.

Publications of the Nebraska Cooperative Extension Service, Lincoln.

Selected climatic maps of the United States from the Environmental Data Service of the Environmental Science Services Administration, U.S. Department of Commerce.

Index

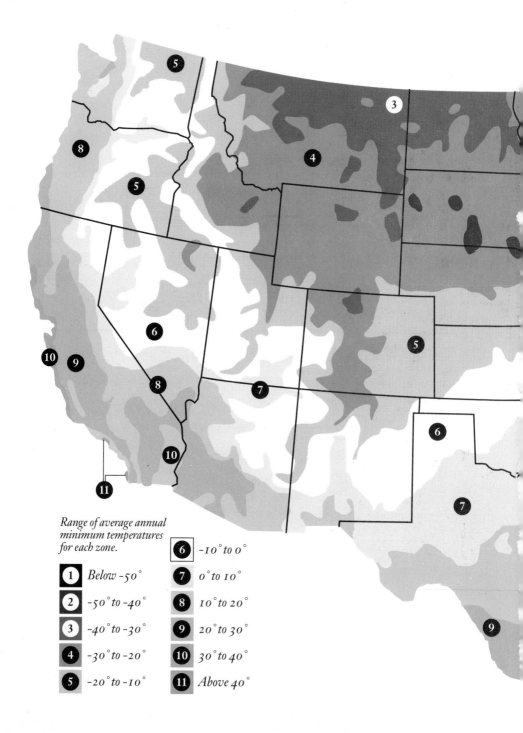

Range of average annual
minimum temperatures
for each zone.

1	Below -50°
2	-50° to -40°
3	-40° to -30°
4	-30° to -20°
5	-20° to -10°

6	-10° to 0°
7	0° to 10°
8	10° to 20°
9	20° to 30°
10	30° to 40°
11	Above 40°